COMMON CORE MATHEMATICS

NEW YORK EDITION

A Story of Ratios

Grade 8, Module 3: Similarity

COMMON CORE™ consider the source

JB JOSSEY-BASS™
A Wiley Brand

ISBN: 978-1-118-81107-8

Printed in the United States of America
FIRST EDITION
PB Printing   10 9 8 7 6 5 4 3 2 1

WELCOME

Dear Teacher,

Thank you for your interest in Common Core's curriculum in mathematics. Common Core is a non-profit organization based in Washington, DC dedicated to helping K-12 public schoolteachers use the power of high-quality content to improve instruction.[1] We are led by a board of master teachers, scholars, and current and former school, district, and state education leaders. Common Core has responded to the Common Core State Standards' (CCSS) call for "content-rich curriculum"[2] by creating new, CCSS-based curriculum materials in mathematics, English Language Arts, history, and (soon) the arts. All of our materials are written by teachers who are among the nation's foremost experts on the new standards.

In 2012 Common Core won three contracts from the New York State Education Department to create a PreKindergarten–12th grade mathematics curriculum for the teachers of that state, and to conduct associated professional development. The book you hold contains a portion of that work. In order to respond to demand in New York and elsewhere, modules of the curriculum will continue to be published, on a rolling basis, as they are completed. This curriculum is based on New York's version of the CCSS (the CCLS, or Common Core Learning Standards). Common Core will be releasing an enhanced version of the curriculum this summer on our website, commoncore.org. That version also will be published by Jossey-Bass, a Wiley brand.

Common Core's curriculum materials are not merely aligned to the new standards, they take the CCSS as their very foundation. Our work in math takes its shape from the expectations embedded in the new standards— including the instructional shifts and mathematical progressions, and the new expectations for student fluency, deep conceptual understanding, and application to real-life context. Similarly, our ELA and history curricula are deeply informed by the CCSS's new emphasis on close reading, increased use of informational text, and evidence-based writing.

Our curriculum is distinguished not only by its adherence to the CCSS. The math curriculum is based on a theory of teaching math that is proven to work. That theory posits that mathematical knowledge is most coherently and

---

1. Despite the coincidence of name, Common Core and the Common Core State Standards are not affiliated. Common Core was established in 2007, prior to the start of the Common Core State Standards Initiative, which was led by the National Governors Association and the Council for Chief State School Officers.

2. *Common Core State Standards for English Language Arts & Literacy in History/Social Studies, Science, and Technical Subjects* (Washington, DC: Common Core State Standards Initiative), 6.

effectively conveyed when it is taught in a sequence that follows the "story" of mathematics itself. This is why we call the elementary portion of this curriculum "A Story of Units," to be followed by "A Story of Ratios" in middle school, and "A Story of Functions" in high school. Mathematical concepts flow logically, from one to the next, in this curriculum. The sequencing has been joined with methods of instruction that have been proven to work, in this nation and abroad. These methods drive student understanding beyond process, to deep mastery of mathematical concepts. The goal of the curriculum is to produce students who are not merely literate, but fluent, in mathematics.

It is important to note that, as extensive as these curriculum materials are, they are not meant to be prescriptive. Rather, they are intended to provide a basis for teachers to hone their own craft through study, collaboration, training, and the application of their own expertise as professionals. At Common Core we believe deeply in the ability of teachers and in their central and irreplaceable role in shaping the classroom experience. We strive only to support and facilitate their important work.

The teachers and scholars who wrote these materials are listed beginning on the next page. Their deep knowledge of mathematics, of the CCSS, and of what works in classrooms defined this work in every respect. I would like to thank Louisiana State University professor of mathematics Scott Baldridge for the intellectual leadership he provides to this project. Teacher and trainer Jill Diniz, who is the lead writer for grades 6–12, has brought extraordinary intelligence and judgment to this work. Jill's ability to thrive in situations in which others would be lucky just to persevere, is uncommon.

Finally, this work owes a debt to project director Nell McAnelly that is so deep I'm confident it never can be repaid. Nell, who leads LSU's Gordon A. Cain Center for STEM Literacy, oversees all aspects of our work for NYSED. She has spent days, nights, weekends, and many cancelled vacations toiling in her efforts to make it possible for this talented group of teacher-writers to produce their best work against impossible deadlines. I'm confident that in the years to come Scott, Robin, and Nell will be among those who will deserve to be credited with putting math instruction in our nation back on track.

Thank you for taking an interest in our work. Please join us at www.commoncore.org.

Lynne Munson
President and Executive Director
Common Core
Washington, DC
October 25, 2013

Common Core's 6-12 Math Staff

Scott Baldridge, Lead Mathematician and Writer
Robin Ramos, Lead Writer, PreKindergarten–5
Ben McCarty, Mathematician

Nell McAnelly, Project Director
Tiah Alphonso, Associate Director
Jennifer Loftin, Associate Director
Catriona Anderson, Curriculum Manager,
    PreKindergarten–5
Jill Diniz, Lead Writer, 9-11 and Curriculum
    Manager

Sixth Grade

Erika Silva, Lead
Debby Grawn
Glenn Gebhard
Krysta Gibbs

Sixth and Seventh Grade

Anne Netter, Lead
Beau Bailey
Saki Milton
Hester Sutton
David Wright
Korinna Sanchez

Seventh Grade

Julie Wortmann, Lead
Joanne Choi
Lori Fanning
Bonnie Hart

Eighth Grade

Stefanie Hassan, Lead
Winnie Gilbert
Sunil Koswatta, Mathematician

Ninth Grade

Miki Alkire
Chris Bejar
Carlos Carrera
Melvin Damaolao
Joe Ferrantelli
Jenny Kim
Athena Leonardo

Rob Michelin
Noam Pillischer
Alex Sczesnak

Tenth Grade

Pia Mohsen, Lead
Bonnie Bergstresser
Ellen Fort
Terrie Poehl

Ninth, Tenth, and Eleventh Grade

Kevin Bluount
Wendy DenBesten
Abe Frankel
Thomas Gaffey
Kay Gleenblatt
Sheri Goings
Pam Goodner
Selena Oswalt
William Rorison
Chris Murcko
Surinder Sandhu
Pam Walker
Darrick Wood

Statistics

Henry Kranendonk, Lead
Michael Allwood
Gail Burrill
Beth Chance
Brian Kotz
Kathy Kritz
Patrick Hopsfensperger
Jerry Moren
Shannon Vinson

Document Management Team

Kristen Zimmerman

Advisors

Richard Askey
Roger Howe
James Madden
Roxy Peck
James Tanton

Table of Contents[1]

Similarity

---

[1] Each lesson is ONE day and ONE day is considered a 45 minute period.

Grade 8 • Module 3

Similarity

OVERVIEW

In Module 3, students learn about dilation and similarity and apply that knowledge to a proof of the Pythagorean Theorem based on the Angle-Angle criterion for similar triangles. The module begins with the definition of dilation, properties of dilations, and compositions of dilations. The instruction regarding dilation in Module 3 is structured similarly to the instruction regarding concepts of basic rigid motions in Module 2. One overarching goal of this module is to replace the common idea of "same shape, different sizes" with a definition of similarity that can be applied to geometric shapes that are not polygons, such as ellipses and circles.

In this module, students describe the effect of dilations on two-dimensional figures in general and using coordinates. Building on prior knowledge of scale drawings (**7.G.A.1**), Module 3 demonstrates the effect dilation has on a figure when the scale factor is greater than zero but less than one (shrinking of figure), equal to one (congruence), and greater than one (magnification of figure). Once students understand how dilation transforms figures in the plane, they examine the effect that dilation has on points and figures in the coordinate plane. Beginning with points, students learn the multiplicative effect that dilation has on the coordinates of the ordered pair. Then students apply the knowledge about points to describe the effect dilation has on figures in the coordinate plane, in terms of their coordinates.

Additionally, Module 3 demonstrates that a two-dimensional figure is similar to another if the second can be obtained from a dilation followed by congruence. Knowledge of basic rigid motions is reinforced throughout the module, specifically when students describe the sequence that exhibits a similarity between two given figures. In Module 2, students used vectors to describe the translation of the plane. Module 3 begins in the same way, but once figures are bound to the coordinate plane, students will describe translations in terms of units left or right and/or units up or down. When figures on the coordinate plane are rotated, the center of rotation is the origin of the graph. In most cases, students will describe the rotation as having center O and degree d, unless the rotation can be easily identified, i.e., a rotation of 90° or 180°. Reflections remain reflections across a line, but when possible, students should identify the line of reflection as the x-axis or y-axis.

It should be noted that congruence, together with similarity, is *the* fundamental concept in planar geometry. It is a concept defined without coordinates. In fact, it is most transparently understood when introduced without the extra conceptual baggage of a coordinate system. This is partly because a coordinate system picks out a preferred point (the origin), which then centers most discussions of rotations, reflections, and translations at or in reference to that point. These discussions are further restricted to only the "nice" rotations, reflections, or translations that are easy to do in a coordinate plane. Restricting to "nice" transformations is a huge mistake mathematically because it is antithetical to the main point that must be made about congruence: that rotations, translations, and reflections are abundant in the plane---that for every point in the plane, there are an *infinite number* of rotations up to 360°, that for every line in the plane

Module 3:   Similarity
Date: 10/15/13

there is a reflection, and for every directed line segment there is a translation. It is this abundance that helps students realize that every congruence transformation (i.e., the act of "picking up a figure" and moving it to another location) can be accomplished through a sequence of translations, rotations, and reflections and further, that similarity is a congruence transformation in addition to dilation.

In Grades 6 and 7, students learned about unit rate, rates in general (**6.RP.A.2**), and how to represent and use proportional relationships between quantities (**7.RP.A.2**, **7.RP.A.3**). In Module 3, students apply this knowledge of proportional relationships and rates to determine if two figures are similar, and if so, by what scale factor one can be obtained from the other. By looking at the effect of a scale factor on the length of a segment of a given figure, students will write proportions to find missing lengths of similar figures.

Module 3 provides another opportunity for students to learn about the Pythagorean Theorem and its applications. With the concept of similarity firmly in place, students are shown a proof of the Pythagorean Theorem that uses similar triangles.

Focus Standards

Understand congruence and similarity using physical models, transparencies, or geometry software.

8.G.A.3	Describe the effect of dilations, translations, rotations, and reflections on two-dimensional figures using coordinates.
8.G.A.4	Understand that a two-dimensional figure is similar to another if the second can be obtained from the first by a sequence of rotations, reflections, translations, and dilations; given two similar two-dimensional figures, describe a sequence that exhibits the similarity between them.
8.G.A.5	Use informal arguments to establish facts about the angle sum and exterior angle of triangles, about the angles created when parallel lines are cut by a transversal, and the angle-angle criterion for similarity of triangles. *For example, arrange three copies of the same triangle so that the sum of the three angles appears to form a line, and give an argument in terms of transversals why this is so.*

Understand and apply the Pythagorean Theorem.

8.G.B.6	Explain a proof of the Pythagorean Theorem and its converse.
8.G.B.7	Apply the Pythagorean Theorem to determine unknown side lengths in right triangles in real-world and mathematical problems in two and three dimensions.

Foundational Standards

Understand ratio concepts and use ratio reasoning to solve problems.

6.RP.A.2   Understand the concept of a unit rate *a/b* associated with a ratio *a:b* with *b≠0*, and use rate language in the context of a ratio relationship. *For example, "This recipe has a ratio of 3 cups of flour to 4 cups of sugar, so there is ¾ cup of flour for each cup of sugar." "We paid $75 for 15 hamburgers, which is a rate of $5 per hamburger."*

Analyze proportional relationships and use them to solve real-world and mathematical problems.

7.RP.A.2   Recognize and represent proportional relationships between quantities.

7.RP.A.3   Use proportional relationships to solve multistep ratio and percent problems. *Examples: simple interest, tax, markups and markdowns, gratuities and commissions, fees, percent increase and decrease, percent error.*

Draw, construct, and describe geometrical figures and describe the relationships between them.

7.G.A.1   Solve problems involving scale drawings of geometric figures, including computing actual lengths and areas from a scale drawing and reproducing a scale drawing at a different scale.

7.G.A.2   Draw (freehand, with ruler and protractor, and with technology) geometric shapes with given conditions. Focus on constructing triangles from three measures of angles or sides, noticing when the conditions determine a unique triangle, more than one triangle, or no triangle.

Focus Standards for Mathematical Practice

MP.6   **Attend to precision**. To communicate precisely, students will use clear definitions in discussions with others and in their own reasoning with respect to similar figures. Students will use the basic properties of dilations to prove or disprove claims about a pair of figures. Students will incorporate their knowledge about basic rigid motions as it relates to similarity, specifically in the description of the sequence that is required to prove two figures are similar.

MP.4   **Model with mathematics**. This module provides an opportunity for students to apply their knowledge of dilation and similarity in real-world applications. Students will use shadow lengths and a known height to find the height of trees, the distance across a lake, and the height of a flagpole.

MP.3   **Construct viable arguments and critiques the reasoning of others**. Many times in this module, students are exposed to the reasoned logic of proofs. Students are called on to make conjectures about the effect of dilations on angles, rays, lines, and segments, and then must evaluate the validity of their claims based on evidence. Students also make conjectures about the effect of dilation on circles, ellipses, and other figures. Students are encouraged to participate in discussions and evaluate the claims of others.

Terminology

New or Recently Introduced Terms

- **Dilation** (Dilation, D, is a transformation of the plane with center O and scale factor r ($r > 0$) if $D(O) = O$ and if $P \neq O$, then the point $D(P)$, to be denoted by Q, is the point on the ray $\overrightarrow{OP}$ so that $|OQ| = r|OP|$. A dilation in the coordinate plane is a transformation that shrinks or magnifies a figure by multiplying each coordinate of the figure by the scale factor.)

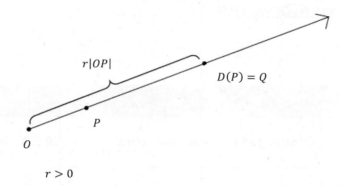

- **Congruence** (A finite composition of basic rigid motions—reflections, rotations, translations—of the plane. Two figures in a plane are *congruent* if there is a congruence that maps one figure onto the other figure.)
- **Similar** (Two figures in the plane are similar if there exists a similarity transformation taking one figure to the other.)
- **Similarity Transformation** (A *similarity transformation*, or *similarity*, is a composition of a finite number of basic rigid motions or dilations. The *scale factor* of a similarity transformation is the product of the scale factors of the dilations in the composition; if there are no dilations in the composition, the scale factor is defined to be 1.)
- **Similarity** (A similarity is an example of a transformation.)

Familiar Terms and Symbols[2]

- Scale Drawing
- Degree-Preserving

---

[2] These are terms and symbols students have seen previously.

Suggested Tools and Representations

- Compass (Required)
- Transparency or patty paper
- Wet or dry erase markers for use with transparency
- Optional: geometry software
- Ruler
- Video that demonstrates Pythagorean Theorem proof using similar triangles:
  http://www.youtube.com/watch?v=QCyvxYLFSfU

Assessment Summary

Assessment Type	Administered	Format	Standards Addressed
Mid-Module Assessment Task	After Topic A	Constructed response with rubric	8.G.A.3
End-of-Module Assessment Task	After Topic B	Constructed response with rubric	8.G.A.3, 8.G.A.4, 8.G.A.5

Mathematics Curriculum

Topic A:

Dilation

8.G.A.3

Focus Standard:	8.G.A.3	Describe the effect of dilations, translations, rotations, and reflections on two-dimensional figures using coordinates.
Instructional Days:	7	
	Lesson 1:	What Lies Behind "Same Shape"? (E)[1]
	Lesson 2:	Properties of Dilations (P)
	Lesson 3:	Examples of Dilations (P)
	Lesson 4:	Fundamental Theorem of Similarity (FTS) (S)
	Lesson 5:	First Consequences of FTS (P)
	Lesson 6:	Dilations on the Coordinate Plane (P)
	Lesson 7:	Informal Proofs of Properties of Dilations (optional) (S)

Topic A begins by demonstrating the need for a precise definition of dilation instead of "same shape, different size" because dilation will be applied to geometric shapes that are not polygons. Students begin their work with dilations off the coordinate plane by experimenting with dilations using a compass and straightedge in order to develop conceptual understanding. It is vital that students have access to these tools in order to develop an intuitive sense of dilation and to prepare for further work in Geometry.

In Lesson 1, dilation is defined, and the role of scale factor is demonstrated through the shrinking and magnification of figures. In Lesson 2, properties of dilations are discussed. As with rigid motions, students learn that dilations map lines to lines, segments to segments, and rays to rays. Students learn that dilations are a degree-preserving transformation. In Lesson 3, students use a compass to perform dilations of figures with the same center and figures with different centers. In Lesson 3, students begin to look at figures that are dilated followed by congruence.

In Lessons 4 and 5, students learn and use the Fundamental Theorem of Similarity (FTS): If in $\triangle ABC$, D is a point on line AB and E is a point on line AC, and $\dfrac{|AB|}{|AD|} = \dfrac{|AC|}{|AE|} = r$, then $\dfrac{|BC|}{|DE|} = r$ and $L_{DE} \parallel L_{BC}$. Students verify this theorem, experimentally, using the lines of notebook paper. In Lesson 6, the work with dilations is tied to the coordinate plane; students use what they learned in Lessons 4 and 5 to conclude that when the

---

[1] Lesson Structure Key: **P**-Problem Set Lesson, **M**-Modeling Cycle Lesson, **E**-Exploration Lesson, **S**-Socratic Lesson

Topic A: Dilation
Date: 10/15/13

center of dilation is the origin, the coordinates of a dilated point is found by multiplying each coordinate of the ordered pair by the scale factor. Students first practice finding the location of dilated points in isolation; then, students locate the dilated points that comprise two-dimensional figures. Lesson 7 provides students with informal proofs of the properties of dilations that they observed in Lesson 2.

Lesson 1: What Lies Behind "Same Shape"?

Student Outcomes

- Students learn the definition of dilation and why "same shape" is not good enough to say two figures are similar.
- Students know that dilations magnify and shrink figures.

Lesson Notes

The goal of this module is to arrive at a precise understanding of the concept of similarity: What does it mean for two geometric figures to have "the same shape but not necessarily the same size"? Note that we introduced the concept of congruence in the last module and are introducing the concept of dilation, presently. Then a similarity (or a similarity transformation) is, by definition, the sequence of a dilation followed by a congruence.

The basic references for this module are: Teaching Geometry According to the Common Core Standards and Pre-Algebra, both by Hung-Hsi Wu. The latter is identical to the document cited on page 92 of the *Common Core State Standards for Mathematics:* Wu, H., "Lecture Notes for the 2009 Pre-Algebra Institute," September 15, 2009.

Classwork

Exploratory Challenge (10 minutes)

Have students examine the following pairs of figures and record their thoughts.

Exploratory Challenge

Two geometric figures are said to be similar if they have the same shape but not necessarily the same size. Using that informal definition, are the following pairs of figures similar to one another? Explain.

Pair A:

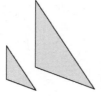

Yes, these figures appear to be similar. They are the same shape, but one is larger than the other, or one is smaller than the other.

Pair B:

No, these figures do not appear to be similar. One looks like a square and the other like a rectangle.

Pair C:

These figures appear to be exactly the same, which means they are congruent.

Pair D:

Yes, these figures appear to be similar. They are both circles, but different sizes.

Pair E:

Yes, these figures appear to be similar. They are the same shape, but different in size.

Pair F:

Yes, these figures appear to be similar. The faces look the same, but they are just different in size.

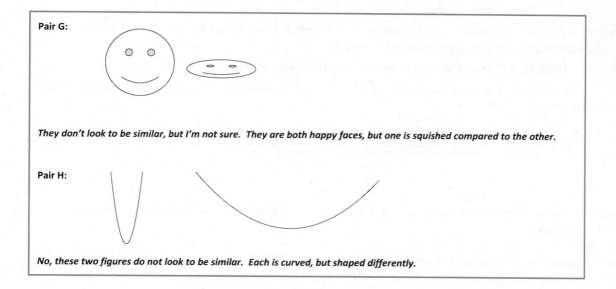

Pair G:

They don't look to be similar, but I'm not sure. They are both happy faces, but one is squished compared to the other.

Pair H:

No, these two figures do not look to be similar. Each is curved, but shaped differently.

Discussion (20 minutes)

- In mathematics, we want to be absolutely sure about what we are saying. Therefore, we need *precise* definitions for similar figures. For example, you may have thought that the figures in Pair G were similar because they are both happy faces. However, a precise definition of similarity tells you that they are in fact NOT similar because the parts of the face are not in proportion. Think about trying to adjust the size of a picture. When you grab from the corner of the photo, everything looks relatively the same, (i.e., it looks to be *in proportion*), but when you grab from the sides, top, or bottom of the photo, the picture does not look quite right (i.e., things are not *in proportion*).

> **Note to Teacher:**
> The embedded .mov file demonstrates what happens to a picture when the corners are grabbed (as opposed to the sides or top). You may choose to demonstrate this in the classroom using a picture of your choice.

- You probably said that the curved figures in Pair H were not similar. However, a precise definition of similarity tells you that in fact they ARE similar. They are shapes called parabolas that you will learn about in Algebra. For now, just know that one of the curved figures has been *dilated* according to a specific factor.

- Now we must discuss what is meant by a transformation of the plane known as dilation. In the next few lessons, we will use dilation to develop a precise definition for similar figures.

> **Scaffolding:**
> Explain to students that the notation $|OP|$ means *the length of the segment OP*.

- **Definition:** A dilation is a transformation of the plane with center O, while scale factor r $(r > 0)$ is a rule that assigns to each point P of the plane a point $Dilation(P)$ so that:

  1. $Dilation(O) = O$, (i.e., a dilation does not move the center of dilation.)

  2. If $P \neq O$, then the point $dilation(P)$, (to be denoted more simply by P') is the point on the ray $\overrightarrow{OP}$ so that $|OP'| = r|OP|$.

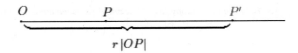

- In other words, a dilation is a rule that moves points in the plane a specific distance, determined by the scale factor r, from a center O.

- In previous grades, you did scale drawings of real-world objects. When a figure shrinks in size, the scale factor r will be less than one but greater than zero (i.e., $0 < r < 1$). In this case, a dilation where $0 < r < 1$, every point in the plane is *pulled toward* the center O proportionally the same amount.

- You may have also done scale drawings of real-world objects where a very small object was drawn larger than it is in real life. When a figure is magnified (i.e., made larger in size), the scale factor r will be greater than 1 (i.e., $r > 1$). In this case, a dilation where $r > 1$, every point in the plane is pushed away from the center O proportionally the same amount.

- If figures shrink in size when the scale factor is $0 < r < 1$, and magnify when the scale factor is $r > 1$, what happens when the scale factor is exactly one? (i.e., $r = 1$)

  - *When the scale factor is $r = 1$, the figure does not change in size. It does not shrink or magnify. It remains congruent to the original figure.*

- What does *proportionally the same amount* mean with respect to the change in size that a dilation causes? Think about this example: If you have a segment, OP, of length 3 cm that is dilated from a center O by a scale factor $r = 4$, how long is the dilated segment OP'?

  - *The dilated segment OP' should be 4 times longer than the original (i.e., 4×3 or 12 cm).*

- For dilation, we think about the measures of the segments accordingly:

  $|OP'| = r|OP|$ The length of the dilated segment OP' is equal to the length of the original segment, OP, multiplied by the scale factor.

- Now think about this example: If you have a segment, OQ, of length 21 cm and it is dilated from a center O by a scale factor $r = \frac{1}{3}$, how long is the dilated segment OQ'?

  - *According to the definition of dilation, the length of the dilated segment is $\frac{1}{3} \times 21$ (i.e., $\frac{1}{3}$ the original length). Therefore, the dilated segment is 7 cm. This makes sense because the scale factor is less than one, so we expect the length of the side to be shrunk.*

- To determine if one object is a dilated version of another, you can measure their individual lengths and check to see that the length of the original figure, multiplied by the scale factor, is equal to the dilated length.

Exercises 1–6 (8 minutes)

Have students check to see if figures are, in fact, dilations and find measures using scale factor.

Exercises 1–6

1.   Given $|OP| = 5$ in.

    a.   If segment OP is dilated by a scale factor $r = 4$, what is the length of segment OP'?

        $|OP'| = 20$ in. because the scale factor multiplied by the length of the original segment is 20, i.e., $4 \times 5 = 20$.

    b.   If segment OP is dilated by a scale factor $r = \frac{1}{2}$, what is the length of segment OP'?

        $|OP'| = 2.5$ in. because the scale factor multiplied by the length of the original segment is 2.5, i.e., $\left(\frac{1}{2}\right) \times 5 = 2.5$.

Use the diagram below to answer Exercises 2–6. Let there be a dilation from center O. Then, $dilation(P) = P'$ and $dilation(Q) = Q'$. In the diagram below, $|OP| = 3$ cm and $|OQ| = 4$ cm as shown.

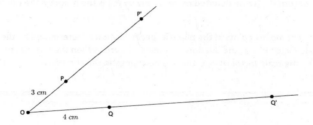

2.   If the scale factor is $r = 3$, what is the length of segment OP' ?

    The length of the segment OP' is 9 cm.

3.   Use the definition of dilation to show that your answer to Exercise 2 is correct.

    $|OP'| = r\,|OP|$; therefore, $|OP'| = 3 \times 3 = 9$ and $|OP'| = 9$.

4.   If the scale factor is $r = 3$, what is the length of segment OQ'?

    The length of the segment OQ' is 12 cm.

5.   Use the definition of dilation to show that your answer to Exercise 4 is correct.

    $|OQ'| = r|OQ|$; therefore, $|OQ'| = 3 \times 4 = 12$ and $|OQ'| = 12$.

6.   If you know that $|OP| = 3$, $|OP'| = 9$, how could you use that information to determine the scale factor?

    Since we know $|OP'| = r|OP|$, we can solve for r: $\dfrac{|OP'|}{|OP|} = r$, which is $\dfrac{9}{3} = r$ or $3 = r$.

	Lesson 1:	What Lies Behind "Same Shape"?
	Date:	10/16/13

Closing (3 minutes)

Summarize, or ask students to summarize, the main points from the lesson:

- We know we need a precise definition for "similar" that includes the use of dilation.
- We know that a dilation will magnify a figure when the scale factor is greater than one and that a dilation will shrink a figure when the scale factor is greater than zero but less than one.
- We know that if we multiply a segment by the scale factor, we will get the length of the dilated segment. (i.e., $|OP'| = r|OP|$)

Lesson Summary

Definition: A dilation is a transformation of the plane with center O, while scale factor r ($r > 0$) is a rule that assigns to each point P of the plane a point $Dilation(P)$ so that:

1. $Dilation(O) = O$, (i.e., a dilation does not move the center of dilation.)

2. If $P \neq O$, then the point $dilation(P)$, (to be denoted more simply by P') is the point on the ray $\overrightarrow{OP}$ so that $|OP'| = r|OP|$.

In other words, a dilation is a rule that moves points in the plane a specific distance, determined by the scale factor r, from a center O. When the scale factor $r > 1$, the dilation magnifies a figure. When the scale factor $0 < r < 1$, the dilation shrinks a figure. When the scale factor $r = 1$, there is no change in the size of the figure, that is, the figure and its image are congruent.

Exit Ticket (4 minutes)

Name _____   Date_____

Lesson 1: What Lies Behind "Same Shape"?

Exit Ticket

1.   Why do we need a better definition for similarity than "same shape, not the same size"?

2.   Use the diagram below. Let there be a dilation from center O with scale factor $r = 3$. Then $dilation(P) = P'$. In the diagram below, $|OP| = 5$ cm. What is $|OP'|$? Show your work.

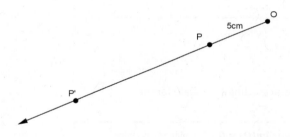

3.   Use the diagram below. Let there be a dilation from center O. Then $dilation(P) = P'$. In the diagram below, $|OP| = 18$ cm and $|OP'| = 9$ cm. What is the scale factor r? Show your work.

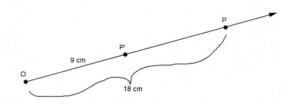

Exit Ticket Sample Solutions

1. **Why do we need a better definition for similarity than "same shape, but not the same size"?**

   We need a better definition that includes dilation and a scale factor because some figures may look to be similar (e.g., the smiley faces), but we cannot know for sure unless we can check the proportionality. Other figures (e.g., the parabolas) may not look similar, but are. We need a definition so that we are not just guessing if they are similar by looking at them.

2. **Use the diagram below. Let there be a dilation from center O with scale factor 3. Then $dilation(P) = P'$. In the diagram below, $|OP| = 5$ cm. What is $|OP'|$? Show your work.**

   Since $|OP'| = r|OP|$

   $|OP'| = 3 \times 5$ cm

   $|OP'| = 15$ cm

3. **Use the diagram below. Let there be a dilation from center O. Then $dilation(P) = P'$. In the diagram below, $|OP| = 18$ cm and $|OP'| = 9$ cm. What is the scale factor r? Show your work.**

   Since $|OP'| = r|OP|$

   9 cm $= r \times 18$ cm

   $\dfrac{1}{2} = r$

Problem Set Sample Solutions

Have students practice using the definition of dilation and finding lengths according to a scale factor.

1. **Let there be a dilation from center O. Then $dilation(P) = P'$ and $dilation(Q) = Q'$. Examine the drawing below. What can you determine about the scale factor of the dilation?**

   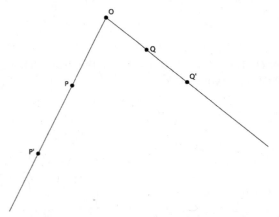

   The scale factor must be greater than one, $r > 1$, because the dilated point is farther from the center than the original point.

2.   Let there be a dilation from center O. Then $dilation(P) = P'$, and $dilation(Q) = Q'$. Examine the drawing below. What can you determine about the scale factor of the dilation?

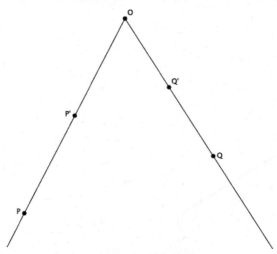

The scale factor must be greater than zero but less than one $(0 < r < 1)$ because the dilated point is closer to the center than the original point.

3.   Let there be a dilation from center O with a scale factor $r = 4$. Then $dilation(P) = P'$ and $dilation(Q) = Q'$. $|OP| = 3.2$ cm and $|OQ| = 2.7$ cm, as shown. Use the drawing below to answer parts (a) and (b).

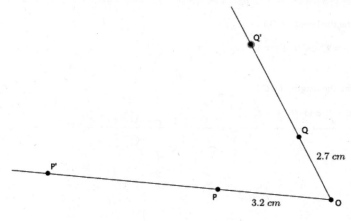

a.   Use the definition of dilation to determine the length of OP'.

$|OP'| = r|OP|$; therefore, $|OP'| = 4 \times (3.2) = 12.8$ and $|OP'| = 12.8$ cm.

b.   Use the definition of dilation to determine the length of OQ'.

$|OQ'| = r|OQ|$; therefore, $|OQ'| = 4 \times (2.7) = 10.8$ and $|OQ'| = 10.8$ cm.

4. Let there be a dilation from center O with a scale factor r. Then $dilation(A) = A'$, $dilation(B) = B'$, and $dilation(C) = C'$. $|OA| = 3$, $|OB| = 15$, $|OC| = 6$, and $|OB'| = 5$ as shown. Use the drawing below to answer parts (a)–(c).

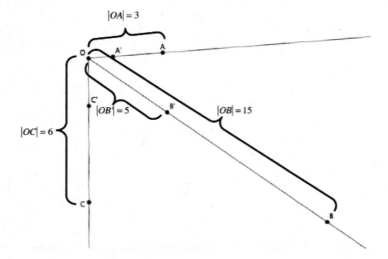

a. Using the definition of dilation with lengths OB and OB', determine the scale factor of the dilation.

$|OB'| = r|OB|$, which means $5 = r \times 15$; therefore, $r = \frac{1}{3}$.

b. Use the definition of dilation to determine the length of OA'.

$|OA'| = \frac{1}{3}|OA|$, therefore, $|OA'| = \frac{1}{3} \times 3 = 1$, and $|OA'| = 1$.

c. Use the definition of dilation to determine the length of OC'.

$|OC'| = \frac{1}{3}|OC|$; therefore, $|OC'| = \frac{1}{3} \times 6 = 2$, and $|OC'| = 2$.

Lesson 2: Properties of Dilations

Student Outcomes

- Students learn how to use a compass and a ruler to perform dilations.
- Students learn that dilations map lines to lines, segments to segments, and rays to rays. Students know that dilations are degree preserving.

Lesson Notes

In this lesson students will become familiar with using a straightedge and compass to perform dilations. Consider having students follow along on their own papers as you work through Examples 1–3 so that students can begin to develop independence with these tools.

Classwork

Discussion (5 minutes)

Ask students to make a conjecture about how dilations will affect lines, segments, and rays.

- Fold a piece of paper into fourths. At the top of each fourth, write *line*, *segment*, *ray*, and *angle* along with a diagram of each. What do you think will happen to each of these after a dilation? Explain.

Have students spend a minute recording their thoughts, then share with a partner, then the whole class. Consider recording the different conjectures on a class chart. Then explain to students that in this lesson we will investigate what happens to each of these figures after our dilation, that is, we will test our conjectures.

Opening Exercise

This is an optional section for those who would like to include a warm-up exercise in their lessons.

Example 1 (6 minutes)

Examples 1–3 demonstrate that dilations map lines to lines and how to use a compass to dilate.

- This example shows that a dilation maps a line to a line. This means that the image of a line, after undergoing a dilation, is also a line. Given line L, we will dilate with a scale factor $r = 2$ from center O. Before we begin, exactly how many lines can be drawn through two points?
  - *Only one line can be drawn through two points.*
- To dilate the line, we will choose two points on L (points P and Q) to dilate. When we connect the dilated images of P and Q (P' and Q') we will have the dilated image of line L, L'.

- First, let's select a center O off the line L and two points P and Q on line L.

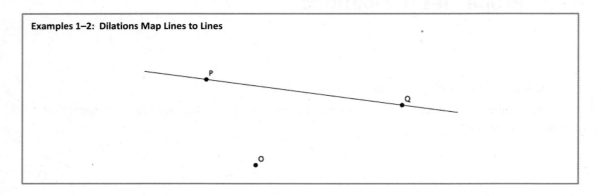

Examples 1–2: Dilations Map Lines to Lines

- Second, we draw rays from center O through each of the points P and Q. We want to make sure that the points O, P and the dilated P, P' lie on the same line (i.e., are collinear). That is what keeps the dilated image "in proportion." Think back to the last lesson where we saw how the size of the picture changed when pulling the corners compared to the sides. Pulling from the corners kept the picture "in proportion." The way we achieve this in diagrams is by drawing rays and making sure that the center, the point, and the dilated point are all on the same line.

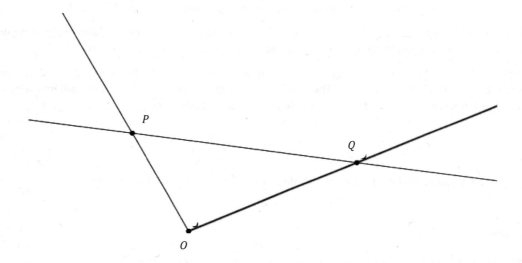

- Next, we use our compass to measure the distance from O to P. Do this by putting the point of the compass on point O and adjust the radius of the compass to draw an arc through point P. Once you have the compass set, move the point of the compass to P and make a mark along the ray (without changing the radius of the compass) to mark P'. Recall that the dilated point P' is the distance $2|OP|$ (i.e., $|OP'| = 2|OP|$). The compass helps us to find the location of P' so that it is exactly twice the length of OP. Use your ruler to prove this to students.

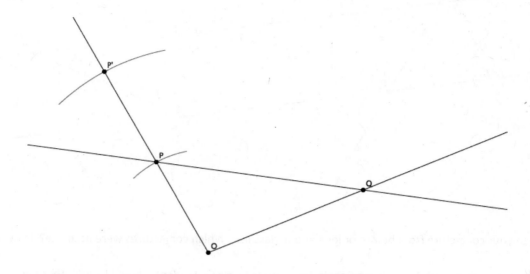

- Next, we repeat this process to locate Q'.

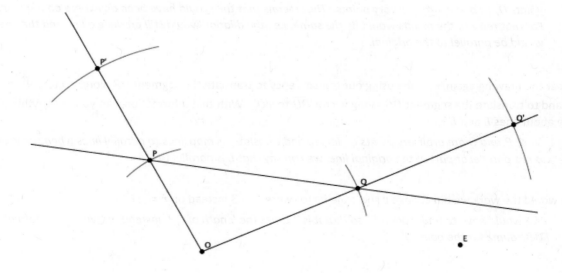

- Finally, connect points P' and Q' to draw line L'.

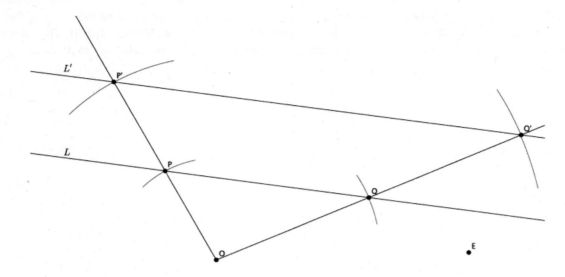

- Return to your conjecture from before or look at our class list. Which conjectures were accurate? How do you know?

  □ *Answers may vary depending on conjectures made by class. Students should identify that the conjecture of a line mapping to a line under a dilation is correct.*

MP.3

- What do you think would happen if we selected a different location for the center or points P and Q?

  □ *Points O, P, and Q are arbitrary points. That means that they could have been anywhere on the plane. For that reason, the results would be the same, i.e., the dilation would still produce a line and the line would be parallel to the original.*

- Look at the drawing again, imagine using our transparency to translate the segment OP along vector $\overrightarrow{OP}$ to PP' and to translate the segment OQ along vector $\overrightarrow{OQ}$ to QQ'. With that information, can you say anything more about lines L and L'?

  □ *Since P and Q are arbitrary points on line L, and translations map lines to parallel lines when the vector is not parallel or part of the original line, we can say that L is parallel to L'.*

- How would the work we did change if the scale factor were $r = 3$ instead of $r = 2$?

  □ *We would have to find a point P' so that it is 3 times the length of OP, instead of twice the length of OP. Same for the point Q'.*

Example 2 (2 minutes)

- Do you think line L would still be a line under a dilation with scale factor $r = 3$? Would the dilated line, L', still be parallel to L? (Allow time for students to talk to their partners and make predictions.)

    - *Yes, it will still be a line and it would still be parallel to line L. The scale factor being three instead of two simply means that we would perform the translation of the points P' and Q' more than once, but the result would be the same.*

- Here is what would happen with scale factor $r = 3$.

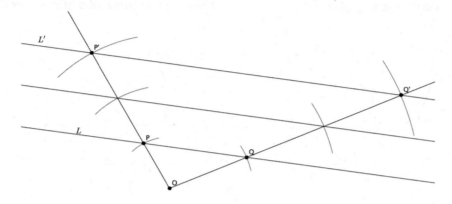

Example 3 (2 minutes)

Example 3: Dilations Map Lines to Lines

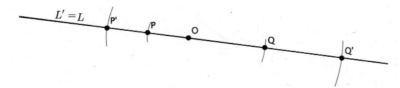

- What would happen if the center O were on line L? (Allow time for students to talk to their partners and make predictions.)

    If the center O were on line L, and we placed points P and Q on L, then the dilations of points P and Q, P' and Q', would also be on L. That means that line L and its dilated image, L', would coincide.

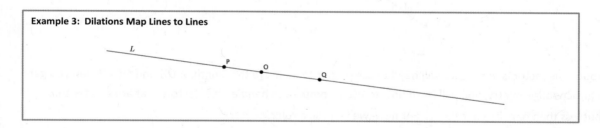

- What we have shown with these three examples is that a line, after a dilation, is still a line. Mathematicians like to say that *dilations map lines to lines*.

	Lesson 2:	Properties of Dilations
	Date:	10/16/13

Example 4 (5 minutes)

Example 4 demonstrates that dilations map rays to rays. It also demonstrates how to use a ruler to dilate with scale factor $r = \frac{1}{2}$. Similar to Example 1, before this example, discuss the conjectures students developed about rays. Also, consider getting students started, then asking them to finish with a partner.

- This example will show that a dilation maps a ray to a ray. Given ray $\overrightarrow{AB}$, we will dilate with a scale factor $r = \frac{1}{2}$ from center O.

- To dilate the ray, we will choose a center O off of the ray. Like before, we will draw rays from center O, through points A and B.

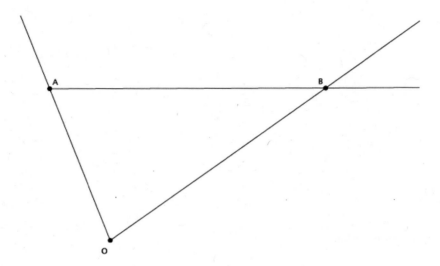

- Since our scale factor is $r = \frac{1}{2}$, we will need to use a ruler to measure the length of OA and OB. When you get into high school geometry, you will learn how to use a compass to handle scale factors that are greater than zero but less than one, like our $r = \frac{1}{2}$. For now, we will use a ruler.

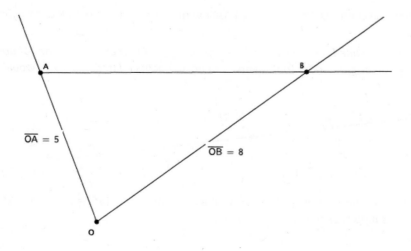

- Since our scale factor is $r = \frac{1}{2}$, we know that the dilated segment, OA', must be equal to $\frac{1}{2}$ the length of OA (i.e., $|OA'| = \frac{1}{2}|OA|$). Then OA' must be $\frac{1}{2} \times 5$; therefore, $|OA'| = 2.5$ cm. What must the length of OB' be?

  - *We know that $|OB'| = \frac{1}{2}|OB|$; therefore, $|OB'| = \frac{1}{2} \times 8 = 4$, and $|OB'| = 4$ cm.*

- Now that we know the lengths of OA' and OB', we will use a ruler to mark off those points on their respective rays.

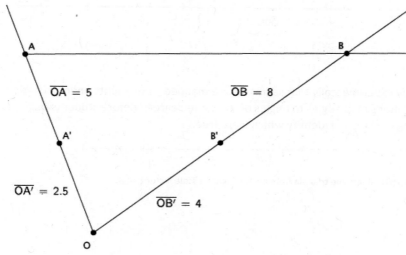

- Finally, we will connect A' to B'. With your partner, evaluate your conjecture. What happened to our ray after the dilation?

  - *When we connect point A' to point B', then we will have the ray $\overrightarrow{A'B'}$.*

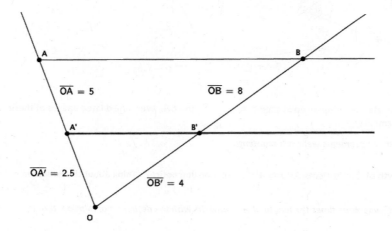

- What do you think would have happened if we selected our center O as a point on the ray $\overrightarrow{AB}$?

  □ *If our center O were on the ray, then the ray $\overrightarrow{AB}$ would coincide with its dilated image $\overrightarrow{A'B'}$, which is similar to what we saw when the line L was dilated from a center O on it.*

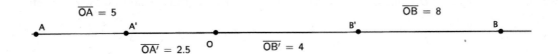

Exercise (15 minutes)

In this Exercise, students will verify experimentally that segments are mapped to segments under a dilation. They will also verify experimentally that dilations map angles to angles of the same degree. Before students begin, revisit the conjectures made at the beginning of class and identify which were true.

Exercise

Given center O and triangle ABC, dilate the triangle from center O with a scale factor $r = 3$.

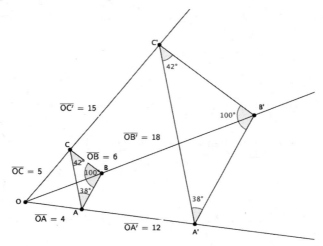

a. Note that the triangle ABC is made up of segments AB, BC, and CA. Were the dilated images of these segments still segments?

   Yes, when dilated, the segments were still segments.

b. Measure the length of the segments AB and $A'B'$. What do you notice? (Think about the definition of dilation.)

   The segment $A'B'$ was three times the length of AB. This fits with the definition of dilation, that is, $|A'B'| = r|AB|$.

c. Verify the claim you made in part (b) by measuring and comparing the lengths of segments BC and $B'C'$ and segments CA and $C'A'$. What does this mean in terms of the segments formed between dilated points?

   This means that dilations affect segments in the same way they do points. Specifically, the lengths of segments are dilated according to the scale factor.

d.   Measure ∠ABC and ∠A′B′C′. What do you notice?

The angles are equal in measure.

e.   Verify the claim you made in part (d) by measuring and comparing angles ∠BCA and ∠B′C′A′ and angles ∠CAB and ∠C′A′B′. What does that mean in terms of dilations with respect to angles and their degrees?

It means that dilations map angles to angles, and the dilation preserves the measure of the angles.

Discussion (5 minutes)

- The exercise you just completed and the examples from earlier in the lesson demonstrate several properties of dilations:

  1. Dilations map lines to lines, rays to rays, and segments to segments.
  2. Dilations map angles to angles of the same degree.

- In this lesson, we have verified experimentally a theorem about dilations. *Theorem: Let a dilation with center O and scale factor r be given. For any two points P and Q in the plane, let P′ = dilation(P) and Q′ = dilation(Q). Then:*

  1. For any P and Q, $|P'Q'| = r|PQ|$.
  2. For any P and Q, the segment joining P to Q is mapped to the segment joining P' and Q' (Exercise 1), the ray from P to Q is mapped to the ray from P' to Q' (Example 4), and the line joining P to Q is mapped to the line joining P' to Q' (Examples 1–3).
  3. Any angle is mapped to an angle of the same degree (Exercise 1).

- We have observed that the length of the dilated line segment is the length of the original segment, multiplied by the scale factor. We have also observed that the measure of an angle remains unchanged after a dilation.

Consider using one (or both) of the above explanations about what dilation does to a line segment and an angle.

Closing (5 minutes)

Summarize, or ask students to summarize, the main points from the lesson:

- We know how to use a compass to dilate when the scale factor $r > 1$. We know how to use a ruler to dilate when the scale factor $0 < r < 1$.
- We know that dilations map lines to lines, rays to rays, and segments to segments.
- We know that dilations map angles to angles of the same degree.

Lesson Summary

Dilations map lines to lines, rays to rays, and segments to segments. Dilations map angles to angles of the same degree.

Exit Ticket (5 minutes)

Name _____   Date_____

Lesson 2: Properties of Dilations

Exit Ticket

1. Given center O and quadrilateral $ABCD$, dilate the figure from center O by a scale factor of $r = 2$. Label the dilated quadrilateral $A'B'C'D'$.

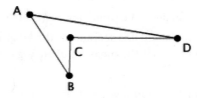

2. Describe what you learned today about what happens to lines, segments, rays, and angles after a dilation.

Exit Ticket Sample Solutions

1. Given center O and quadrilateral $ABCD$, dilate the figure from center O by a scale factor of $r = 2$. Label the dilated quadrilateral $A'B'C'D'$.

   Sample student work shown below. Verify that students have magnified the image $ABCD$.

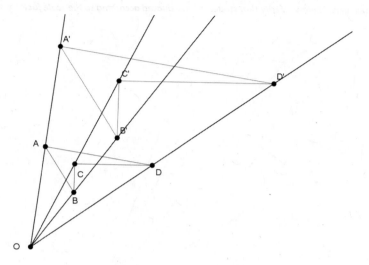

2. Describe what you learned today about what happens to lines, segments, rays, and angles after a dilation.

   We learned that a dilation will map a line to a line, a segment to a segment, a ray to a ray, and an angle to angle. Further, the length of the dilated line segment will be exactly r (the scale factor) times the length of the original segment. Also, the measure of a dilated angle will remain unchanged compared to the original angle.

Problem Set Sample Solutions

Students practice dilating figures with different scale factors.

1. Use a ruler to dilate the following figure from center O, with scale factor $r = \frac{1}{2}$.

    The dilated figure is shown in red below. Verify that students have dilated according to the scale factor $r = \frac{1}{2}$.

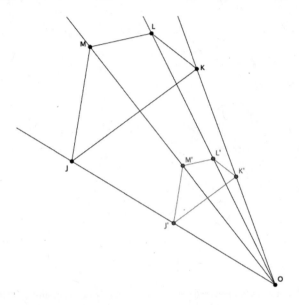

2. Use a compass to dilate the figure $ABCDE$ from center O, with scale factor $r = 2$.

    The figure in red, below, shows the dilated image of $ABCDE$.

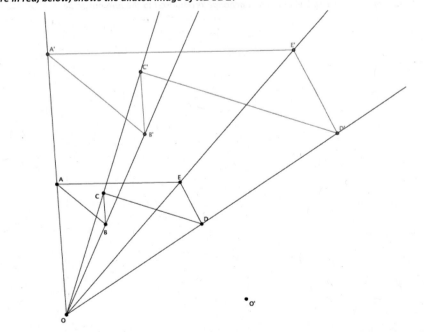

a.   Dilate the same figure, $ABCDE$, from a new center, O', with scale factor $r = 2$. Use double primes to distinguish this image from the original ($A''B''C''D''E''$).

The figure in blue, below, shows the dilated figure $A''B''C''D''E''$.

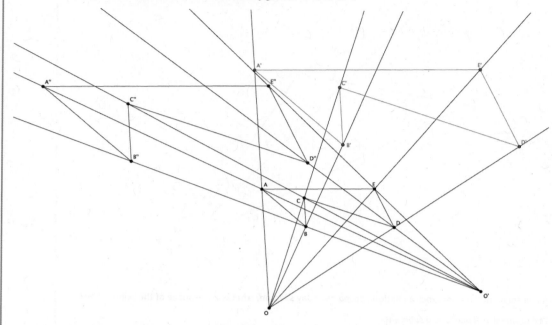

b.   What rigid motion, or sequence of rigid motions, would map $A''B''C''D''E''$ to $A'B'C'D'E'$?

A translation along vector $\overrightarrow{A''A'}$ (or any vector that connects a point of $A''B''C''D''E''$ and its corresponding point of $A'B'C'D'E'$) would map the figure $A''B''C''D''E''$ to $A'B'C'D'E'$.

The image below (with rays removed for clarity) shows the vector $\overrightarrow{A''A'}$.

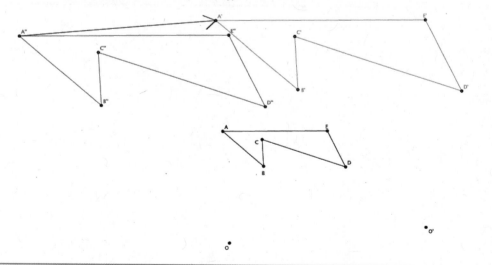

3. Given center O and triangle ABC, dilate the figure from center O by a scale factor of $r = \frac{1}{4}$. Label the dilated triangle $A'B'C'$.

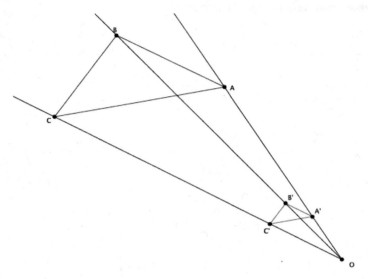

a. A line segment AB undergoes a dilation. Based on today's lesson, what will the image of the segment be?

The segment will dilate as a segment.

b. Angle $\angle GHI$ measures 78°. After a dilation, what will the measure of $\angle G'H'I'$ be? How do you know?

The measure of angle $\angle G'H'I'$ will be 78°. Dilations preserve angle measure, so it will remain the same size as $\angle GHI$.

Lesson 3: Examples of Dilations

Student Outcomes

- Students know that dilations map circles to circles and ellipses to ellipses with the same shape.
- Students know that to shrink or magnify a dilated figure back to its original size from center O with scale factor r you must dilate the figure by a scale factor of $\frac{1}{r}$.

Classwork

Opening Exercise

This is an optional section for those who would like to include a warm-up exercise in their lessons.

Example 1 (8 minutes)

Ask students to (a) describe how they would plan to dilate a circle and (b) conjecture about what the result will be when they dilate a circle. Consider asking them to collaborate with a partner and to share their plans and conjectures with the class. Then, you may have students attempt to dilate the circle on their own, based on their plans. As necessary, show students how to dilate a curved figure, namely, circle A.

- We want to find out how many points we will need to dilate in order to develop an image of Circle A, from center O at the origin of the graph, with scale factor $r = 3$.

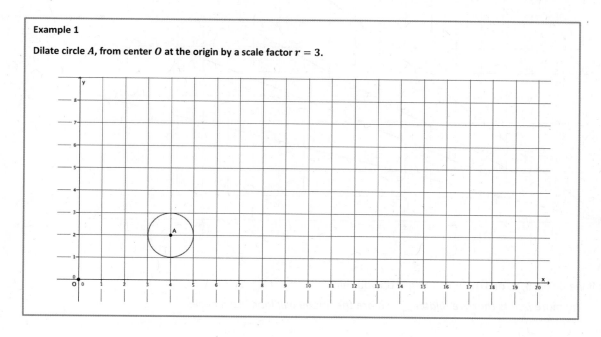

Example 1

Dilate circle A, from center O at the origin by a scale factor $r = 3$.

- Will 3 points be enough? Let's try.
- (Show a picture of 3 dilated points). If we connect these 3 dilated points, what image will we get?
  - *With just 3 points, the image will look like a triangle.*

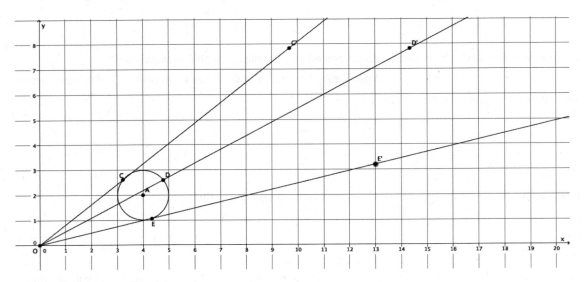

- What if we dilate a fourth point? Will that be enough? Let's try.
- (Show picture of 4 dilated points). If we connect these 4 dilated points, what image will we get?
  - *With 4 points, the image will look like a quadrilateral.*

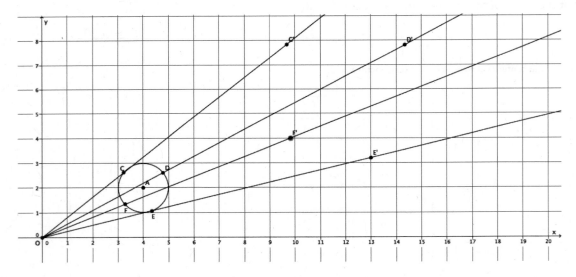

- What if we dilate 5, 6, or 10 points? What do you think?
  - *The more points that are dilated, the more the image will look like a circle.*

- (Show the picture with many dilated points).

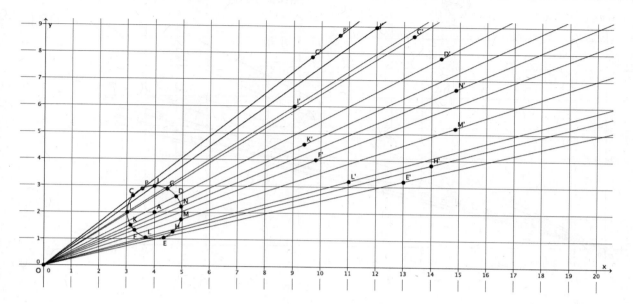

- Notice that the shape of the dilated image is now unmistakably a circle. Dilations map circles to circles, so it is important that when we dilate a circle we choose our points carefully.

- Would we have an image that looked like a circle if all of the points we dilated were located on just one part of the circle? For example, what if all of our points were located on just the top half of the circle? Would the dilated points produce an image of the circle?

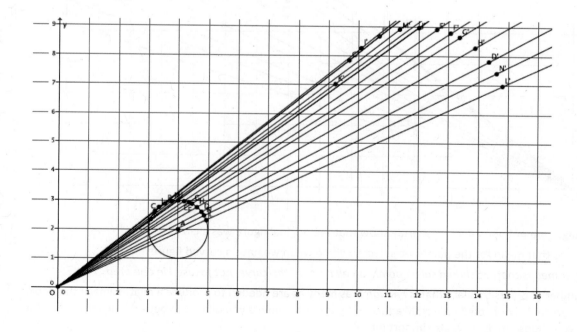

▪ Or, consider the image when we select points just on the lower half of the circle:

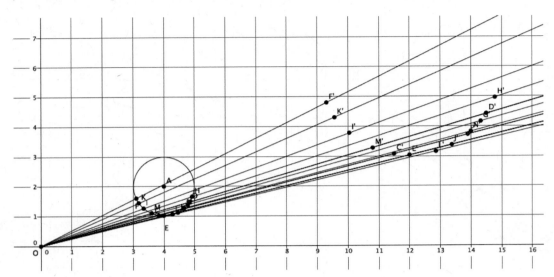

▪ Consider the image when the points are focused on just the sides of the circle:

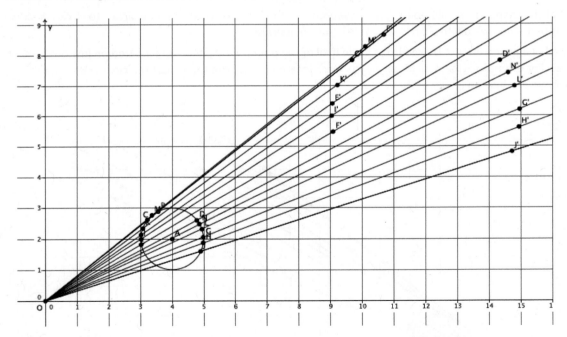

▪ The images are not *good enough* to truly show that the original figure was a circle.

▪ What does that mean for the points we select to dilate when we have a curved figure?

    ▫ *It means that we should select points on all parts of the curve, not focused in one area.*

▪ The number of points to dilate that is *enough* is as many as are needed to produce a dilated image that looks like the original. For curved figures, like this circle, the more points you dilate the better. The location of the points you choose to dilate is also important.

Exercises 1–2 (10 minutes)

Prior to this exercise, ask students to make a conjecture about what figure will result when we dilate an ellipse. Similarly, ask them to develop a plan for how they will perform the dilation. Then have students dilate an ellipse on the coordinate plane.

Exercises 1–2

1. Dilate ellipse E, from center O at the origin of the graph, with scale factor $r = 2$. Use as many points as necessary to develop the dilated image of ellipse E.

    Dilated image of E is shown in red below. Verify that students have dilated enough points to get an image that resembles an ellipse.

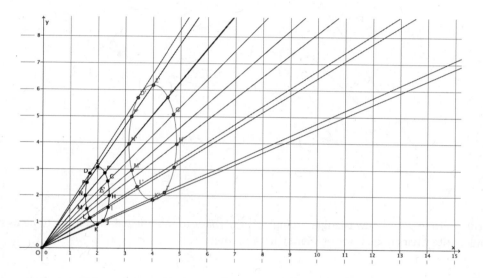

2. What shape was the dilated image?

    The dilated image was an ellipse. Dilations map ellipses to ellipses.

Lesson 3:	Examples of Dilations
Date:	10/16/13

Example 2 (4 minutes)

- In the picture below, we have a triangle ABC, that has been dilated from center O, by a scale factor of $r = \frac{1}{3}$. It is noted by $A'B'C'$.

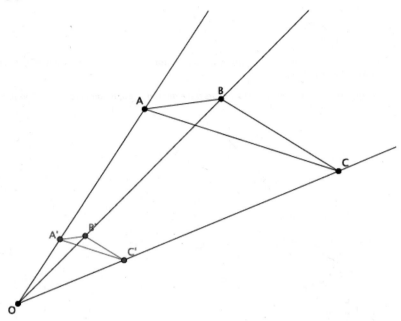

Ask students what we can do to map this new triangle, triangle $A'B'C'$, back to the original. Tell them to be as specific as possible. Students should write their conjectures or share with a partner.

- Let's use the definition of dilation and some side lengths to help us figure out how to map triangle $A'B'C'$ back onto triangle ABC. How are the lengths $|OA'|$ and $|OA|$ related?
  - *We know by the definition of dilation that $|OA'| = r|OA|$.*
- We know that $r = \frac{1}{3}$. Let's say that the length of OA is 6 units (we can pick any number, but 6 will make it easy for us to compute). What is the length of OA'?
  - *Since $|OA'| = \frac{1}{3}|OA|$, and we are saying that the length of OA is 6, then $|OA'| = \frac{1}{3} \times 6 = 2$, and $|OA'| = 2$ units.*

- Now since we want to dilate triangle $A'B'C'$ to the size of triangle ABC, we need to know what scale factor r is required so that $|OA| = r|OA'|$. What scale factor should we use and why?
  - *We need a scale factor $r = 3$ because we want $|OA| = r|OA'|$. Using the lengths from before, we have $6 = r \times 2$. Therefore, $r = 3$.*
- Now that we know the scale factor, what precise dilation would map triangle $A'B'C'$ onto triangle ABC?
  - *A dilation from center O with scale factor $r = 3$.*

Example 3 (4 minutes)

- In the picture below we have a triangle DEF, that has been dilated from center O, by a scale factor of $r = 4$. It is noted by $D'E'F'$.

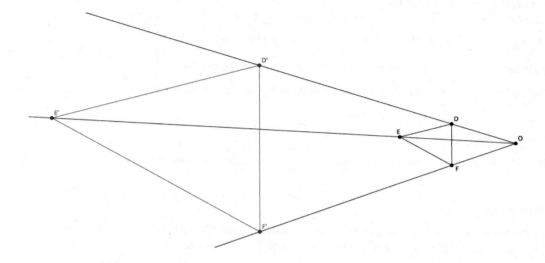

- Based on the example we just did, make a conjecture about how we could map this new triangle $\triangle\, D'E'F'$ back onto the original triangle.

Let students attempt to prove their conjectures on their own or with a partner. If necessary, use the scaffolding questions that follow.

- What's the difference between this problem and the last?
    - *This time the scale factor is greater than one, so we will need to shrink triangle $D'E'F'$ to the size of triangle DEF.*
- We know that $r = 4$. Let's say that the length of OF is 3 units. What is the length of OF'?
    - *Since $|OF'| = r|OF|$ and we are saying that the length of OF is 3, then $|OF'| = 4 \times 3 = 12$, and $|OF'| = 12$ units.*
- Now, since we want to dilate triangle $D'E'F'$ to the size of triangle DEF, we need to know what scale factor r is required so that $|OF| = r|OF'|$. What scale factor should we use and why?
    - *We need a scale factor $r = \frac{1}{4}$ because we want $|OF| = r|OF'|$. Using the lengths from before, we have $3 = r \times 12$. Therefore, $r = \frac{1}{4}$.*
- What precise dilation would make triangle $D'E'F'$ the same size as triangle DEF?
    - *A dilation from center O with scale factor $r = \frac{1}{4}$ would make triangle $D'E'F'$ the same size as triangle DEF.*

Discussion (4 minutes)

- In the last two problems, we needed to figure out the scale factor r that would bring a dilated figure back to the size of the original. In one case, the figure was dilated by a scale factor $r = \frac{1}{3}$ and to take the dilated figure back to the original size we needed to magnify it by a scale factor $r = 3$. In the other case, the figure was dilated by a scale factor $r = 4$ and to take the dilated figure back to the original size we needed to shrink it by a scale factor $r = \frac{1}{4}$. Is there any relationship between the scale factors in each case?

  - *The scale factors of 3 and $\frac{1}{3}$ are reciprocals of one another and so are 4 and $\frac{1}{4}$.*

- If a figure is dilated from a center O by a scale factor $r = 5$, what scale factor would shrink it back to its original size?

  - *A scale factor of $\frac{1}{5}$.*

MP.8

- If a figure is dilated from a center O by a scale factor $= \frac{2}{3}$, what scale factor would shrink it back to its original size?

  - *A scale factor of $\frac{3}{2}$.*

- Based on these examples and the two triangles we examined, determine a general rule or way of determining how to find the scale factor that will map a dilated figure back to its original size.

Give students time to write and talk with their partners. Lead a discussion that results in the crystallization of the rule below.

- To shrink or magnify a dilated figure from center O with scale factor r back to its original size you must dilate the figure by a scale factor of $\frac{1}{r}$.

Exercise 3 (5 minutes)

Allow students to work in pairs to describe sequences that map one figure onto another.

---

3. Triangle ABC has been dilated from center O by a scale factor of $r = \frac{1}{4}$ denoted by triangle $A'B'C'$. Using a ruler, verify that it would take a scale factor of $r = 4$ from center O to map triangle $A'B'C'$ onto triangle ABC.

   Verify that students have measured the lengths of segments from center O to each of the dilated points. Then verify that students have multiplied each of the lengths by 4 to see that it really is the length of the segments from center O to the original points.

   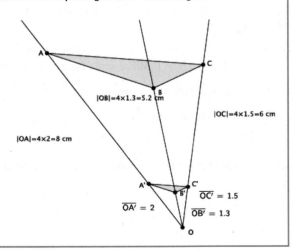

   $|OB| = 4 \times 1.3 = 5.2$ cm

   $|OC| = 4 \times 1.5 = 6$ cm

   $|OA| = 4 \times 2 = 8$ cm

   $\overline{OC'} = 1.5$

   $\overline{OA'} = 2$

   $\overline{OB'} = 1.3$

Lesson 3:   Examples of Dilations
Date: 10/16/13

40

Closing (5 minutes)

Summarize, or ask students to summarize, the main points from the lesson:

- We know that to dilate curved figures, we need to use a lot of points spread throughout the figure; therefore, we focused on the curves to produce a good image of the original figure.

- We know that if a figure is dilated by scale factor r, to bring the dilated figure back to the original size we must dilate it by a scale factor of $\frac{1}{r}$. For example, if a scale factor is $r = 4$, then to bring a dilated figure back to the original size, we must dilate it by a scale factor $r = \frac{1}{4}$.

Lesson Summary

Dilations map circles to circles and ellipses to ellipses.

If a figure is dilated by scale factor r, to bring the dilated figure back to the original size we must dilate it by a scale factor of $\frac{1}{r}$. For example, if a scale factor is $r = 4$, then to bring a dilated figure back to the original size, we must dilate it by a scale factor $r = \frac{1}{4}$.

Exit Ticket (5 minutes)

Name _____   Date_____

Lesson 3: Examples of Dilations

Exit Ticket

1. Dilate circle A from center O by a scale factor $= \frac{1}{2}$. Make sure to use enough points to make a good image of the original figure.

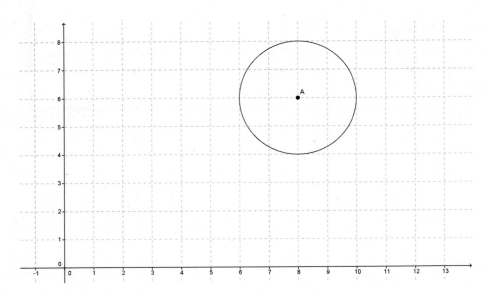

2.   What scale factor would magnify the dilated circle back to the original size of circle A? How do you know?

Exit Ticket Sample Solutions

1. Dilate circle A from center O by a scale factor $= \frac{1}{2}$. Make sure to use enough points to make a good image of the original figure.

   Student work shown below. Verify that students used enough points to produce an image similar to the original.

   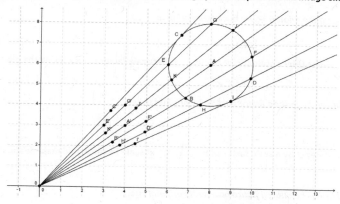

2. What scale factor would magnify the dilated circle back to the original size of circle A?

   A scale factor of $r = 2$ would bring the dilated circle back to the size of circle A. Since the circle was dilated by a scale factor of $r = \frac{1}{2}$, then to bring it back to its original size you must dilate by a scale factor that is the reciprocal of $\frac{1}{2}$, which is 2.

Problem Set Sample Solutions

Students practice dilating a curved figure and stating the scale factor that would bring a dilated figure back to its original size.

1. Dilate the figure from center O by a scale factor $r = 2$. Make sure to use enough points to make a good image of the original figure.

   Sample student work shown below. Verify that students used enough points to produce an image similar to the original.

   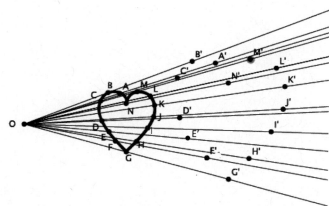

2. Describe the process for selecting points when dilating a curved figure.

When dilating a curved figure, you have to make sure to use a lot of points to produce a decent image of the original figure. You also have to make sure that the points you choose are not all concentrated in just one part of the figure.

3. A triangle ABC was dilated from center O by a scale factor of $r = 5$. What scale factor would shrink the dilated figure back to the original size?

A scale factor of $r = \frac{1}{5}$ would bring the dilated figure back to its original size.

4. A figure has been dilated from center O by a scale factor of $r = \frac{7}{6}$. What scale factor would shrink the dilated figure back to the original size?

A scale factor of $r = \frac{6}{7}$ would bring the dilated figure back to its original size.

5. A figure has been dilated from center O by a scale factor of $r = \frac{3}{10}$. What scale factor would magnify the dilated figure back to the original size?

A scale factor of $r = \frac{10}{3}$ would bring the dilated figure back to its original size.

Lesson 4: Fundamental Theorem of Similarity (FTS)

Student Outcomes

- Students experimentally verify the properties related to the Fundamental Theorem of Similarity (FTS).

Lesson Notes

The goal of this activity is to show students the properties of the Fundamental Theorem of Similarity (FTS), in terms of dilation. FTS states that given a dilation from center O, and points P and Q (points O, P, Q are not collinear), the segments formed when you connect P to Q, and P' to Q', are parallel. More surprising is that $|P'Q'| = r|PQ|$. That is, the segment PQ, even though it was not dilated as points P and Q were, dilates to segment $P'Q'$ and the length of $P'Q'$ is the length of PQ multiplied by the scale factor. The picture that follows is what the end product of the activity should look like. Also, consider showing the diagram (without the lengths of segments), and ask students to make conjectures about the relationships between the lengths of segments PQ and $P'Q'$.

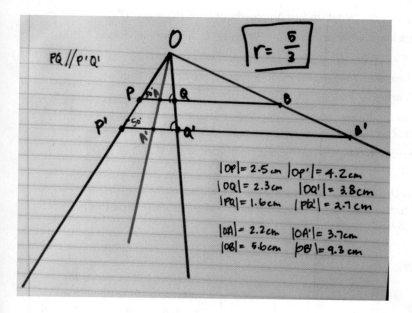

Classwork

Discussion (30 minutes)

For this discussion, students will need a piece of lined paper, a cm ruler, a protractor, and a four-function (or scientific) calculator.

- The last few days have focused on dilation. We now want to use what we know about dilation to come to some conclusions about the concept of similarity in general.

- A regular piece of notebook paper can be a great tool for discussing similarity. What do you notice about the lines on the notebook paper?
  - *The lines on the notebook paper are parallel, that is, they never intersect.*
- Keep that information in mind as we proceed through this activity. On the first line of your paper, mark a point O. We will use this as our center.
- From point O, draw a ray $\overrightarrow{OP}$. Mark the point P a few lines down from the center. Now, choose a P' farther down the ray, also on one of the lines of the notebook paper. For example, you may have placed point P, 3 lines down from the center, and point P', 5 lines down from the center.
- Use the definition of dilation to describe the lengths along this ray.
  - *By definition of dilation, $|OP'| = r|OP|$.*
- Recall that we can calculate the scale factor using the following computation: $\dfrac{|OP'|}{|OP|} = r$. In my example, the scale factor $r = \dfrac{5}{3}$ because OP' is 5 lines from the center, and OP is 3 lines down. On the top of your paper, write down the scale factor that you have used.
- Now draw another ray, $\overrightarrow{OQ}$. Use the same scale factor to mark points Q and Q'. In my example, I would place Q, 3 lines down, and Q', 5 lines down from the center.
- Now connect point P to point Q, and point P' to point Q'. What do you notice about lines PQ and $P'Q'$?
  - *The lines PQ and $P'Q'$ fall on the notebook lines, which means that PQ and $P'Q'$ are parallel lines.*
- Use your protractor to measure angles $\angle OPQ$ and $\angle OP'Q'$. What do you notice and why is it so?
  - *Angles $\angle OPQ$ and $\angle OP'Q'$ are equal in measure. They must be equal in measure because they are corresponding angles of parallel lines (PQ and $P'Q'$) cut by a transversal (ray $\overrightarrow{OP}$).*
- (Consider asking students to write their answers to the following question in their notebooks and to justify their answers.) Now, without using your protractor, what can you say about angles $\angle OQP$ and $\angle OQ'P'$?
  - *These angles are also equal for the same reason; they are corresponding angles of parallel lines (PQ and $P'Q'$) cut by a transversal (ray $\overrightarrow{OQ}$).*
- Use your cm ruler to measure the lengths OP and OP'. By definition of dilation, we expect $|OP'| = r|OP|$ (that is, we expect the length of OP' to be equal to the scale factor times the length of OP). Verify that this is true. Do the same for lengths OQ and OQ'.

  - *Sample of what student work may look like:*

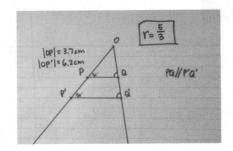

Note to Teacher:

A cm ruler will be easier for students to come up with a precise measurement. Also, let students know that it is okay if their measurements are off by a tenth of a cm because that difference can be attributed to human error.

- Bearing in mind that we have dilated from center O, points P and Q along their respective rays. Do you expect the segments PQ and $P'Q'$ to have the relationship $|P'Q'| = r|PQ|$?

  □ *(Some students may say yes. If they do, ask for a convincing argument. At this point they have knowledge of dilating segments, but that is not what we have done here. We have dilated points and then connected them to draw the segments.)*

- Measure the segments PQ and $P'Q'$ to see if they have the relationship $|P'Q'| = r|PQ|$.

- It should be somewhat surprising that in fact, segments PQ and $P'Q'$ enjoy the same properties as the segments that we actually dilated.

- Now mark a point A on line PQ, between points P and Q. Draw a ray from center O through point A and then mark A' on the line $P'Q'$. Do you think $|P'A'| = r|PA|$? Measure the segments and use your calculator to check.

  □ *Students should notice that these new segments also have the same properties as the dilated segments.*

- Now, mark a point B on the line PQ, but this time not on the segment PQ (i.e., not between points P and Q). Again, draw the ray from center O through point B and mark the point B' on the line $P'Q'$. Select any segment, AB, PB, QB, and verify that it has the same property as the others.

  □ *Sample of what student work may look like:*

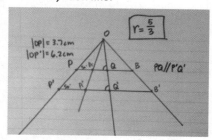

- Will this always happen, no matter the scale factor or placement of points $P, Q, A,$ and B?

  □ *Yes, I believe this is true. One main reason is that everyone in class probably picked different points and I'm sure many of us used different scale factors.*

- Describe the rule or pattern that we have discovered in your own words.

Encourage students to write and collaborate with a partner to answer this question. Once students have finished their work, lead a discussion that crystallizes the information in the theorem that follows.

- We have just experimentally verified the properties of the Fundamental Theorem of Similarity (FTS) in terms of dilation. Namely, that the parallel line segments connecting dilated points are related by the same scale factor as the segments that are dilated.

  Theorem: Given a dilation with center O and scale factor r, then for any two points P and Q in the plane so that $O, P,$ and Q are not collinear, the lines PQ and $P'Q'$ are parallel, where $P' = dilation(P)$ and $Q' = dilation(Q)$, and furthermore, $|P'Q'| = r|PQ|$.

Ask students to paraphrase the theorem in their own words or offer them the following version of the theorem: FTS states that given a dilation from center O, and points P and Q (points O, P, Q are not on the same line), the segments formed when you connect P to Q, and P' to Q', are parallel. More surprising is the fact that the segment PQ, even though it was not dilated as points P and Q were, dilates to segment $P'Q'$ and the length of $P'Q'$ is the length of PQ multiplied by the scale factor.

- Now that we are more familiar with properties of dilations and similarity, we will begin using these properties in the next few lessons to do things like verify similarity of figures.

Exercise (5 minutes)

Exercise

1.   In the diagram below, points R and S have been dilated from center O, by a scale factor of $r = 3$.

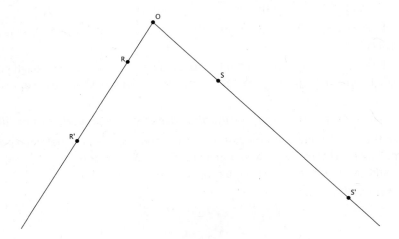

a.   If the length of $|OR| = 2.3$ cm, what is the length of $|OR'|$?

$|OR'| = 3(2.3) = 6.9$ *cm*

b.   If the length of $|OS| = 3.5$ cm, what is the length of $|OS'|$?

$|OS'| = 3(3.5) = 10.5$ *cm*

c.   Connect the point R to the point S and the point R' to the point S'. What do you know about lines RS and $R'S'$?

The lines RS and R'S' are parallel.

d.   What is the relationship between the length of RS and the length of $R'S'$?

The length of R'S' will be equal to the length of RS, times the scale factor of 3 (i.e., $|R'S'| = 3|RS|$).

e.   Identify pairs of angles that are equal in measure. How do you know they are equal?

$\angle ORS = \angle OR'S'$ and $\angle OSR = \angle OS'R'$. They are equal because they are corresponding angles of parallel lines cut by a transversal.

Closing (5 minutes)

Summarize, or ask students to summarize, the main points from the lesson:

- We know that the following is true: If $|OP'| = r|OP|$ and $|OQ'| = r|OQ|$, then $|P'Q'| = r|PQ|$. In other words, under a dilation from a center with scale factor r, a segment multiplied by the scale factor results in the length of the dilated segment.

- We also know that the lines PQ and $P'Q'$ are parallel.

- We verified the Fundamental Theorem of Similarity in terms of dilation using an experiment with notebook paper.

> **Lesson Summary**
>
> **Theorem:** Given a dilation with center O and scale factor r, then for any two points P and Q in the plane so that O, P, and Q are not collinear, the lines PQ and $P'Q'$ are parallel, where $P' = dilation(P)$ and $Q' = dilation(Q)$, and furthermore, $|P'Q'| = r|PQ|$.

Exit Ticket (5 minutes)

Name _____   Date_____

Lesson 4: Fundamental Theorem of Similarity (FTS)

Exit Ticket

Steven sketched the following diagram on graph paper. He dilated points B and C from point O. Answer the following questions based on his drawing:

1. What is the scale factor r? Show your work.

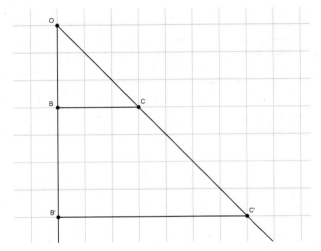

2. Verify the scale factor with a different set of segments.

3. Which segments are parallel? How do you know?

4. Are $\angle OBC = \angle OB'C'$ right angles? How do you know?

Exit Ticket Sample Solutions

1. **What is the scale factor r? Show your work.**

    $|OB'| = r|OB|$
    $7 = r \times 3$
    $\dfrac{7}{3} = r$

2. **Verify the scale factor with a different set of segments.**

    $|B'C'| = r|BC|$
    $7 = r \times 3$
    $\dfrac{7}{3} = r$

3. **Which segments are parallel? How do you know?**

    Segments BC and $B'C'$ are parallel since they lie on the grid lines of the paper, which are parallel.

4. **Are $\angle OBC = \angle OB'C'$ right angles? How do you know?**

    The grid lines on graph paper are perpendicular, and since perpendicular lines form right angles, $\angle OBC = \angle OB'C'$ are right angles.

Problem Set Sample Solutions

Students verify that the Fundamental Theorem of Similarity holds true when the scale factor r is $0 < r < 1$.

1. **Use a piece of notebook paper to verify the Fundamental Theorem of Similarity for a scale factor r that is $0 < r < 1$.**

    ✓   Mark a point O on the first line of notebook paper.

    ✓   Draw a ray, $\overrightarrow{OP}$. Mark the point P on a line, several lines down from the center. Mark the point P' on the ray, and on a line of the notebook paper, closer to O than you placed point P. This ensures that you have a scale factor that is $0 < r < 1$. Write your scale factor at the top of the notebook paper.

    ✓   Draw another ray, $\overrightarrow{OQ}$, and mark the points Q and Q' according to your scale factor.

    ✓   Connect points P and Q. Then, connect points P' and Q'.

    ✓   Place a point A on line PQ between points P and Q. Draw ray $\overrightarrow{OA}$. Mark the point A' at the intersection of line $P'Q'$ and ray $\overrightarrow{OA}$.

Sample student work shown in the picture below:

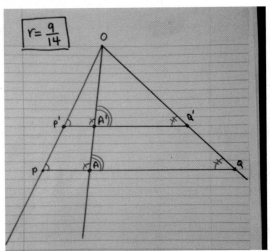

a.　Are lines PQ and $P'Q'$ parallel lines? How do you know?

Yes, the lines PQ and $P'Q'$ are parallel. The notebook lines are parallel and these lines fall on the notebook lines.

b.　Which, if any, of the following pairs of angles are equal? Explain.

　　i.　　$\angle OPQ$ and $\angle OP'Q'$

　　ii.　　$\angle OAQ$ and $\angle OA'Q'$

　　iii.　$\angle OAP$ and $\angle OA'P'$

　　iv.　$\angle OQP$ and $\angle OQ'P'$

All four pairs of angles are equal because each pair of angles are corresponding angles of parallel lines cut by a transversal. In each case, the parallel lines are PQ and $P'Q'$ and the transversal is their respective ray.

c.　Which, if any, of the following statements are true? Show your work to verify or dispute each statement.

　　i.　　$|OP'| = r|OP|$

　　ii.　　$|OQ'| = r|OQ|$

　　iii.　$|P'A'| = r|PA|$

　　iv.　$|A'Q'| = r|AQ|$

All four of the statements are true. Verify that students have shown that the length of the dilated segment was equal to the scale factor multiplied by the original segment length.

d.　Do you believe that the Fundamental Theorem of Similarity (FTS) is true even when the scale factor is $0 < r < 1$. Explain.

Yes, because I just experimentally verified the properties of FTS for when the scale factor is $0 < r < 1$.

2.   Caleb sketched the following diagram on graph paper. He dilated points B and C from center O.

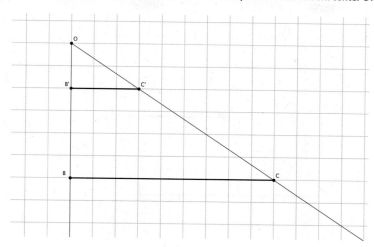

a.   What is the scale factor r? Show your work.

$$|OB'| = r|OB|$$
$$2 = r \times 6$$
$$\frac{2}{6} = r$$
$$\frac{1}{3} = r$$

b.   Verify the scale factor with a different set of segments.

$$|B'C'| = r|BC|$$
$$3 = r \times 9$$
$$\frac{3}{9} = r$$
$$\frac{1}{3} = r$$

c.   Which segments are parallel? How do you know?

Segment BC and $B'C'$ are parallel. They lie on the lines of the graph paper, which are parallel.

d.   Which angles are equal in measure? How do you know?

$\angle OB'C' = \angle OBC$, and $\angle OC'B' = \angle OCB$ because they are corresponding angles of parallel lines cut by a transversal.

3.   Points B and C were dilated from center O.

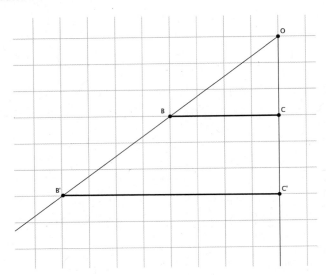

a.   **What is the scale factor r? Show your work.**

$$|OC'| = r|OC|$$
$$6 = r \times 3$$
$$\frac{6}{3} = r$$
$$2 = r$$

b.   **If the length of $|OB| = 5$, what is the length of $|OB'|$?**

$$|OB'| = r|OB|$$
$$|OB'| = 2 \times 5$$
$$|OB'| = 10$$

c.   **How does the perimeter of triangle OBC compare to the perimeter of triangle $OB'C'$?**

The perimeter of triangle OBC is 12 units and the perimeter of triangle $OB'C'$ is 24 units.

d.   **Did the perimeter of triangle $OB'C' = r \times$ (perimeter of triangle OBC)? Explain.**

Yes, the perimeter of triangle $OB'C'$ was twice the perimeter of triangle OBC, which makes sense because the dilation increased the length of each segment by a scale factor of 2. That means that each side of triangle $OB'C'$ was twice as long as each side of triangle OBC.

Lesson 5: First Consequences of FTS

Student Outcomes

- Students verify the converse of the Fundamental Theorem of Similarity experimentally.
- Students apply the Fundamental Theorem of Similarity to find the location of dilated points on the plane.

Classwork

Concept Development (5 minutes)

Begin by having students restate (in their own words) the Fundamental Theorem of Similarity that they learned in the last lesson.

- The Fundamental Theorem of Similarity states:

  Given a dilation with center O and scale factor r, then for any two points P and Q in the plane so that O, P, and Q are not collinear, the lines PQ and $P'Q'$ are parallel, where $P' = dilation(P)$ and $Q' = dilation(Q)$, and furthermore, $|P'Q'| = r|PQ|$.

The paraphrased version from the last lesson was: FTS states that given a dilation from center O, and points P and Q (points O, P, and Q are not on the same line), the segments formed when you connect P to Q, and P' to Q', are parallel. More surprising is the fact that the segment PQ, even though it was not dilated as points P and Q were, dilates to segment $P'Q'$ and the length of $P'Q'$ is the length of PQ multiplied by the scale factor.

- The converse of this theorem is also true. That is, *if lines PQ and $P'Q'$ are parallel, and $|P'Q'| = r|PQ|$, then from a center O, $P' = dilation(P)$, $Q' = dilation(Q)$, and $|OP'| = r|OP|$ and $|OQ'| = r|OQ|$.*

The converse of a theorem begins with the conclusion and produces the hypothesis. FTS concludes that lines are parallel and the length of $P'Q'$ is the length of PQ multiplied by the scale factor. The converse of FTS begins with the statement that the lines are parallel and the length of $P'Q'$ is the length of PQ multiplied by the scale factor. It ends with us knowing that the points P' and Q' are dilations of points P and Q by scale factor r and their respective segments, OP' and OQ' have lengths that are the scale factor multiplied by the original lengths of OP and OQ. Consider providing students with some simple examples of converses, and discuss whether or not the converses are true. For example, "If it is raining, then I have an umbrella." And its converse: "If I have an umbrella, then it is raining." In this case, the converse is not necessarily true. An example where the converse is true can be: "If we turn the faucet on, then water comes out" and the converse is "If water comes out, then the faucet is on."

- The converse of the theorem is basically the work we did in the last lesson, but backwards. In the last lesson, we knew about dilated points and found out that the segments between the points, P, Q, and their dilations P', Q', were dilated according the same scale factor, i.e., $|P'Q'| = r|PQ|$. We also discovered that the lines containing those segments were parallel, i.e., $PQ \parallel P'Q'$. The converse states that we are given parallel lines, PQ and $P'Q'$, where a segment, PQ, in one line is dilated by scale factor r to a segment, $P'Q'$, in the other line. With that knowledge, we can say something about the center of dilation and the relationship between segments OP' and OP, as well as segments OQ' and OQ.

In Exercise 1 below, students are given the information in the converse of FTS, i.e., $PQ \parallel P'Q'$ and $|P'Q'| = r|PQ|$. Students then verify the conclusion of the converse of FTS by measuring lengths of segments and their dilated images to make sure that they have the properties stated, i.e., $|OP'| = r|OP|$ and $|OQ'| = r|OQ|$.

Consider showing the diagram below and asking students to make conjectures about the relationship between OP' and OP, as well as OQ' and OQ. You can record the conjectures and possibly have the class vote on which they believe to be true.

In the diagram below, the lines containing segments PQ and $P'Q'$ are parallel, and the length of $P'Q'$ is equal to the length of PQ multiplied by the scale factor r, dilated from center O.

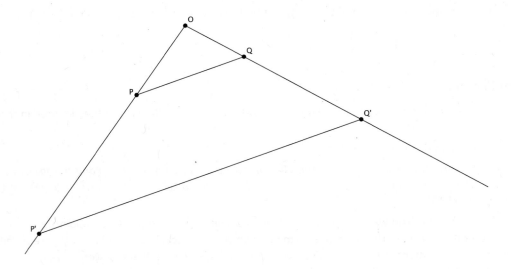

Exercise 1 (5 minutes)

Have students verify experimentally the validity of the converse of the theorem. They can work independently or in pairs.

Exercise 1

1. **In the diagram below, points P and Q have been dilated from center O by scale factor r. $PQ \parallel P'Q'$, $|PQ| = 5$ cm, and $|P'Q'| = 10$ cm.**

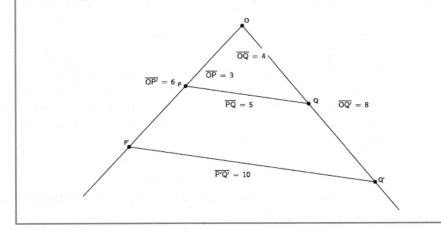

Scaffolding:

If students need help getting started, have them review the activity from Lesson 4. Ask what they should do to find the center O. Students should say: draw lines through PP' and QQ', the point of intersection is the center O.

a.   **Determine the scale factor r.**

According to FTS, $|P'Q'| = r|PQ|$. Therefore, $10 = r \times 5$, so $r = 2$.

b.   **Locate the center O of dilation. Measure the segments to verify that $|OP'| = r|OP|$ and $|OQ'| = r|OQ|$. Show your work below.**

Center O and measurements shown above.

$$|OP'| = r|OP|$$ $$|OQ'| = r|OQ|$$
$$6 = 2 \times 3$$ $$8 = 2 \times 4$$
$$6 = 6$$ $$8 = 8$$

Example 1 (5 minutes)

- Now that we know FTS and the converse of FTS in terms of dilations, we will practice using them to find the coordinates of points and dilated points on a plane. We will begin simply.

- In the diagram we have center O and ray $\overrightarrow{OA}$. We want to find the coordinates of point A'. We are given that the scale factor of dilation is $r = 2$.

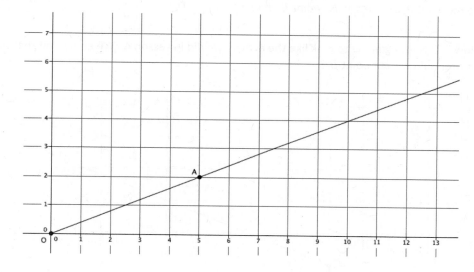

- To find A' we could use a ruler or compass to measure $|OA|$, but now that we know about FTS, we can do this another way. First, we should look for parallel lines that will help us locate point A'. How can we use the coordinate plane to ensure parallel lines?

  □ *We could use the vertical or horizontal lines of the coordinate plane to ensure lines are parallel. The coordinate plane is set up so that the lines never intersect. You could also think of those lines as translations of the x-axis and y-axis. Therefore, we are guaranteed to have parallel lines.*

- Let's use the x-axis as one of our rays. (Show picture below). Where should we place a point, B, on the ray along the x-axis?

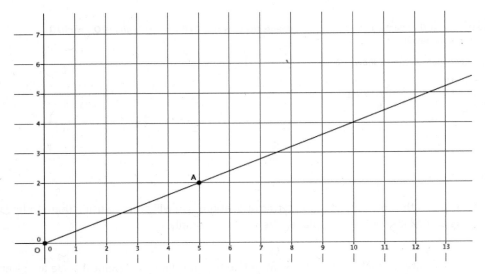

- □ *Since we are using the lines on the coordinate plane to verify parallelism, we should place point B directly below point A, on the x-axis. Point B should be at $(5, 0)$.*

- (Show picture below.) This is beginning to look like the activity we did in Lesson 4. We know that that scale factor $r = 2$. Where should we put point B'?

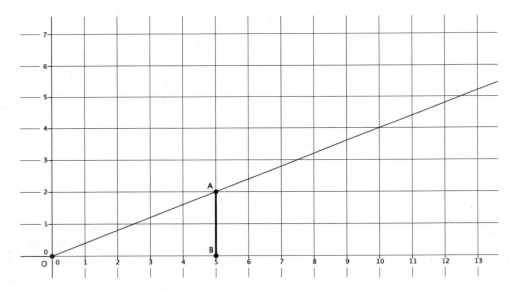

- □ *It is clear that the length of $|OB| = 5$; therefore, $|OB'| = 2 \times 5$, so the point B' should be placed at $(10, 0)$.*

- (Show picture below.) Now that we know the location of B', using FTS, what do we expect to be true about the lines containing segments AB and $A'B'$?

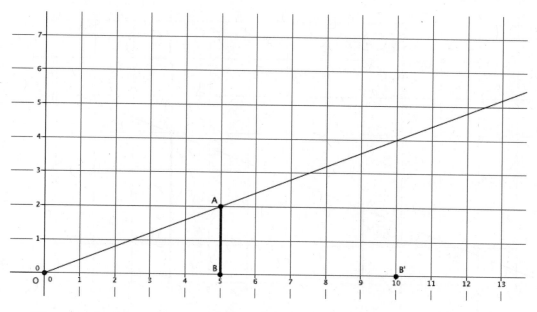

- We expect the lines containing segments AB and $A'B'$ to be parallel.

- (Show picture below.) Then what is the location of point A'?

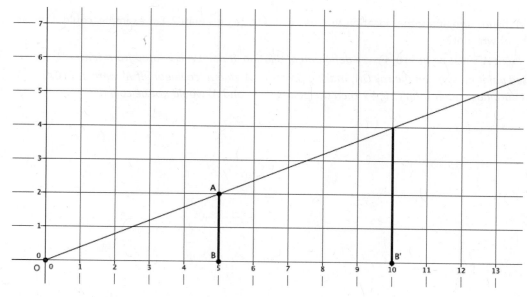

- Point A' will be located at $(10, 4)$.

- (Show picture below.) Could point A' be located anywhere else? Specifically, could A' have a different x-coordinate? Why or why not?

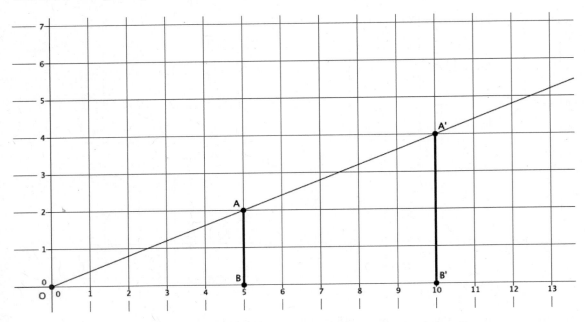

  - No. Point A' must be at $(10, 4)$. If it had another x-coordinate then lines AB and $A'B'$ would not be parallel.

- Could point A' be located at another location that has 10 as its x-coordinate? For example, could A' be at $(10, 5)$? Why or why not?

  - No. Point A' must be at $(10, 4)$. By definition of dilation, if point A is dilated from center O, then the dilated point must be on the ray $\overrightarrow{OA}$, making points O, A, and A' collinear. If A' were at $(10, 5)$ or at any coordinate other than $(10, 4)$, then the points O, A, and A' would not be collinear.

Exercise 2 (3 minutes)

Students work independently to find the location of point A' on the coordinate plane.

Exercise 2

2. In the diagram below, you are given center O and ray $\overrightarrow{OA}$. Point A is dilated by a scale factor $r = 4$. Use what you know about FTS to find the location of point A'.

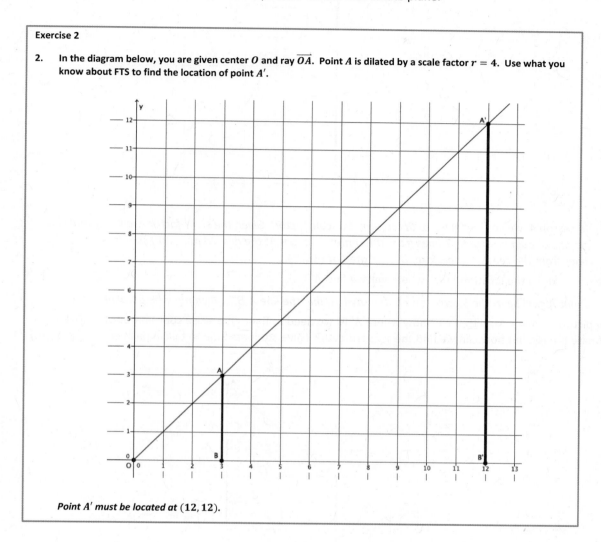

Point A' must be located at $(12, 12)$.

Example 2 (6 minutes)

▪ In the diagram we have center O and ray $\overrightarrow{OA}$. We are given that the scale factor of dilation is $r = \frac{11}{7}$. We want to find the precise coordinates of point A'. Based on our previous work, we know exactly how to begin. Draw a ray $\overrightarrow{OB}$ along the x-axis and mark a point B, directly below point A, on the ray $\overrightarrow{OB}$. (Show picture below.) The question now is: How do we locate B'? Think about our work from Lesson 4.

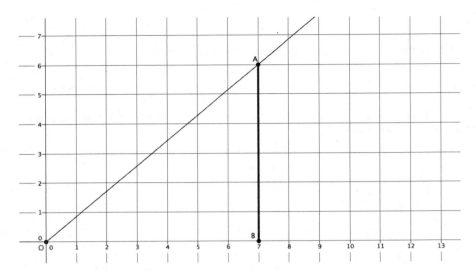

- In Lesson 4, we counted lines to determine the scale factor. Given the scale factor, we know that the point B should be exactly 7 lines from the center O, and that the dilated point, B', should be exactly 11 lines from the center. Therefore, B' is located at (11, 0).

- Now that we know the location of B', where will we find A'?

  - Point A' will be at the intersection of the ray $\overrightarrow{OA}$, and the line A'B', which must be parallel to AB.

- (Show picture below.) Now that we know where A' is, we need to find the precise coordinates of it. The x-coordinate is easy, but how can we find the y-coordinate? (Give students time to talk in pairs or small groups.)

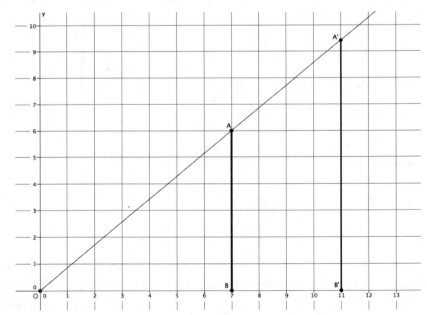

- The y-coordinate will be the exact length of the segment A'B'. To find that length, we can use what we know about the length of AB and the scale factor since $|A'B'| = r|AB|$.

- The length of A'B' will give us the y-coordinate. Then $|A'B'| = \frac{11}{7} \times 6 = \frac{66}{7} \approx 9.4$. That means that the location of A' is (11, 9.4).

Exercise 3 (4 minutes)

Students work independently or in pairs to find the location of point A' on the coordinate plane.

Exercise 3

3. In the diagram below, you are given center O and ray $\overrightarrow{OA}$. Point A is dilated by a scale factor $r = \frac{5}{12}$. Use what you know about FTS to find the location of point A'.

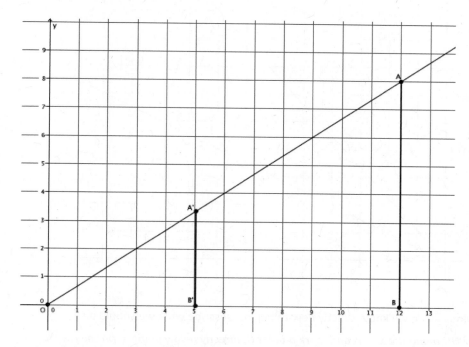

The x-coordinate of A' is 5. The y-coordinate will be equal to the length of segment $A'B'$. Since $|A'B'| = r|AB|$, then $|A'B'| = \frac{5}{12} \times 8 = \frac{40}{12} \approx 3.3$. The location of A' is $(5, 3.3)$.

Example 3 (8 minutes)

- In the diagram below we have center O and rays $\overrightarrow{OA}$ and $\overrightarrow{OB}$. We are given that the scale factor of dilation is $r = \frac{5}{8}$. We want to find the precise coordinates of points A' and B'.

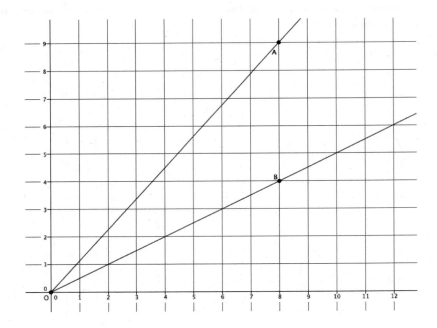

- Based on our previous work, we know exactly how to begin. Describe what we should do.

  □ *Draw a ray $\overrightarrow{OC}$ along the x-axis and mark a point C, directly below point A, on the ray $\overrightarrow{OC}$.*

▪ (Show picture below.) Based on our work in Lesson 4, and our knowledge of FTS, we know that points B and B' along ray $\overrightarrow{OB}$ enjoy the same properties we have been using in the last few problems. Let's begin by finding the coordinates of A'. What should we do first?

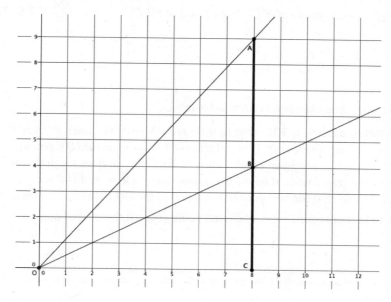

  ▫ First, we need to place the points $'$, B', and C' on their respective rays by using the scale factor. Since the scale factor $r = \frac{5}{8}$, A', B', and C' will have an x-coordinate of 5. (Also, it is 5 lines from the center.)

▪ (Show picture below.) Let's first find the coordinates of A'. What do we need to do to find the y-coordinate of A'?

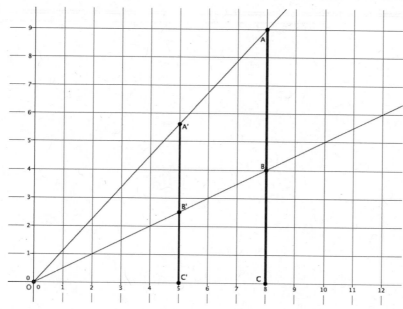

  ▫ The y-coordinate of A' will be the length of the segment $A'C'$. We can calculate that length by using what we know about segment AC and the scale factor.

- The y-coordinate of A' is $|A'C'| = r|AC| = \frac{5}{8} \times 9 = \frac{45}{8} \approx 5.6$. Then the location of A' is $(5, 5.6)$.
- Work with a partner to find the y-coordinate of B'.

  □ *The y-coordinate of B' is the length of $B'C'$. Then $|B'C'| = r|BC| = \frac{5}{8} \times 4 = \frac{20}{8} = 2.5$. The location of B' is $(5, 2.5)$.*

Closing (4 minutes)

Summarize, or ask students to summarize, the main points from the lesson:

- We experimentally verified the converse of FTS. That is, if we are given parallel lines, PQ and $P'Q'$, and know $|P'Q'| = r|PQ|$, then we know from a center O, $P' = dilation(P)$, $Q' = dilation(Q)$, and $|OP'| = r|OP|$ and $|OQ'| = r|OQ|$. In other words, if we are given parallel lines PQ and $P'Q'$, and we know that the length of $P'Q'$ is equal to PQ multiplied by the scale factor, then we also know that the length of OP' is equal to OP multiplied by the scale factor, and that the length of OQ' is equal to the OQ multiplied by the scale factor.
- We know how to use FTS to find the coordinates of dilated points, even if the dilated point is not on an intersection of graph lines.

Lesson Summary

Converse of the Fundamental Theorem of Similarity:

If lines PQ and $P'Q'$ are parallel, and $|P'Q'| = r|PQ|$, then from a center O, $P' = dilation(P)$, $Q' = dilation(Q)$, and $|OP'| = r|OP|$ and $|OQ'| = r|OQ|$.

To find the coordinates of a dilated point, we must use what we know about FTS, dilation, and scale factor.

Exit Ticket (5 minutes)

| **Lesson 5:** | First Consequences of FTS |
| **Date:** | 10/16/13 |

Name _____   Date_____

Lesson 5: First Consequences of FTS

Exit Ticket

In the diagram below, you are given center O and ray $\overrightarrow{OA}$. Point A is dilated by a scale factor $r = \frac{6}{4}$. Use what you know about FTS to find the location of point A'.

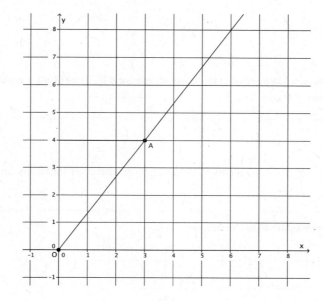

Exit Ticket Sample Solutions

In the diagram below, you are given center O and ray $\overrightarrow{OA}$. Point A is dilated by a scale factor $r = \frac{6}{4}$. Use what you know about FTS to find the location of point A'.

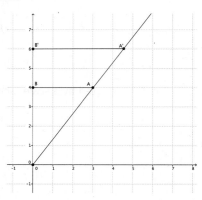

The y-coordinate of A' is 6. The x-coordinate will be equal to the length of segment $A'B'$. Since $|A'B'| = r|AB|$, then $|A'B'| = \frac{6}{4} \times 3 = \frac{18}{4} = 4.5$. The location of A' is $(4.5, 6)$.

Problem Set Sample Solutions

Students practice using the first consequences of FTS in terms of dilated points and their locations on the coordinate plane.

1. Dilate point A, located at $(3, 4)$ from center O, by a scale factor $r = \frac{5}{3}$.

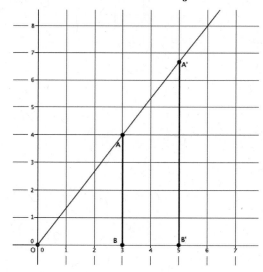

What is the precise location of point A'?

The y-coordinate of point A' will be the length of $A'B'$. Since $|A'B'| = r|AB|$, then $|A'B'| = \frac{5}{3} \times 4 = \frac{20}{3} \approx 6.7$. The location of point A' is $(5, 6.7)$.

2. Dilate point A, located at $(9, 7)$ from center O, by a scale factor $r = \frac{4}{9}$. Then dilate point B, located at $(9, 5)$ from center O, by a scale factor of $r = \frac{4}{9}$. What are the coordinates of A' and B'? Explain.

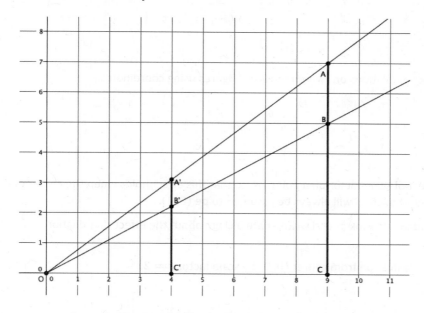

The y-coordinate of point A' will be the length of $A'C'$. Since $|A'C'| = r|AC|$, then $|A'C'| = \frac{4}{9} \times 7 = \frac{28}{9} \approx 3.1$. The location of point A' is $(4, 3.1)$. The y-coordinate of point B' will be the length of $B'C'$. Since $|B'C'| = r|BC|$, then $|B'C'| = \frac{4}{9} \times 5 = \frac{20}{9} \approx 2.2$. The location of point B' is $(4, 2.2)$.

3. Explain how you used the Fundamental Theorem of Similarity in Problems 1 and 2.

Using what I knew about scale factor, I was able to determine the placement of points A' and B', but I didn't know the actual coordinates. So, one of the ways that FTS was used was actually in terms of the converse of FTS. I had to make sure I had parallel lines. Since the lines of the coordinate plane guarantee parallel lines, I knew that $|A'C'| = r|AC|$. Then since I knew the length of AC and the scale factor, I could find the precise location of A'. The precise location of B' was found in a similar way, but using $|B'C'| = r|BC|$.

Lesson 6: Dilations on the Coordinate Plane

Student Outcomes

- Students describe the effect of dilations on two-dimensional figures using coordinates.

Classwork

Example 1 (7 minutes)

Students learn the multiplicative effect of scale factor on a point. Note that this effect holds when the center of dilation is the origin. In this lesson, the center of dilation will always be assumed to be $(0,0)$.

Show the diagram below and ask students to look at and write/share a claim about the effect that dilation has on the coordinates of dilated points.

- The graph below represents a dilation from center $(0,0)$ by scale factor $r = 2$.

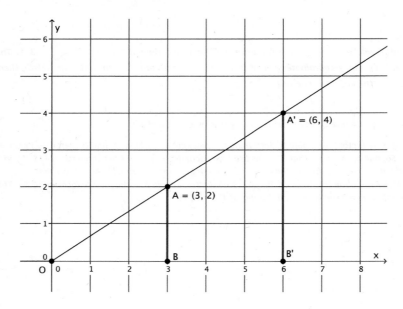

Show them the second diagram below so students can check if their claim was correct. Give students time to verify the claim that they made about the above graph, with the one below. Then have students share their claims with the class. Use the discussion that follows to crystallize what students observed.

- The graph below represents a dilation from center $(0, 0)$ by scale factor $r = 4$.

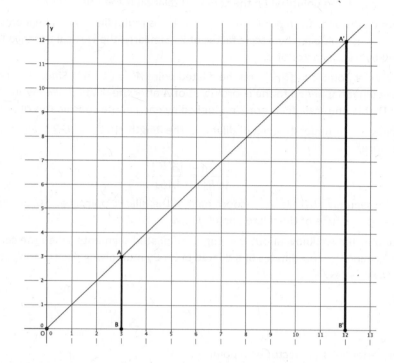

- In Lesson 5 we found the location of a dilated point by using the knowledge of dilation and scale factor, as well as the lines of the coordinate plane to ensure equal angles to find the coordinates of the dilated point. For example, we were given the point $A = (5, 2)$ and told the scale factor of dilation was $r = 2$. We created the following picture and determined the location of A' to be $(10, 4)$.

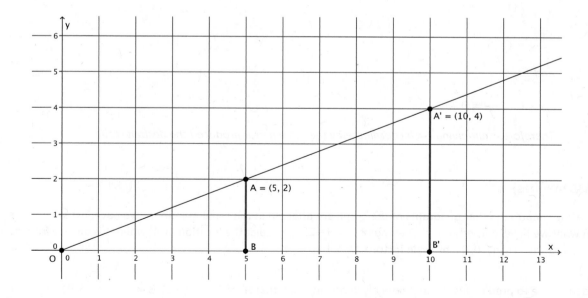

- We can use this information, and the observations we made at the beginning of class, to develop a shortcut for finding the coordinates of dilated points when the center of dilation is the origin.

- Notice that the horizontal distance from the y-axis to point A was multiplied by a scale factor of 2. That is, the x-coordinate of point A was multiplied by a scale factor of 2. Similarly, the vertical distance from the x-axis to point A was multiplied by a scale factor of 2.

- Here are the coordinates of point $A = (5, 2)$ and the dilated point $A' = (10, 4)$. Since the scale factor was 2, we can more easily see what happened to the coordinates of A after the dilation if we write the coordinates of A' as $(2 \times 5, 2 \times 2)$. That is, the scale factor of 2 multiplied by each of the coordinates of point A to get A'.

MP.8

- The reasoning goes back to our understanding of dilation. The length $r|OB| = |OB'|$, and the length $r|AB| = |A'B'|$; therefore,

$$ r = \frac{|OB'|}{|OB|} = \frac{|A'B'|}{|AB|} $$

where the length of the segment $|OB'|$ is the x-coordinate of the dilated point, i.e., 10, and the length of the segment $|A'B'|$ is the y-coordinate of the dilated point, i.e., 4.

In other words, based on what we know about the lengths of dilated segments, when the center of dilation is the origin, we can determine the coordinates of a dilated point by multiplying each of the coordinates in the original point by the scale factor.

Example 2 (3 minutes)

Students learn the multiplicative effect of scale factor on a point.

- Let's look at another example from Lesson 5. We were given the point $A = (7, 6)$, and asked to find the location of the dilated point A' when $r = \frac{11}{7}$. Our work on this problem led us to coordinates of $(11, 9.4)$ for point A'. Verify that we would get the same result if we multiply each of the coordinates of point A by the scale factor.

  □ $A' = \left(\frac{11}{7} \times 7, \frac{11}{7} \times 6\right)$

  $\frac{11}{7} \times 7 = 11$

  and

  $\frac{11}{7} \times 6 = \frac{66}{7} = 9.4$

  Therefore, multiplying each coordinate by the scale factor produced the desired result.

Example 3 (5 minutes)

- The coordinates in other quadrants of the graph are affected in the same manner as we have just seen. Based on what we have learned so far, given point $A = (-2, 3)$, predict the location of A' when A is dilated from a center at the origin, $(0, 0)$, by scale factor $r = 3$.

Provide students time to predict, justify, and possibly verify, in pairs, that $A' = (3 \times (-2), 3 \times 3) = (-6, 9)$. Verify the fact on the coordinate plane, or have students share their verification with the class.

- As before, mark a point B on the x-axis. Then, $|OB'| = 3|OB|$. Where is B' located?

  □ *Since the length of $|OB| = 2$, then $|OB'| = 3 \times 2 = 6$. But we are looking at a distance to the left of zero; therefore, the location of B' is $(-6, 0)$.*

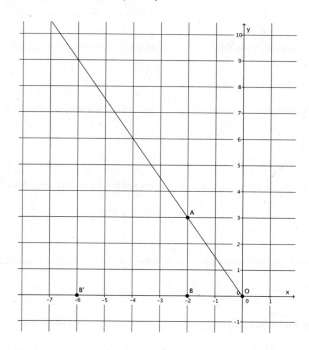

- Now that we know where B' is, we can easily find the location of A'. It will be on the ray $\overrightarrow{OA}$, but at what location?

  □ *The location of $A' = (-6, 9)$, as desired.*

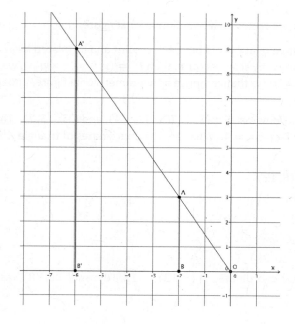

Exercises 1–5 (5 minutes)

Students complete Exercises 1–5 independently.

Exercises 1–5

1. Point $A = (7, 9)$ is dilated from the origin by scale factor $r = 6$. What are the coordinates of point A'?

   $A' = (6 \times 7, 6 \times 9) = (42, 54)$

2. Point $B = (-8, 5)$ is dilated from the origin by scale factor $r = \frac{1}{2}$. What are the coordinates of point B'?

   $B' = \left(\frac{1}{2} \times (-8), \frac{1}{2} \times 5\right) = \left(-4, \frac{5}{2}\right)$

3. Point $C = (6, -2)$ is dilated from the origin by scale factor $r = \frac{3}{4}$. What are the coordinates of point C'?

   $C' = \left(\frac{3}{4} \times 6, \frac{3}{4} \times (-2)\right) = \left(\frac{9}{2}, -\frac{3}{2}\right)$

4. Point $D = (0, 11)$ is dilated from the origin by scale factor $r = 4$. What are the coordinates of point D'?

   $D' = (4 \times 0, 4 \times 11) = (0, 44)$

5. Point $E = (-2, -5)$ is dilated from the origin by scale factor $r = \frac{3}{2}$. What are the coordinates of point E'?

   $E' = \left(\frac{3}{2} \times (-2), \frac{3}{2} \times (-5)\right) = \left(-3, -\frac{15}{2}\right)$

Example 4 (4 minutes)

Students learn the multiplicative effect of scale factor on a two dimensional figure.

- Now that we know the multiplicative relationship between a point and its dilated location (i.e., if point $P = (p_1, p_2)$ is dilated from the origin by scale factor r, then $P' = (r \times p_1, r \times p_2)$), we can quickly find the coordinates of any point, including those that comprise a two-dimensional figure, under a dilation of any scale factor.

- For example, triangle ABC has coordinates $A = (2, 3), B = (-3, 4)$, and $C = (5, 7)$. The triangle is being dilated from the origin with scale factor $r = 4$. What are the coordinates of triangle $A'B'C'$?

- First, find the coordinates of A'.
  - $A' = (4 \times 2, 4 \times 3) = (8, 12)$

- Next, locate the coordinates of B'.
  - $B' = (4 \times (-3), 4 \times 4) = (-12, 16)$

- Finally, locate the coordinates of C'.
  - $C' = (4 \times 5, 4 \times 7) = (20, 28)$

- Therefore, triangle $A'B'C'$ will have coordinates of $(8, 12), (-12, 16)$, and $(20, 28)$, respectively.

Lesson 6: Dilations on the Coordinate Plane
Date: 10/16/13

Example 5 (4 minutes)

Students learn the multiplicative effect of scale factor on a two-dimensional figure.

- Parallelogram $ABCD$ has coordinates of $(-2, 4)$, $(4, 4)$, $(2, -1)$, and $(-4, -1)$, respectively. Find the coordinates of Parallelogram $A'B'C'D'$ after a dilation from the origin with a scale factor $r = \frac{1}{2}$.

    □ $A' = \left(\frac{1}{2} \times (-2), \frac{1}{2} \times 4\right) = (-1, 2)$

    □ $B' = \left(\frac{1}{2} \times 4, \frac{1}{2} \times 4\right) = (2, 2)$

    □ $C' = \left(\frac{1}{2} \times 2, \frac{1}{2} \times (-1)\right) = \left(1, -\frac{1}{2}\right)$

    □ $D' = \left(\frac{1}{2} \times (-4), \frac{1}{2} \times (-1)\right) = \left(-2, -\frac{1}{2}\right)$

- Therefore, parallelogram $A'B'C'D'$ will have coordinates of $(-1, 2)$, $(2, 2)$, $\left(1, -\frac{1}{2}\right)$, and $\left(-2, -\frac{1}{2}\right)$, respectively.

Exercises 6–8 (9 minutes)

Students complete Exercises 6–8 independently.

Exercises 6–8

6. The coordinates of triangle ABC are shown on the coordinate plane below. The triangle is dilated from the origin by scale factor $r = 12$. Identify the coordinates of the dilated triangle $A'B'C'$.

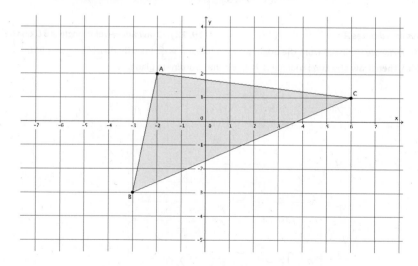

Point $A = (-2, 2)$, then $A' = (12 \times (-2), 12 \times 2) = (-24, 24)$

Point $B = (-3, -3)$, then $B' = (12 \times (-3), 12 \times (-3)) = (-36, -36)$

Point $C = (6, 1)$, then $C' = (12 \times 6, 12 \times 1) = (72, 12)$

The coordinates of $\triangle A'B'C'$ are $(-24, 24)$, $(-36, -36)$, and $(72, 12)$, respectively.

 **COMMON CORE** | Lesson 6: | Dilations on the Coordinate Plane
| Date: | 10/16/13

7. Figure $DEFG$ is shown on the coordinate plane below. The figure is dilated from the origin by scale factor $r = \frac{2}{3}$. Identify the coordinates of the dilated figure $D'E'F'G'$, then draw and label figure $D'E'F'G'$ on the coordinate plane.

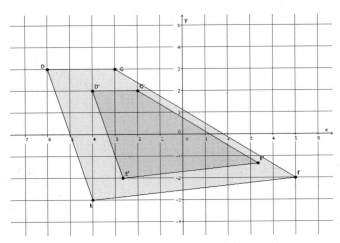

Point $D = (-6, 3)$, then $D' = \left(\frac{2}{3} \times (-6), \frac{2}{3} \times 3\right) = (-4, 2)$

Point $E = (-4, -3)$, then $E' = \left(\frac{2}{3} \times (-4), \frac{2}{3} \times (-3)\right) = \left(-\frac{8}{3}, -2\right)$

Point $F = (5, -2)$, then $F' = \left(\frac{2}{3} \times 5, \frac{2}{3} \times (-2)\right) = \left(\frac{10}{3}, -\frac{4}{3}\right)$

Point $G = (-3, 3)$, then $G' = \left(\frac{2}{3} \times (-3), \frac{2}{3} \times 3\right) = (-2, 2)$

The coordinates of figure $D'E'F'G'$ are $(-4, 2)$, $\left(-\frac{8}{3}, -2\right)$, $\left(\frac{10}{3}, -\frac{4}{3}\right)$, and $(-2, 2)$, respectively.

8. The triangle ABC has coordinates $A = (3, 2)$, $B = (12, 3)$, and $C = (9, 12)$. Draw and label triangle ABC on the coordinate plane. The triangle is dilated from the origin by scale factor $r = \frac{1}{3}$. Identify the coordinates of the dilated triangle $A'B'C'$, then draw and label triangle $A'B'C'$ on the coordinate plane.

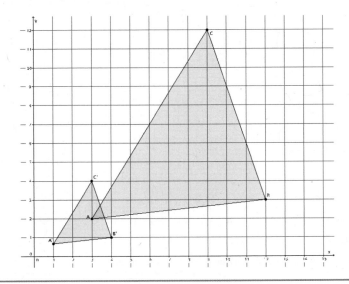

> **Point A = (3, 2)**, then $A' = \left(\frac{1}{3} \times 3, \frac{1}{3} \times 2\right) = \left(1, \frac{2}{3}\right)$
>
> **Point B = (12, 3)**, then $B' = \left(\frac{1}{3} \times 12, \frac{1}{3} \times 3\right) = (4, 1)$
>
> **Point C = (9, 12)**, then $C' = \left(\frac{1}{3} \times 9, \frac{1}{3} \times 12\right) = (3, 4)$
>
> **The coordinates of △ A'B'C' are** $\left(1, \frac{2}{3}\right)$, **(4, 1), and (3, 4), respectively.**

Closing (4 minutes)

Summarize, or ask students to summarize, the main points from the lesson:

- We know that we can calculate the coordinates of a dilated point given the coordinates of the original point and the scale factor.

- To find the coordinates of a dilated point we must multiply both the x-coordinate and the y-coordinate by the scale factor of dilation.

- If we know how to find the coordinates of a dilated point, we can find the location of a dilated triangle or other two dimensional figure.

Lesson Summary

Dilation has a multiplicative effect on the coordinates of a point in the plane. Given a point (x, y) in the plane, a dilation from the origin with scale factor r moves the point (x, y) to $(r \times x, r \times y)$.

For example, if a point $(3, -5)$ in the plane is dilated from the origin by a scale factor of $r = 4$, then the coordinates of the dilated point are $(4 \times 3, 4 \times (-5)) = (12, -20)$.

Exit Ticket (4 minutes)

Name _____   Date _____

Lesson 6: Dilations on the Coordinate Plane

Exit Ticket

1. The point $A = (7, 4)$ is dilated from the origin by a scale factor $r = 3$. What are the coordinates of A'?

2. The triangle ABC, shown on the coordinate plane below, is dilated from the origin by scale factor $r = \frac{1}{2}$. What is the location of triangle $A'B'C'$? Draw and label it on the coordinate plane.

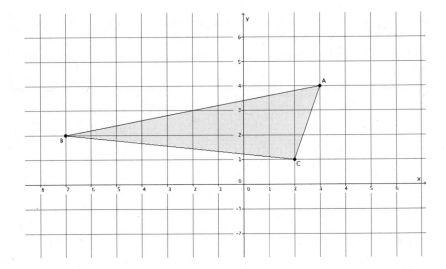

Exit Ticket Sample Solutions

1. The point $A = (7, 4)$ is dilated from the origin by a scale factor $r = 3$. What are the coordinates of A'?

   Point $A = (7, 4)$, then $A' = (3 \times 7, 3 \times 4) = (21, 12)$.

2. The triangle ABC, shown on the coordinate plane below, is dilated from the origin by scale factor $r = \frac{1}{2}$. What is the location of triangle $A'B'C'$?

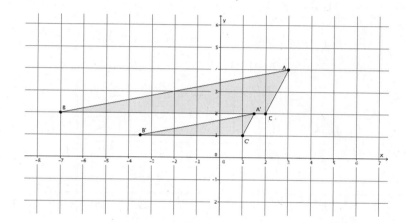

   Point $A = (3, 4)$, then $A' = \left(\frac{1}{2} \times 3, \frac{1}{2} \times 4\right) = \left(\frac{3}{2}, 2\right)$.

   Point $B = (-7, 2)$, then $B' = \left(\frac{1}{2} \times (-7), \frac{1}{2} \times 2\right) = \left(-\frac{7}{2}, 1\right)$.

   Point $C = (2, 2)$, then $C' = \left(\frac{1}{2} \times 2, \frac{1}{2} \times 2\right) = (1, 1)$.

   The coordinates of $\triangle A'B'C'$ are $\left(\frac{3}{2}, 2\right)$, $\left(-\frac{7}{2}, 1\right)$, and $(1, 1)$, respectively.

Problem Set Sample Solutions

Students practice finding the coordinates of dilated points of two-dimensional figures.

1. Triangle ABC is shown on the coordinate plane below. The triangle is dilated from the origin by scale factor $r = 4$. Identify the coordinates of the dilated triangle $A'B'C'$.

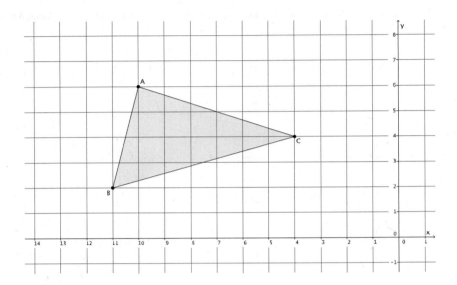

Point $A = (-10, 6)$, then $A' = (4 \times (-10), 4 \times 6) = (-40, 24)$.

Point $B = (-11, 2)$, then $B' = (4 \times (-11), 4 \times 2) = (-44, 8)$.

Point $C = (-4, 4)$, then $C' = (4 \times (-4), 4 \times 4) = (-16, 16)$.

The coordinates of $\triangle A'B'C'$ are $(-40, 24), (-44, 8)$, and $(-16, 16)$, respectively.

2. Triangle ABC is shown on the coordinate plane below. The triangle is dilated from the origin by scale factor $r = \frac{5}{4}$. Identify the coordinates of the dilated triangle $A'B'C'$.

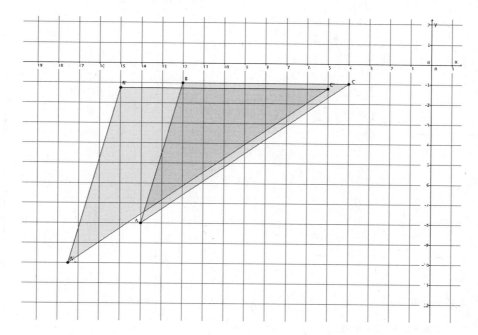

Point $A = (-14, -8)$, then $A' = \left(\frac{5}{4} \times (-14), \frac{5}{4} \times (-8)\right) = \left(-\frac{35}{2}, -10\right)$.

Point $B = (-12, -1)$, then $B' = \left(\frac{5}{4} \times (-12), \frac{5}{4} \times (-1)\right) = \left(-15, -\frac{5}{4}\right)$.

Point $C = (-4, -1)$, then $C' = \left(\frac{5}{4} \times (-4), \frac{5}{4} \times (-1)\right) = \left(-5, -\frac{5}{4}\right)$.

The coordinates of $\triangle A'B'C'$ are $\left(-\frac{35}{2}, -10\right)$, $\left(-15, -\frac{5}{4}\right)$, and $\left(-5, -\frac{5}{4}\right)$, respectively.

3. The triangle ABC has coordinates $A = (6, 1)$, $B = (12, 4)$, and $C = (-6, 2)$. The triangle is dilated from the origin by a scale factor $r = \frac{1}{2}$. Identify the coordinates of the dilated triangle $A'B'C'$.

Point $A = (6, 1)$, then $A' = \left(\frac{1}{2} \times 6, \frac{1}{2} \times 1\right) = \left(3, \frac{1}{2}\right)$.

Point $B = (12, 4)$, then $B' = \left(\frac{1}{2} \times 12, \frac{1}{2} \times 4\right) = (6, 2)$.

Point $C = (-6, 2)$, then $C' = \left(\frac{1}{2} \times (-6), \frac{1}{2} \times 2\right) = (-3, 1)$.

The coordinates of $\triangle A'B'C'$ are $\left(3, \frac{1}{2}\right)$, $(6, 2)$, and $(-3, 1)$, respectively.

4. Figure $DEFG$ is shown on the coordinate plane below. The figure is dilated from the origin by scale factor $r = \frac{3}{2}$. Identify the coordinates of the dilated figure $D'E'F'G'$, then draw and label figure $D'E'F'G'$ on the coordinate plane.

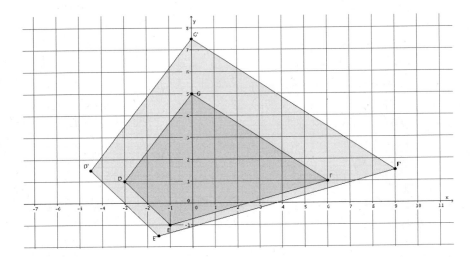

Point $D = (-3, 1)$, then $D' = \left(\frac{3}{2} \times (-3), \frac{3}{2} \times 1\right) = \left(-\frac{9}{2}, \frac{3}{2}\right)$.

Point $E = (-1, -1)$, then $E' = \left(\frac{3}{2} \times (-1), \frac{3}{2} \times (-1)\right) = \left(-\frac{3}{2}, -\frac{3}{2}\right)$.

Point $F = (6, 1)$, then $F' = \left(\frac{3}{2} \times 6, \frac{3}{2} \times 1\right) = \left(9, \frac{3}{2}\right)$.

Point $G = (0, 5)$, then $G' = \left(\frac{3}{2} \times 0, \frac{3}{2} \times 5\right) = \left(0, \frac{15}{2}\right)$.

The coordinates of figure $D'E'F'G'$ are $\left(-\frac{9}{2}, \frac{3}{2}\right)$, $\left(-\frac{3}{2}, -\frac{3}{2}\right)$, $\left(9, \frac{3}{2}\right)$, and $\left(0, \frac{15}{2}\right)$, respectively.

5. Figure $DEFG$ has coordinates $D = (1, 1)$, $E = (7, 3)$, $F = (5, -4)$, and $G = (-1, -4)$. The figure is dilated from the origin by scale factor $r = 7$. Identify the coordinates of the dilated figure $D'E'F'G'$.

Point $D = (1, 1)$, then $D' = (7 \times 1, 7 \times 1) = (7, 7)$.

Point $E = (7, 3)$, then $E' = (7 \times 7, 7 \times 3) = (49, 21)$.

Point $F = (5, -4)$, then $F' = \left(7 \times 5, 7 \times (-4)\right) = (35, -28)$.

Point $G = (-1, -4)$, then $G' = \left(7 \times (-1), 7 \times (-4)\right) = (-7, -28)$.

The coordinates of figure $D'E'F'G'$ are $(7, 7), (49, 21), (35, -28)$ and $(-7, -28)$, respectively.

Lesson 7: Informal Proofs of Properties of Dilations

Student Outcomes

- Students know an informal proof of why dilations are degree-preserving transformations.
- Students know an informal proof of why dilations map segments to segments, lines to lines, and rays to rays.

Lesson Notes

These properties were first introduced in Lesson 2. In this lesson, students think about the mathematics behind why those statements are true in terms of an informal proof developed through a Socratic Discussion. This lesson is optional.

Classwork

Discussion (15 minutes)

Begin by asking students to brainstorm what we already know about dilations. Accept any reasonable responses. Responses should include the basic properties of dilations, for example: lines map to lines, segments to segments, rays to rays, etc. Students should also mention that dilations are degree-preserving. Let students know that in this lesson they will informally prove why the properties are true.

- In previous lessons we learned that dilations are degree-preserving transformations. Now we want to develop an informal proof as to why the theorem is true:

  Theorem: Dilations preserve the degrees of angles.

- We know that dilations map angles to angles. Let there be a dilation from center O and scale factor r. Given $\angle PQR$, we want to show that if $P' = dilation(P)$, $Q' = dilation(Q)$, and $R' = dilation(R)$, then $|\angle PQR| = |\angle P'Q'R'|$. In other words, when we dilate an angle, the measure of the angle remains unchanged. Take a moment to draw a picture of the situation. (Give students a couple of minutes to prepare their drawings. Instruct them to draw an angle on the coordinate plane and to use the multiplicative property of coordinates learned in the previous lesson.)

  > *Scaffolding:*
  >
  > Provide more explicit directions, such as: "Draw an angle PQR and dilate it from a center O to create an image, angle $P'Q'R'$."

  - *(Have students share their drawings). Sample drawing below:*

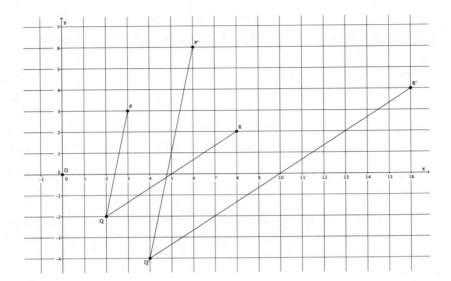

- Could line $Q'P'$ be parallel to line QP?

    □ *Yes. Based on what we know about the Fundamental Theorem of Similarity, since $P' = dilation(P)$ and $Q' = dilation(Q)$, then we know that line $Q'P'$ is parallel to line QP.*

- Could line $Q'P'$ intersect line QR?

    □ *Yes, if we extend the ray $\overrightarrow{Q'P'}$ it will intersect line QR.*

- Could line $Q'P'$ be parallel to line QR?

    □ *No. Based on what we know about the Fundamental Theorem of Similarity, line QR and line $Q'R'$ are supposed to be parallel. In the last module, we learned that there is only one line that is parallel to a given line going through a specific point. Since line $Q'P'$ and line $Q'R'$ have a common point, Q', only one of those lines can be parallel to line QR.*

- Now that we are sure that line $Q'P'$ intersects line QR, mark that point of intersection on your drawing (extend rays if necessary). Let's call that point of intersection point B.

    □ *Sample student drawing below:*

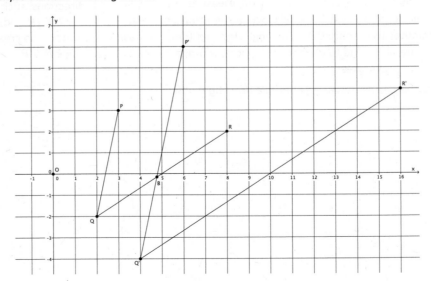

- At this point, we have all the information that we need to show that $|\angle PQR| = |\angle P'Q'R'|$. (Give students several minutes in small groups to discuss possible proofs for why $|\angle PQR| = |\angle P'Q'R'|$.)

    □ *We know that when parallel lines are cut by a transversal, then their alternate interior angles are equal in measure. Looking first at parallel lines $Q'P'$ and QP, we have transversal, QB. Then, alternate interior angles are equal (i.e., $|\angle Q'BQ| = |\angle PQR|$). Now, looking at parallel lines $R'Q'$ and RQ, we have transversal, $Q'B$. Then, alternate interior angles are equal (i.e., $|\angle P'Q'R'| = |\angle Q'BQ|$). We have the two equalities, $|\angle P'Q'R'| = |\angle Q'BQ|$ and $|\angle Q'BQ| = |\angle PQR|$, where within each equality is the angle $\angle Q'BQ$. Therefore, $|\angle PQR| = |\angle P'Q'R'|$.*

> **Scaffolding:**
>
> Remind students what we know about angles that have a relationship to parallel lines. They may need to review their work from Topic C of Module 2. Also, students may use protractors to measure the angles as an alternative way of verifying the result.

Sample drawing below:

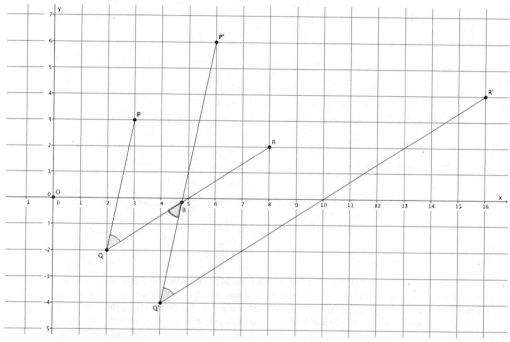

- Using FTS, and our knowledge of angles formed by parallel lines cut by a transversal, we have proven that dilations are degree-preserving transformations.

Exercise (5 minutes)

Following this demonstration, give students the option of either (a) summarizing what they learned from the demonstration or (b) writing a proof as shown in Exercise 1.

Exercise

Use the diagram below to prove the theorem: *Dilations preserve the degrees of angles.*

Let there be a dilation from center O with scale factor r. Given $\angle PQR$, show that since $P' = dilation(P)$, $Q' = dilation(Q)$, and $R' = dilation(R)$, then $|\angle PQR| = |\angle P'Q'R'|$. That is, show that the image of the angle after a dilation has the same measure, in degrees, as the original.

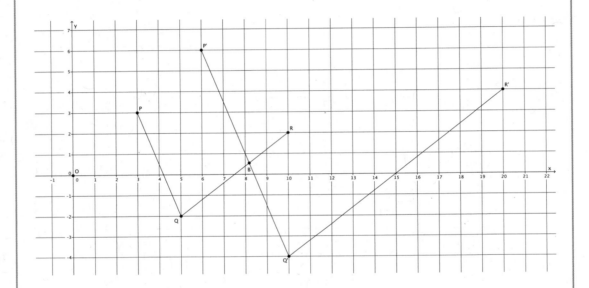

Using FTS, we know that line $P'Q'$ is parallel to PQ, and that line $Q'R'$ is parallel to QR. We also know that there exists just one line through a given point, parallel to a given line. Therefore, we know that $Q'P'$ must intersect QR at a point. We know this because there is already a line that goes through point Q' that is parallel to QR, and that line is $Q'R'$. Since $Q'P'$ cannot be parallel to $Q'R'$, it must intersect it. We will let the intersection of $Q'P'$ and QR be named point B. Alternate interior angles of parallel lines cut by a transversal are equal in measure. Parallel lines QR and $Q'R'$ are cut by transversal $Q'B$. Therefore, the alternate interior angles $\angle P'Q'R'$ and $\angle Q'BQ$ are equal. Parallel lines $Q'P'$ and QP are cut by transversal QB. Therefore, the alternate interior angles $\angle PQR$ and $\angle Q'BQ$ are equal. Since angle $\angle P'Q'R'$ and angle $\angle PQR$ are equal to $\angle QB'Q$, then $|\angle PQR| = |\angle P'Q'R'|$.

Example 1 (5 minutes)

In this example, students verify that dilations map lines to lines.

- On the coordinate plane, mark two points: A and B. Connect the points to make a line; make sure you go beyond the actual points to show that it is a line and not just a segment. Now, use what you know about the multiplicative property of dilation on coordinates to dilate the points by some scale factor. Label the images of the points. What do you have when you connect A' to B'?

Have several students share their work with the class. Make sure each student explains that the dilation of line AB is the line $A'B'$. Sample student work shown below.

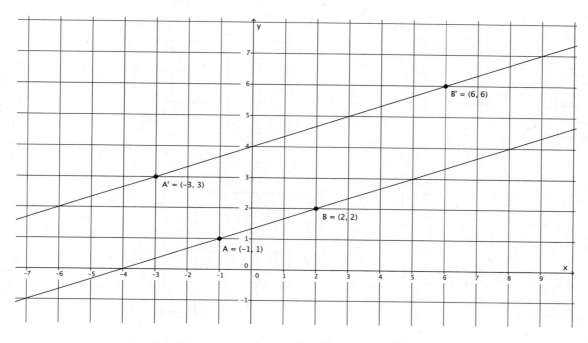

- Each of us selected different points and different scale factors. Therefore, we have informally shown that dilations map lines to lines.

Example 2 (5 minutes)

In this example, students verify that dilations map segments to segments.

- On the coordinate plane, mark two points: A and B. Connect the points to make a segment. This time, make sure you do not go beyond the marked points. Now, use what you know about the multiplicative property of dilation on coordinates to dilate the points by some scale factor. Label the images of the points. What do you have when you connect A' to B'?

Have several students share their work with the class. Make sure each student explains that the dilation of segment AB is the segment $A'B'$. Sample student work shown below.

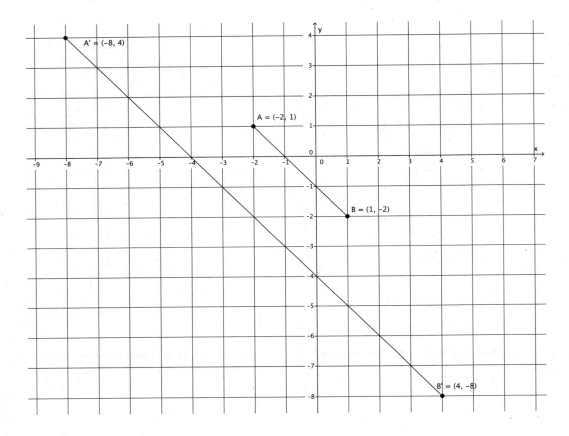

- Each of us selected different points and different scale factors. Therefore, we have informally shown that dilations map segments to segments.

Example 3 (5 minutes)

In this example, students verify that dilations map rays to rays.

- On the coordinate plane, mark two points: A and B. Connect the points to make a ray; make sure you go beyond point B to show that it is a ray. Now, use what you know about the multiplicative property of dilation on coordinates to dilate the points by some scale factor. Label the images of the points. What do you have when you connect A' to B'?

Have several students share their work with the class. Make sure each student explains that the dilation of ray AB is the ray $A'B'$. Sample student work shown below.

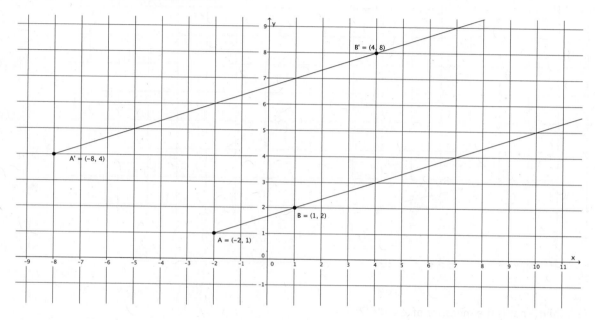

- Each of us selected different points and different scale factors. Therefore, we have informally shown that dilations map rays to rays.

Closing (5 minutes)

Summarize, or ask students to summarize, the main points from the lesson:

- We know an informal proof for dilations being degree-preserving transformations that uses the definition of dilation, the Fundamental Theorem of Similarity, and the fact that there can only be one line through a point that is parallel to a given line.

- We informally verified that dilations of segments map to segments, dilations of lines map to lines, and dilations of rays map to rays.

Exit Ticket (5 minutes)

Name _____   Date_____

Lesson 7: Informal Proofs of Properties of Dilations

Exit Ticket

Dilate $\angle ABC$ with center O and scale factor $r = 2$. Label the dilated angle $\angle A'B'C'$.

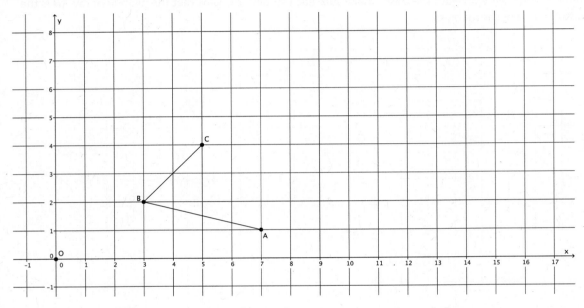

1.   If $\angle ABC = 72°$, then what is the measure of $\angle A'B'C'$?

2.   If segment AB is 2 cm. What is the measure of line $A'B'$?

3.   Which segments, if any, are parallel?

Exit Ticket Sample Solutions

Dilate $\angle ABC$ with center O and scale factor $r = 2$. Label the dilated angle $\angle A'B'C'$.

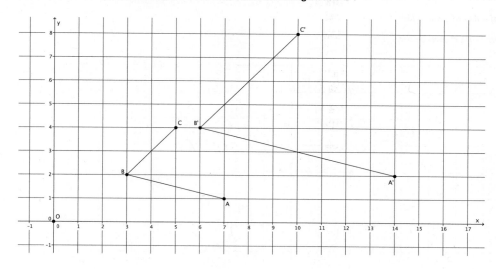

1. If $\angle ABC = 72°$, then what is the measure of $\angle A'B'C'$?

   Since dilations preserve angles, then $\angle ABC = 72°$.

2. If segment AB is 2 cm. What is the measure of line $A'B'$?

   The length of segment $A'B'$ is 4 cm.

3. Which segments, if any, are parallel?

   Since dilations map segments to parallel segments, then $AB \parallel A'B'$, and $BC \parallel B'C'$.

Problem Set Sample Solutions

1. A dilation from center O by scale factor r of a line maps to what? Verify your claim on the coordinate plane.

   The dilation of a line maps to a line.

   Sample student work shown below.

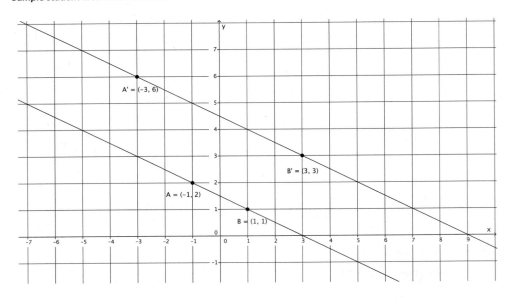

2. A dilation from center O by scale factor r of a segment maps to what? Verify your claim on the coordinate plane.

   The dilation of a segment maps to a segment.

   Sample student work shown below.

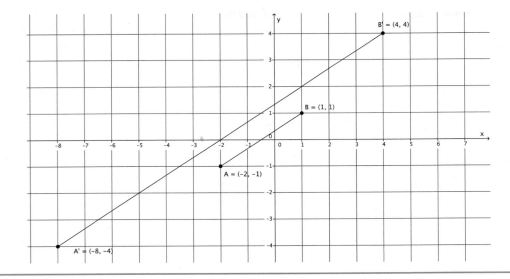

3. A dilation from center O by scale factor r of a ray maps to what? Verify your claim on the coordinate plane.

The dilation of a ray maps to a ray.

Sample student work shown below.

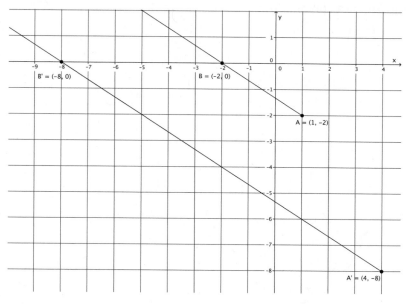

4. **Challenge Problem:**

Prove the theorem: *A dilation maps lines to lines.*

Let there be a dilation from center O with scale factor r so that $P' = dilation(P)$ and $Q' = dilation(Q)$. Show that line PQ maps to line $P'Q'$ (i.e., that dilations map lines to lines). Draw a diagram, and then write your informal proof of the theorem. (Hint: This proof is a lot like the proof for segments. This time, let U be a point on line PQ, that is not between points P and Q.)

Sample student drawing and response below:

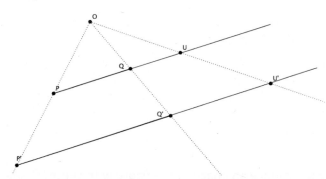

Let U be a point on line PQ. By definition of dilation, we also know that $U' = dilation(U)$. We need to show that U' is a point on line $P'Q'$. If we can, then we have proven that a dilation maps lines to lines.

By definition of dilation and FTS, we know that $\dfrac{|OP'|}{|OP|} = \dfrac{|OQ'|}{|OQ|}$ and that line PQ is parallel to $P'Q'$. Similarly, we know that $\dfrac{|OQ'|}{|OQ|} = \dfrac{|OU'|}{|OU|} = r$ and that line QU is parallel to line $Q'U'$. Since U is a point on line PQ, then we also know that line PQ is parallel to line $Q'U'$. But we already know that PQ is parallel to $P'Q'$. Since there can only be one line that passes through Q' that is parallel to line PQ, then line $P'Q'$ and line $Q'U'$ must coincide. That places the dilation of point U, U' on the line $P'Q'$, which proves that dilations map lines to lines.

Name _____   Date _____

1. Use the figure below to complete parts (a) and (b).

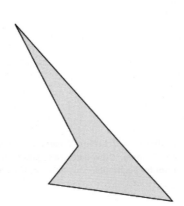

a. Use a compass and ruler to produce an image of the figure with center O and scale factor $r = 2$.

b. Use a ruler to produce an image of the figure with center O and scale factor $r = \frac{1}{2}$.

2. Use the diagram below to answer the questions that follow.

Let D be the dilation with center O and scale factor $r > 0$ so that $D(P) = P'$ and $D(Q) = Q'$.

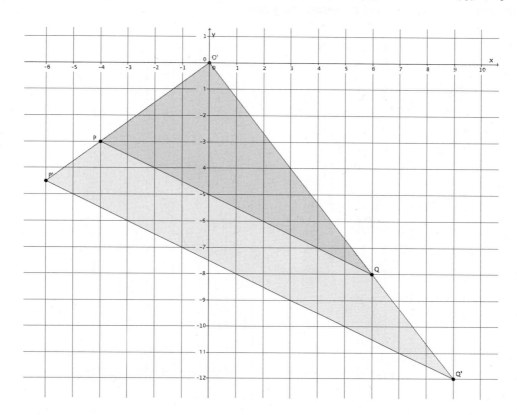

a. Use lengths $|OQ| = 10$ units and $|OQ'| = 15$ units, to determine the scale factor r, of dilation D. Describe how to determine the coordinates of P' using the coordinates of P.

b. If $|OQ| = 10$ units, $|OQ'| = 15$ units, and $|P'Q'| = 11.2$ units, determine the length of $|PQ|$. Round your answer to the tenths place, if necessary.

3. Use a ruler and compass, as needed, to answer parts (a) and (b).

a. Is there a dilation D with center O that would map figure $PQRS$ to figure $P'Q'R'S'$? If yes, describe the dilation in terms of coordinates of corresponding points.

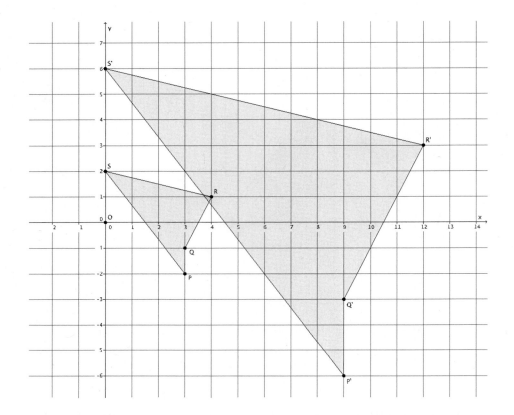

b.   Is there a dilation D with center O that would map figure $PQRS$ to figure $P'Q'R'S'$?   If yes, describe the dilation in terms of coordinates of corresponding points.

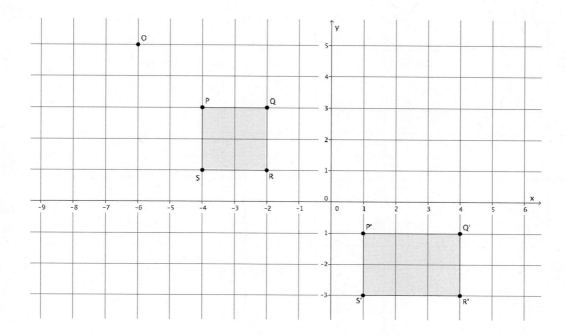

c.   Triangle ABC is located at points $A = (-4, 3)$, $B = (3, 3)$, and $C = (2, -1)$ and has been dilated from the origin by a scale factor of 3. Draw and label the vertices of triangle ABC. Determine the coordinates of the dilated triangle $A'B'C'$ and draw and label it on the coordinate plane.

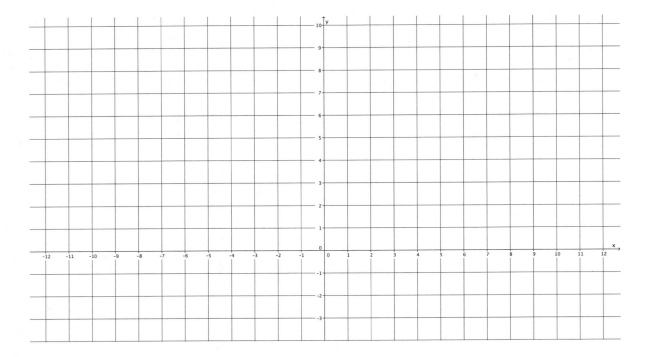

A Progression Toward Mastery

Assessment Task Item		STEP 1 Missing or incorrect answer and little evidence of reasoning or application of mathematics to solve the problem.	STEP 2 Missing or incorrect answer but evidence of some reasoning or application of mathematics to solve the problem.	STEP 3 A correct answer with some evidence of reasoning or application of mathematics to solve the problem, or an incorrect answer with substantial evidence of solid reasoning or application of mathematics to solve the problem.	STEP 4 A correct answer supported by substantial evidence of solid reasoning or application of mathematics to solve the problem.
1	a 8.G.A.3	Student did not use compass and ruler to dilate the figure, i.e., the dilated figure is drawn free hand or not drawn. Student used an incorrect or no scale factor. The dilated figure is smaller than the original figure. The corresponding segments are not parallel.	Student may or may not have used a compass and/or ruler to dilate the figure, i.e., some of the work was done by free hand. The dilated figure is larger than the original figure. Student may or may not have solid or dotted rays drawn from the center O through most of the vertices. Student may have used an incorrect scale factor for parts of the dilated figure, i.e., the length from the center O to all dilated vertices is not two times the length from the center to the corresponding vertices. Some of the corresponding segments are parallel.	Student used a compass to dilate the figure, evidenced by arcs on the figure to measure the appropriate lengths. The dilated figure is larger than the original figure. Student has solid or dotted rays drawn from the center O through most of the vertices. Student may have used an incorrect scale factor for parts of the dilated figure, i.e., the length from the center O to all dilated vertices is not two times the length from the center to the corresponding vertices. Most of the corresponding segments are parallel.	Student used a compass to dilate the figure, evidenced by arcs on the figure to measure the appropriate lengths. The dilated figure is larger than the original figure. Student has solid or dotted rays drawn from the center O through all of the vertices. The length from the center O to all dilated vertices is two times the length from the center to the corresponding vertices. All of the corresponding segments are parallel.
	b 8.G.A.3	Student did not use a ruler to dilate the figure, i.e., the dilated figure is drawn free hand or not drawn.	Student may or may not have used a ruler to dilate the figure, i.e., parts of the work were done by free hand.	Student used a ruler to dilate the figure. The dilated figure is smaller than the original figure.	Student used a ruler to dilate the figure. The dilated figure is smaller than the original figure.

Module 3: Similarity
Date: 10/16/13

99

		Student used an incorrect or no scale factor. The dilated figure is larger than the original figure. The corresponding segments are not parallel.	The dilated figure is smaller than the original figure. Student may or may not have solid or dotted rays drawn from the center O through most of the vertices. Student may have used an incorrect scale factor for parts of the dilated figure, e.g., the length from the center O to all dilated vertices is not one half of the length from the center to the corresponding vertices. Some of the corresponding segments are parallel.	Student has solid or dotted rays drawn from the center O through most of the vertices. Student may have used an incorrect scale factor for parts of the dilated figure, e.g., the length from the center O to all dilated vertices is not one half of the length from the center to the corresponding vertices. Most of the corresponding segments are parallel.	Student has solid or dotted rays drawn from the center O through all of the vertices. The length from the center O to all dilated vertices is one half of the length from the center to the corresponding vertices. All of the corresponding segments are parallel.
2	**a** **8.G.A.3**	Student did not attempt the problem. Student may or may not have calculated the scale factor correctly.	Student used the definition of dilation with the given side lengths to calculate the scale factor. Student may have made calculation errors when calculating the scale factor. Student may or may not have attempted to find the coordinates of P'.	Student used the definition of dilation with the given side lengths to calculate the scale factor $r = 1.5$ or equivalent. Student determined the coordinates of point P', but did not explain or relate it to scale factor and point P.	Student used the definition of dilation with the given side lengths to calculate the scale factor $r = 1.5$ or equivalent. Student explained that the coordinates of P' are found by multiplying the coordinates of P by the scale factor. Student determined the coordinates of $Q' = (-6, -4.5)$.
	b **8.G.A.3**	Student did not attempt the problem. Student wrote a number for the length of $|PQ|$ without showing any work as to how he/she arrived at the answer.	Student may have inverted one of the fractions of the equal ratios leading to an incorrect answer. Student may have made a calculation error in finding the length of $|PQ|$. Student did not answer the question in a complete sentence.	Student correctly set up ratios to find the length of $|PQ|$. Student may have made a rounding error in stating the length. Student did not answer the question in a complete sentence or did not include units in the answer.	Student correctly set up ratios to find the length of $|PQ|$. Student correctly identified the length of $|PQ| \approx 7.5$ units. Student answered the question in a complete sentence and identified the units.

Module 3:   Similarity
Date: 10/16/13

3	a 8.G.A.3	Student did not attempt the problem. Student wrote a number for scale factor without showing any work or providing an explanation for how the scale factor was determined. Student did not describe the dilation.	Student made an error in calculation leading to an incorrect scale factor. Student did not describe the dilation in terms of coordinates of corresponding points.	Student may have identified the scale factor of dilation as $r = \frac{1}{3}$ instead of $r = 3$. Student attempted to describe the dilation with some evidence of mathematical vocabulary and/or reasoning.	Student correctly identified the scale factor as $r = 3$. Student clearly described the dilation in terms of the coordinates of at least one pair of corresponding points. There is strong evidence of mathematical reasoning and use of related vocabulary.
	b 8.G.A.3	Student did not attempt the problem. Student answered with yes or no only. Student did not give any explanation or reasoning.	Student answered yes or no. Student explanation and/or reasoning is not based on mathematics, e.g., "doesn't look like there is." Student attempted to solve problem by showing measurements. Student may or may not have attempted to solve problem by drawing in a solid or dotted ray from center O through one vertex, e.g., from center O through P and P'.	Student answered no correctly. Student used mathematical vocabulary in the explanation. Basis for explanation relies heavily on the diagram, e.g., "look at drawing." Student attempted to solve problem by drawing a solid or dotted ray from center O through one or more vertex, e.g., from center O through P and P'.	Student answered no correctly. Student used mathematical vocabulary in the explanation. Explanation included the fact that the corresponding vertices and center O must be on the same line, e.g., "center O, P, and P' would be on the same ray if a dilation was possible." Student drew solid or dotted rays from center O through multiple vertices. Diagram enhanced explanation.
	c 8.G.A.3	Student did not attempt the problem. Student may have drawn $\triangle ABC$ using incorrect coordinates, or student did not label coordinates correctly.	Student correctly drew and labeled $\triangle ABC$. Student may or may not have identified the correct coordinates of the dilated points. For example, student may have only multiplied one coordinate of each ordered pair to determine location of image point. Student may have placed the image of $\triangle ABC$ at the wrong coordinates.	Student correctly drew and labeled $\triangle ABC$. Student may have minor calculation errors when identifying the coordinates of A', B', C'. For example, student multiplied -4 and 3 and wrote 12. Student drew and labeled $\triangle A'B'C'$ using the incorrect coordinates that were calculated.	Student correctly drew and labeled $\triangle ABC$. Student correctly identified the image of the points as $A' = (-12, 9)$, $B' = (9,9)$, and $C' = (6, -3)$. Student correctly drew and labeled $\triangle A'B'C'$.

Name _____   Date _____

1. Use the figure below to complete parts (a) and (b).

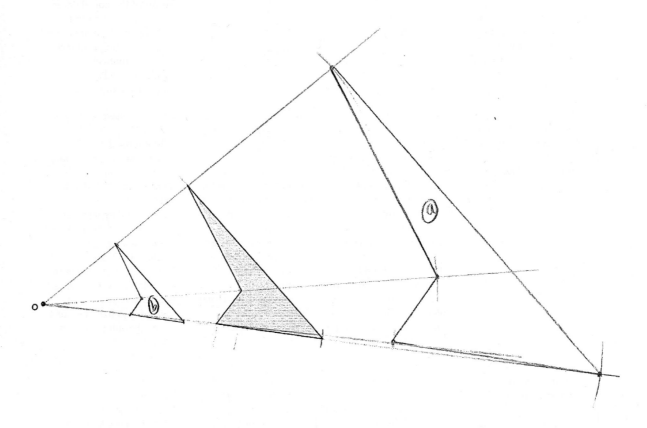

a. Use a compass and ruler to produce an image of the figure with center O and scale factor, $r = 2$.

b. Use a ruler to produce an image of the figure with center O and scale factor, $r = \frac{1}{2}$.

2. Use the diagram below to answer the questions that follow.

Let D be the dilation with center O and scale factor $r > 0$ so that $D(P) = P'$ and $D(Q) = Q'$.

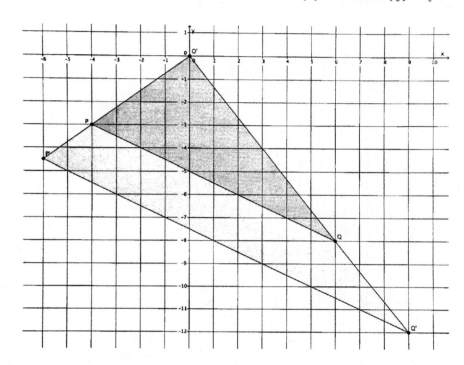

a. Use lengths $|OQ| = 10$ units and $|OQ'| = 15$ units, to determine the scale factor r, of dilation D. Describe how to determine the coordinates of P' using the coordinates of P.

$|OQ|r = |OQ'|$

$r = \dfrac{|OQ'|}{|OQ|}$

$r = \dfrac{15}{10}$

$r = \dfrac{3}{2}$

THE SCALE FACTOR IS $r = \dfrac{3}{2}$.

SINCE THE COORDINATES OF $P = (-4, -3)$ THE COORDINATES OF THE DILATED POINT P' WILL BE THE SCALE FACTOR TIMES THE COORDINATES OF P. THEREFORE $P' = \left(\frac{3}{2} \times (-4), \frac{3}{2} \times (-3)\right) = (-6, -4.5)$.

b. If $|OQ| = 10$ units, $|OQ'| = 15$ units, and $|P'Q'| = 11.2$ units, determine the length of $|PQ|$. Round your answer to the tenths place, if necessary.

$\dfrac{15}{10} = \dfrac{11.2}{|PQ|}$

$15(|PQ|) = 112$

$|PQ| = \dfrac{112}{15} \approx 7.5$

THE LENGTH OF PQ IS ABOUT 7.5 UNITS

3. Use a ruler and compass, as needed, to answer parts (a) and (b).

   a. Is there a dilation D with center O that would map figure $PQRS$ to figure $P'Q'R'S'$? If yes, describe the dilation in terms of coordinates of corresponding points.

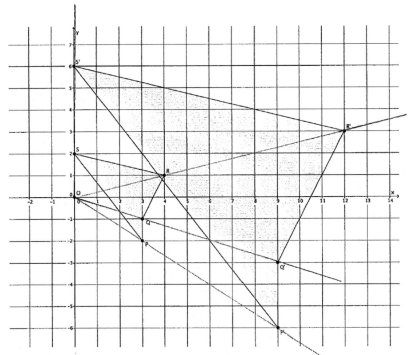

$P = (3, -2)$ $P' = (9, -6)$

$Q = (3, -1)$ $Q' = (9, -3)$

$R = (4, 1)$ $R' = (12, 3)$

$S = (0, 2)$ $S' = (0, 6)$

YES, THERE IS A DILATION D WITH CENTER O THAT MAPS PQRS TO PQ'R'S'. THE SCALE FACTOR IS 3. THE IMAGE OF EACH POINT IS 3 TIMES THE COORDINATES OF THE ORIGINAL IMAGE. FOR EXAMPLE, $P = (3, 2)$ AND $P' = (3 \times 3, 3 \times (-2)) = (9, -6)$.

b. Is there a dilation D with center O that would map figure $PQRS$ to figure $P'Q'R'S'$? If yes, describe the dilation in terms of coordinates of corresponding points.

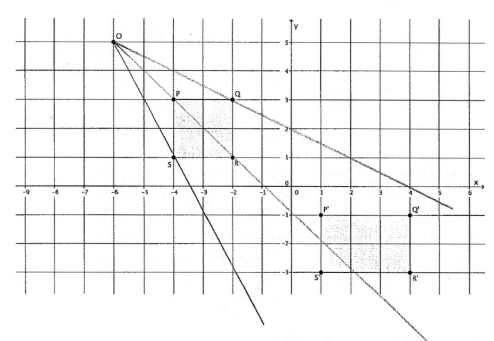

NO, THERE IS NOT A DILATION D THAT WILL MAP
PQRS TO P'Q'R'S! A DILATION WILL MOVE A POINT, S, TO
ITS IMAGE S' ON THE RAY $\overrightarrow{OS}$. IN THE PICTURE ABOVE
O, S, S' ARE NOT ON THE SAME RAY. A SIMILAR
STATEMENT CAN BE MADE FOR POINTS P, Q, AND R. THEREFORE,
THERE IS NO DILATION THAT MAPS PQRS TO P'Q'R'S!

c. Triangle △ ABC is located at points $A = (-4, 3)$, $B = (3, 3)$ and $C = (2, -1)$ has been dilated from the origin by a scale factor of 3. Draw and label the vertices of △ ABC. Determine the coordinates of the dilated triangle, △ $A'B'C'$ and draw and label it on the coordinate plane.

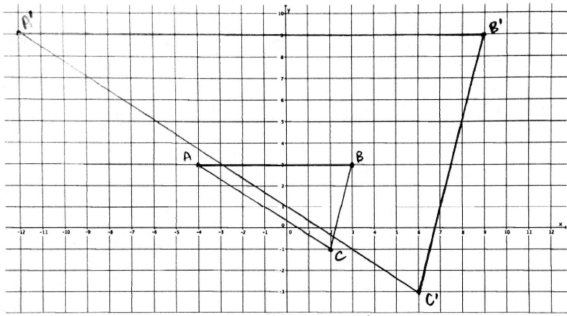

$A = (-4, 3)$ $A' = (-4 \times 3, 3 \times 3) = (-12, 9)$

$B = (3, 3)$ $B' = (3 \times 3, 3 \times 3) = (9, 9)$

$C = (2, -1)$ $C' = (2 \times 3, -1 \times 3) = (6, -3)$

Mathematics Curriculum

Topic B:
Similar Figures

8.G.A.4, 8.G.A.5

Focus Standard:	8.G.A.4	Understand that a two-dimensional figure is similar to another if the second can be obtained from the first by a sequence of rotations, reflections, translations, and dilations; given two similar two-dimensional figures, describe a sequence that exhibits the similarity between them.
	8.G.A.5	Use informal arguments to establish facts about the angle sum and exterior angle of triangles, about the angles created when parallel lines are cut by a transversal, and the angle-angle criterion for similarity of triangles. *For example, arrange three copies of the same triangle so that the sum of the three angles appears to form a line, and give an argument in terms of transversals why this is so.*
Instructional Days:	5	
Lesson 8:	Similarity (P)[1]	
Lesson 9:	Basic Properties of Similarity (E)	
Lesson 10:	Informal Proof of Angle-Angle Criterion (S)	
Lesson 11:	More About Similar Triangles (P)	
Lesson 12:	Modeling with Similarity (M)	

Topic B begins with the definition of similarity and the properties of similarities. In Lesson 8, students learn that similarities map lines to lines, change the length of segments by factor r, and are degree-preserving. In Lesson 9, additional properties about similarity are investigated; first, students learn that congruence implies similarity (e.g., congruent figures are also similar). Next, students learn that similarity is symmetric (e.g., if figure A is similar to figure B, then figure B is similar to figure A) and transitive (e.g., if figure A is similar to figure B, and figure B is similar to figure C, then figure A is similar to figure C.) Finally, students learn about similarity with respect to triangles.

Lesson 10 provides students with an informal proof of the angle-angle criterion for similarity of triangles. Lesson 10 also provides opportunities for students to use the AA criterion to determine if a pair of triangles is

---

[1] Lesson Structure Key: **P**-Problem Set Lesson, **M**-Modeling Cycle Lesson, **E**-Exploration Lesson, **S**-Socratic Lesson

similar. In Lesson 11, students use what they know about similar triangles and dilation to find an unknown side length of one triangle. Since students know that similar triangles have side lengths that are equal in ratio (specifically equal to the scale factor), students verify whether or not a pair of triangles is similar by comparing their corresponding side lengths.

In Lesson 12, students apply their knowledge of similar triangles and dilation to real world situations. For example, students use the height of a person and the height of his shadow to determine the height of a tree. Students may also use their knowledge to determine the distance across a lake, the height of a building, and the height of a flagpole.

Lesson 8: Similarity

Student Outcomes

- Students know the definition of similar and why dilation alone is not enough to determine similarity.
- Given two similar figures, students describe the sequence of a dilation and a congruence that would map one figure onto the other.

Lesson Notes

In Module 2, students used vectors to describe the translation of the plane. Now in Topic B, figures are bound to the coordinate plane, and students will describe translations in terms of units left or right and/or units up or down. When figures on the coordinate plane are rotated, the center of rotation is the origin of the graph. In most cases, students will describe the rotation as having center O and degree d unless the rotation can be easily identified, i.e., a rotation of $90°$ or $180°$. Reflections remain reflections across a line, but when possible, students should identify the line of reflection as the x-axis or y-axis.

It should be noted that congruence, together with similarity, is *the* fundamental concept in planar geometry. It is a concept defined without coordinates. In fact, it is most transparently understood when introduced without the extra conceptual baggage of a coordinate system. This is partly because a coordinate system picks out a preferred point (the origin), which then centers most discussions of rotations, reflections, and translations at or in reference to that point. They are then further restricted to only the "nice" rotations/reflections/translations that are easy to do in a coordinate plane. Restricting to "nice" transformations is a huge mistake mathematically because it is antithetical to the main point that must be made about congruence: that rotations, translations, and reflections are abundant in the plane—that for every point in the plane, there are an *infinite number* of rotations up to $360°$, that for every line in the plane there is a reflection, and for every directed line segment there is a translation. It is this abundance that helps students realize that every congruence transformation (i.e., the act of "picking up a figure" and moving it to another location) can be accomplished through a sequence of translations, rotations, and reflections, and further, that similarity is a congruence transformation in addition to dilation.

Classwork

Concept Development (5 minutes)

- A dilation alone is not enough to state that two figures are similar. Consider the following pair of figures:

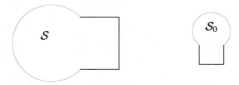

- Do these figures look similar?
    - *Yes, they look like the same shape, but they are different in size.*

- ■ How could you prove that they are similar? What would you need to do?

  - □ *We would need to show that they could become the same size by dilating one of the figures.*

- ■ Would we be able to dilate one figure so that it was the same size as the other?

  - □ *Yes, we could dilate to make them the same size by using the appropriate scale factor.*

- ■ We could make them the same size, but would a dilation alone map figure S onto S_0?

  - □ *No, a dilation alone would not map S onto S_0.*

- ■ What else should we do to map figure S onto S_0?

  - □ *We would have to perform a translation and a rotation to map S onto S_0.*

- ■ That is precisely why a dilation alone is not enough to define similarity. Two figures are said to be similar if one can be mapped onto the other using a dilation followed by a congruence (a sequence of basic rigid motions) or a congruence followed by a dilation.

Example 1 (5 minutes)

Example 1

In the picture below we have a triangle ABC, that has been dilated from center O, by a scale factor of $r = \frac{1}{2}$. It is noted by $A'B'C'$. We also have triangle $A''B''C''$, which is congruent to triangle $A'B'C'$ (i.e., $\triangle A'B'C' \cong \triangle A''B''C''$).

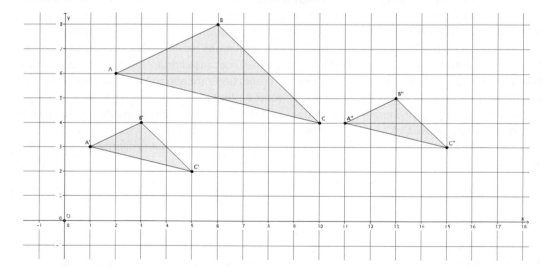

Describe the sequence that would map triangle $A''B''C''$ onto triangle ABC.

- ■ Based on the definition, how could we show that triangle $A''B''C''$ is similar to triangle ABC?

  - □ *To show that $\triangle A''B''C'' \sim \triangle ABC$, we need to describe a dilation followed by a congruence.*

> *Scaffolding:*
>
> Remind students of the work they did in Lesson 3 to bring dilated figures back to their original size.

- ▪ We want to describe a sequence that would map triangle $A''B''C''$ onto triangle ABC. There is no clear way to do this so let's begin with something simpler: How can we map triangle $A'B'C'$ onto triangle ABC? That is, what is the precise dilation that would make triangle $A'B'C'$ the same size as triangle ABC?

  - ▫ *A dilation from center O with scale factor $r = 2$.*

- ▪ Remember, our goal was to describe how to map triangle $A''B''C''$ onto triangle ABC. What precise dilation would make triangle $A''B''C''$ the same size as triangle ABC?

  - ▫ *A dilation from center O with scale factor $r = 2$ would make* triangle $A''B''C''$ the same size as triangle ABC.

- ▪ (Show the picture below with the dilated triangle $A''B''C''$ noted by $A'''B'''C'''$.) Now that we know how to make triangle $A''B''C''$ the same size as triangle ABC, what rigid motion(s) should we use to actually map triangle $A''B''C''$ onto triangle ABC? Have we done anything like this before?

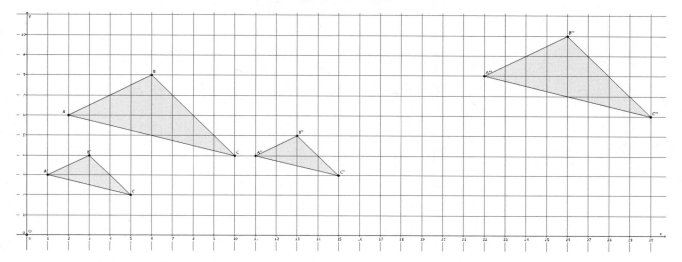

  - ▫ *Number 2 of the problem set from Lesson 2 was like this. That is, we had two figures dilated by the same scale factor in different locations on the plane. To get one to map to the other, we just translated along a vector.*

- ▪ Now that we have an idea of what needs to be done, let's describe the translation in terms of coordinates. How many units and in which direction will we need to translate so that triangle $A'''B'''C'''$ maps to triangle ABC?

  - ▫ *We need to translate triangle $A'''B'''C'''$ 20 units to the left, and 2 units down.*

- ▪ Let's use precise language to describe how to map triangle $A''B''C''$ onto triangle ABC. We will need information about the dilation and the translation.

  - ▫ *The sequence that would map* triangle $A''B''C''$ onto triangle ABC is as follows: Dilate triangle $A''B''C''$ from center O by scale factor $r = 2$. Then translate the dilated triangle 20 units to the left and 2 units down.

- ▪ Since we were able to map triangle $A''B''C''$ onto triangle ABC with a dilation followed by a congruence, we can write that triangle $A''B''C''$ is similar to triangle ABC, in notation, $\triangle A''B''C'' \sim \triangle ABC$.

Example 2 (5 minutes)

▪ In the picture below, we have a triangle DEF, that has been dilated from center O, by scale factor $r = 3$. It is noted by $D'E'F'$. We also have a triangle $D''E''F''$, which is congruent to triangle $D'E'F'$ (i.e., $\triangle\, D'E'F' \cong \triangle\, D''E''F''$).

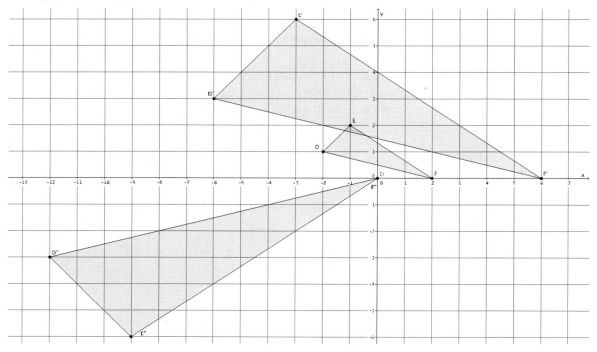

▪ We want to describe a sequence that would map triangle $D''E''F''$ onto triangle DEF. This is similar to what we did in the last example. Can someone summarize the work we did in the last example?

    □ *First, we figured out what scale factor r would make the triangles the same size. Then, we used a translation to map the magnified figure onto the original triangle.*

▪ What is the difference between this problem and the last?

    □ *This time the scale factor is greater than one, so we will need to shrink triangle $D''E''F''$ to the size of triangle DEF. Also, it appears as if a translation alone will not map one triangle onto another.*

▪ Now, since we want to dilate triangle $D''E''F''$ to the size of triangle DEF, we need to know what scale factor r is required so that $|OF| = r|OF''|$. What scale factor do you think we should use and why?

    □ *We need a scale factor $r = \frac{1}{3}$ because we want $|OF| = r|OF''|$.*

▪ What precise dilation would make triangle $D''E''F''$ the same size as triangle DEF?

    □ *A dilation from center O with scale factor $r = \frac{1}{3}$ would make triangle $D''E''F''$ the same size as triangle DEF.*

- (Show the picture below with the dilated triangle $D''E''F''$ noted by $D'''E'''F'''$.) Now, we should use what we know about rigid motions to map the dilated version of triangle $D''E''F''$ onto triangle DEF. What should we do first?

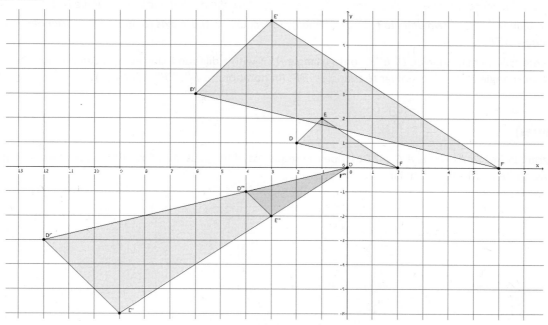

  - *We should translate triangle $D'''E'''F'''$ 2 units to the right.*

- (Show the picture below, the translated triangle in noted in red.) What should we do next (refer to the translated triangle as the red triangle)?

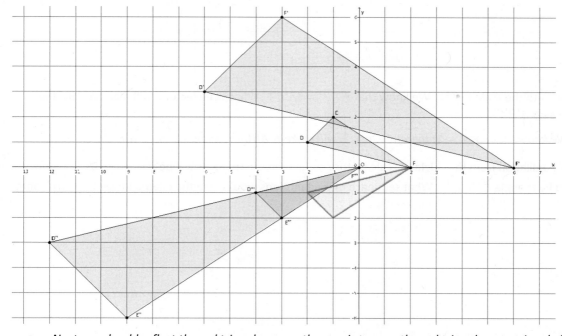

  - *Next, we should reflect the red triangle across the x-axis to map the red triangle onto triangle DEF.*

- Use precise language to describe how to map triangle $D''E''F''$ onto triangle DEF.
  - *The sequence that would map triangle DEF onto triangle DEF is as follows: Dilate triangle $D''E''F''$ from center O by scale factor $r = \frac{1}{3}$. Then translate the dilated image of triangle $D''E''F''$, noted by $D'''E'''F'''$ two units to the right. Finally, reflect across the x-axis to map the red triangle onto triangle DEF.*
- Since we were able to map triangle $D''E''F''$ onto triangle DEF with a dilation followed by a congruence, we can write that triangle $D''E''F''$ is similar to triangle DEF. (In notation: $\triangle D''E''F'' \sim \triangle DEF$.)

Example 3 (3 minutes)

- In the diagram below, $\triangle ABC \sim \triangle A'B'C'$. Describe the sequence of the dilation followed by a congruence that would prove these figures to be similar.

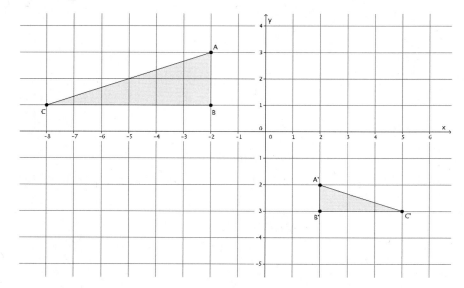

- Let's begin with the scale factor. We know that $r|AB| = |A'B'|$. What scale factor r will make $\triangle ABC$ the same size as $\triangle A'B'C'$?
  - *We know that $r \times 2 = 1$; therefore, $r = \frac{1}{2}$ will make $\triangle ABC$ the same size as $\triangle A'B'C'$.*
- If we apply a dilation from the origin of scale factor $r = \frac{1}{2}$, then the triangles will be the same size (as shown and noted by triangle $A''B''C''$). What sequence of rigid motions would map the dilated image of $\triangle ABC$ onto $\triangle A'B'C'$?

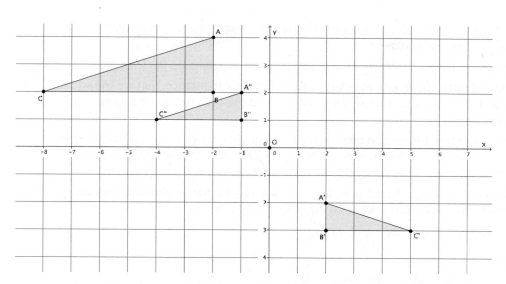

- □ *We could translate the dilated image of △ ABC, △ A″B″C″, 3 units to the right and 4 units down, then reflect the triangle across line A′B′.*
- ■ The sequence that would map △ ABC onto △ A′B′C′ to prove the figures similar is: A dilation from the origin by scale factor $r = \frac{1}{2}$, followed by the translation of the dilated version of △ ABC 3 units to the right and 4 units down, followed by the reflection across line A′B′.

Example 4 (5 minutes)

- ■ In the diagram below, we have two similar figures. Using the notation, we have △ ABC ~ △ DEF. We want to describe the sequence of the dilation followed by a congruence that would prove these figures to be similar.

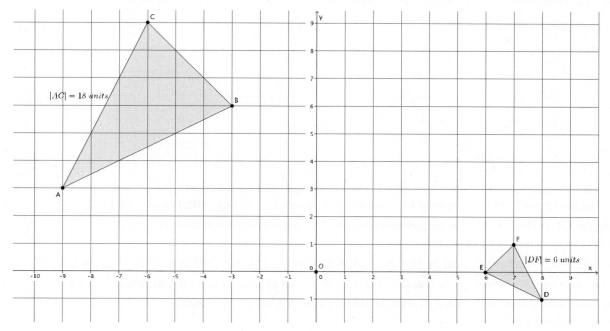

- First, we need to describe the dilation that would make the triangles the same size. What information do we have to help us describe the dilation?

  - *Since we know the length of side AC and side DF, we can determine the scale factor.*

- Can we use any two sides to calculate the scale factor? Assume, for instance, that we know that side AC is 18 units in length and side EF is 2 units in length. Could we find the scale factor using those two sides, AC and EF? Why or why not?

  - *No. We need more information about corresponding sides. Sides AC and DF are the longest sides of each triangle (they are also opposite the obtuse angle in the triangle). Side AC does not correspond to side EF. If we knew the length of BC, we could use BC and EF.*

- Now that we know that we *can* find the scale factor if we have information about corresponding sides, how would we calculate the scale factor if we were mapping $\triangle\ ABC$ onto $\triangle\ DEF$?

  - *$|DF| = r|AC|$, then $6 = r \times 18$, and $r = \frac{1}{3}$.*

- If we were mapping $\triangle\ DEF$ onto $\triangle\ ABC$, what would the scale factor be?

  - *$|AC| = r|DF|$, then $18 = r \times 6$, and $r = 3$.*

- What is the precise dilation that would map $\triangle\ ABC$ onto $\triangle\ DEF$?

  - *Dilate $\triangle\ ABC$ from center O, by scale factor $r = \frac{1}{3}$.*

- (Show the picture below with the dilated triangle noted as $\triangle\ A'B'C'$.) Now we have to describe the congruence. Work with a partner to determine the sequence of rigid motions that would map $\triangle\ ABC$ onto $\triangle\ DEF$.

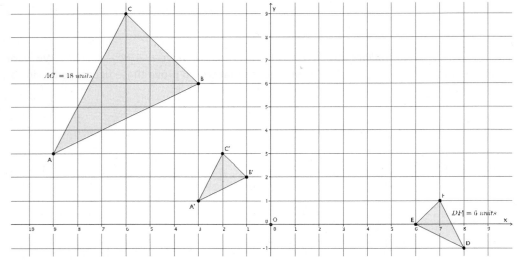

  - *Translate the dilated version of $\triangle\ ABC$ 7 units to the right and 2 units down. Then, rotate d degrees around point E, so that segment B'C' maps onto segment EF. Finally, reflect across line EF.*

Note that "d degrees" refers to a rotation by an appropriate number of degrees to exhibit similarity. Students may choose to describe this number of degrees in other ways.

- The sequence of a dilation followed by a congruence that proves $\triangle\ ABC \sim \triangle\ DEF$ is as follows: Dilate $\triangle\ ABC$ from center O by scale factor $r = \frac{1}{3}$. Translate the dilated version of $\triangle ABC$ 7 units to the right and 2 units down. Next, rotate around point E d degrees so that *segment B'C' maps onto segment EF, then reflect the triangle across line EF.*

| **Lesson 8:** | Similarity |
| **Date:** | 10/16/13 |

Example 5 (3 minutes)

- Knowing that a sequence of a dilation followed by a congruence defines similarity also helps determine if two figures are, in fact, similar. For example, would a dilation map triangle ABC onto triangle DEF? That is, is $\triangle ABC \sim \triangle DEF$?

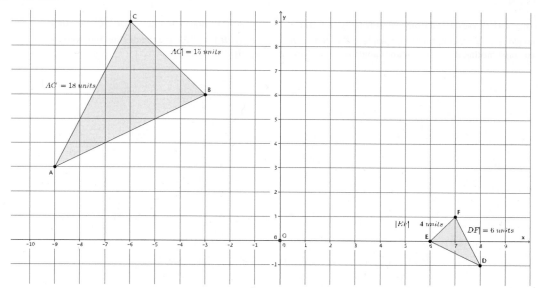

- *No, by FTS, we expect the corresponding sides lengths to be in proportion and equal to the scale factor. If we compare side AC to side DF, and BC to EF, then we get $\dfrac{18}{6} \neq \dfrac{15}{4}$.*

- *Therefore, the triangles are not similar, because a dilation will not map one to the other.*

Example 6 (3 minutes)

- Again, knowing that a dilation followed by a *congruence* defines similarity also helps determine if two figures are, in fact, similar. For example, would a dilation map Figure A onto Figure A'? That is, is *Figure $A \sim$ Figure A'*?

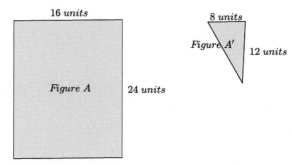

- *No, even though we could say that the corresponding sides are in proportion, there exists no single rigid motion or sequence of rigid motions that would map a four-sided figure to a three-sided figure. Therefore, the figures do not fulfill the congruence part of the definition for similarity, and Figure A is not similar to Figure A'.*

Exercises 1–4 (10 minutes)

Allow students to work in pairs to describe sequences that map one figure onto another.

Exercises 1–4

1. Triangle ABC was dilated from center O by scale factor $r = \frac{1}{2}$. The dilated triangle is noted by $A'B'C'$. Another triangle $A''B''C''$ is congruent to triangle $A'B'C'$ (i.e., $\triangle A''B''C'' \cong \triangle A'B'C'$). Describe the dilation followed by the basic rigid motion that would map triangle $A''B''C''$ onto triangle ABC.

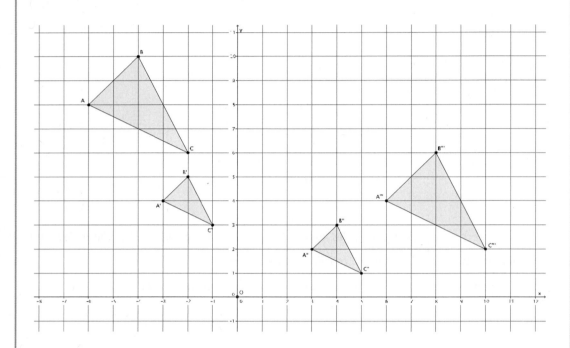

Triangle $A''B''C''$ will need to be dilated from center O, by scale factor $r = 2$ to bring it to the same size as triangle ABC. This will produce a triangle noted by $A'''B'''C'''$. Next, triangle $A'''B'''C'''$ will need to be translated 4 units up and 12 units left. The dilation followed by the translation will map triangle $A''B''C''$ onto triangle ABC.

2. Describe the sequence that would show $\triangle ABC \sim \triangle A'B'C'$.

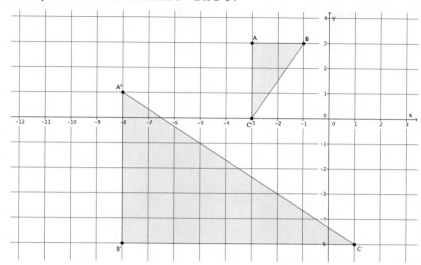

Since $r|AB| = |A'B'|$, then $r \times 2 = 6$ and $r = 3$. A dilation from the origin by scale factor $r = 3$ will make $\triangle ABC$ the same size as $\triangle A'B'C'$. Then, a translation of the dilated image of $\triangle ABC$ ten units right and five units down, followed by a rotation of 90 degrees around point C' will map $\triangle ABC$ onto $\triangle A'B'C'$, proving the triangles to be similar.

3. Are the two triangles shown below similar? If so, describe the sequence that would prove $\triangle ABC \sim \triangle A'B'C'$. If not, state how you know they are not similar.

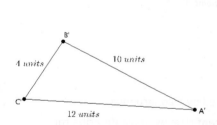

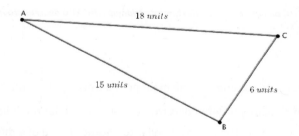

Yes, triangle $\triangle ABC \sim \triangle A'B'C'$. The corresponding sides are in proportion, and equal to the scale factor:

$$\frac{10}{15} = \frac{4}{6} = \frac{12}{18} = \frac{2}{3} = r.$$

To map triangle ABC onto triangle $A'B'C'$, dilate triangle ABC from center O, by scale factor $r = \frac{2}{3}$. Then, translate triangle ABC along vector $\overrightarrow{AA'}$. Next, rotate triangle ABC d degrees around point A.

4. Are the two triangles shown below similar? If so, describe the sequence that would prove △ ABC ~ △ $A'B'C'$. If not, state how you know they are not similar.

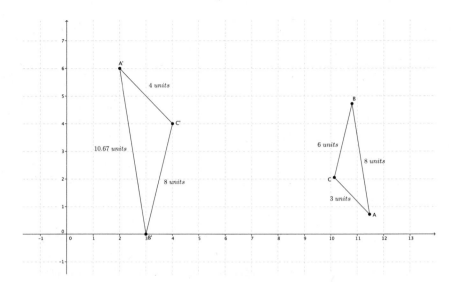

Yes, triangle △ ABC ~ △ $A'B'C'$. The corresponding sides are in proportion and equal to the scale factor:

$$\frac{4}{3} = \frac{8}{6} = \frac{4}{3} = 1.3\overline{3}; \ \frac{10.67}{8} = 1.33375; \ therefore, \ r = 1.33 \cong \frac{4}{3}.$$

To map triangle ABC onto triangle $A'B'C'$, dilate triangle ABC from center O, by scale factor $r = \frac{4}{3}$. Then, translate triangle ABC along vector $\overrightarrow{AA'}$. Next, rotate triangle ABC 180 degrees around point A'.

Closing (5 minutes)

Summarize, or ask students to summarize, the main points from the lesson:

- We know that similarity is defined as the sequence of a dilation, followed by a congruence.
- To show that a figure in the plane is similar to another figure of a different size, we must describe the sequence of a dilation, followed by a congruence (one or more rigid motions), that maps one figure onto another.

> **Lesson Summary**
>
> Similarity is defined as mapping one figure onto another as a sequence of a dilation followed by a congruence (a sequence of rigid motions).
>
> The notation, $\triangle ABC \sim \triangle A'B'C'$, means that $\triangle ABC$ is similar to $\triangle A'B'C'$.

Exit Ticket (5 minutes)

Lesson 8:	Similarity
Date:	10/16/13

Name _____   Date_____

Lesson 8: Similarity

Exit Ticket

In the picture below, we have a triangle DEF that has been dilated from center O, by scale factor $r = \frac{1}{2}$. The dilated triangle is noted by $D'E'F'$. We also have a triangle $D''EF$, which is congruent to triangle DEF (i.e., $\triangle DEF \cong \triangle D''EF$). Describe the sequence of a dilation followed by a congruence (of one or more rigid motions) that would map triangle $D'E'F'$ onto triangle $D''EF$.

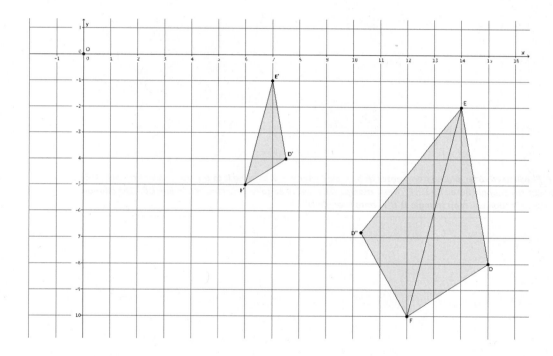

Exit Ticket Sample Solutions

In the picture below we have a triangle DEF that has been dilated from center O, by scale factor $r = \frac{1}{2}$. The dilated triangle is noted by $D'E'F'$. We also have a triangle $D''EF$, which is congruent to triangle DEF (i.e., $\triangle DEF \cong D''EF$). Describe the sequence of a dilation, followed by a congruence (of one or more rigid motions), that would map triangle $D'E'F'$ onto triangle $''EF$.

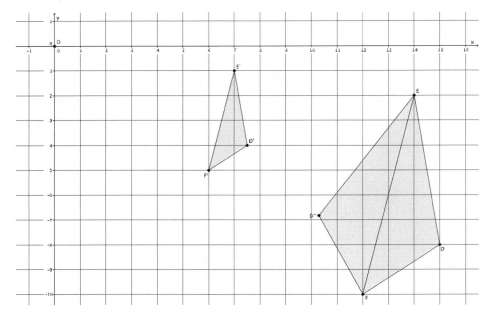

Triangle $D'E'F'$ will need to be dilated from center O, by scale factor $r = 2$ to bring it to the same size as triangle DEF. This will produce the triangle noted by DEF. Next, triangle DEF will need to be reflected across line EF. The dilation followed by the reflection will map triangle $D'E'F'$ onto triangle $D''EF$.

Problem Set Sample Solutions

Students practice dilating a curved figure and describing a sequence of a dilation followed by a congruence that maps one figure onto another.

1. In the picture below, we have a triangle DEF, that has been dilated from center O, by scale factor $r = 4$. It is noted by $D'E'F'$. We also have a triangle $D''E''F''$, which is congruent to triangle $D'E'F'$ (i.e., $\triangle D'E'F' \cong \triangle D''E''F''$). Describe the sequence of a dilation, followed by a congruence (of one or more rigid motions), that would map triangle $D''E''F''$ onto triangle DEF.

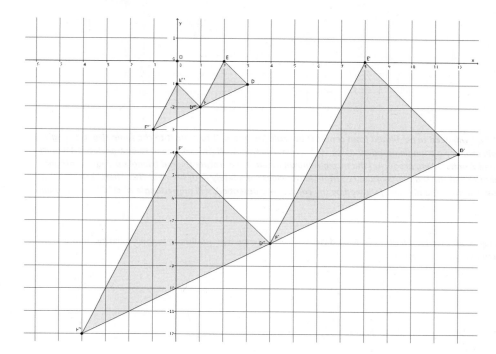

First, we must dilate triangle $D''E''F''$ by scale factor $r = \frac{1}{4}$ to shrink it to the size of triangle DEF. Next, we must translate the dilated triangle, noted by $D'''E'''F'''$, one unit up and two units to the right. This sequence of the dilation followed by the translation, would map triangle $D''E''F''$ onto triangle DEF.

2. Triangle ABC was dilated from center O by scale factor $r = \frac{1}{2}$. The dilated triangle is noted by $A'B'C'$. Another triangle $A''B''C''$ is congruent to triangle $A'B'C'$ (i.e., $\triangle A''B''C'' \cong \triangle A'B'C'$). Describe the dilation followed by the basic rigid motion that would map triangle $A''B''C''$ onto triangle ABC.

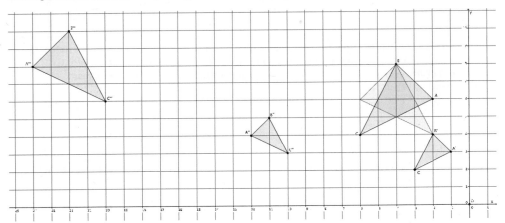

Triangle $A''B''C''$ will need to be dilated from center O by scale factor $r = 2$ to bring it to the same size as triangle ABC. This will produce a triangle noted by $A'''B'''C'''$. Next, triangle $A'''B'''C'''$ will need to be translated 18 units to the right and 2 units down, producing the triangle shown in red. Next, rotate the red triangle d degrees around point B, so that one of the segments of the red triangle coincides completely with segment BC. Then, reflect the red triangle across line BC. The dilation, followed by the congruence described, will map triangle $A''B''C''$ onto triangle ABC.

3. Are the two figures shown below similar? If so, describe the sequence that would prove the similarity. If not, state how you know they are not similar.

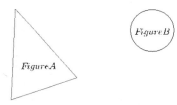

No, these figures are not similar. There is no single rigid motion, or sequence of rigid motions, that would map Figure A onto Figure B.

4. Triangle ABC is similar to triangle $A'B'C'$, (i.e, $\triangle ABC \sim \triangle A'B'C'$). Prove the similarity by describing the sequence that would map triangle $A'B'C'$ onto triangle ABC.

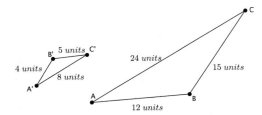

The scale factor that would magnify triangle $A'B'C'$ to the size of triangle ABC is $r = 3$. The sequence that would prove the similarity of the triangles is a dilation from center O by a scale factor of $r = 3$, followed by a translation along vector $\overrightarrow{A'A}$ and, finally, a reflection across line AC.

5. Are the two figures shown below similar? If so, describe the sequence that would prove $\triangle ABC \sim \triangle A'B'C'$. If not, state how you know they are not similar.

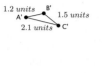

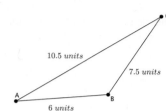

Yes, the triangles are similar. The scale factor that triangle ABC has been dilated is $r = \frac{1}{5}$. The sequence that proves the triangles are similar is as follows: dilate triangle $A'B'C'$ from center O by scale factor $r = 5$, then translate triangle $A'B'C'$ along vector $\overrightarrow{C'C}$, next, rotate triangle $A'B'C'$ d degrees around point C and, finally, reflect triangle $A'B'C'$ across line AC.

6. Describe the sequence that would show $\triangle ABC \sim \triangle A'B'C'$.

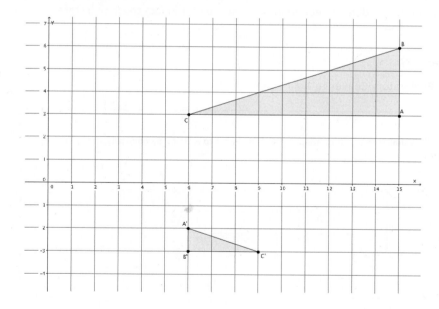

Since $r|AB| = |A'B'|$, then $r \times 3 = 1$, and $r = \frac{1}{3}$. A dilation from the origin by scale factor $r = \frac{1}{3}$ will make $\triangle ABC$ the same size as $\triangle A'B'C'$. Then, a translation of the dilated image of $\triangle ABC$ four units down and one unit to the right, followed by a reflection across line $A'B'$ will map $\triangle ABC$ onto $\triangle A'B'C'$, proving the triangles to be similar.

Lesson 9: Basic Properties of Similarity

Student Outcomes

- Students know that similarity is both a symmetric and a transitive relation.

Classwork

Concept Development (3 minutes)

- If we say that one figure, S, is similar to another figure S', i.e., $S \sim S'$, can we also say that $S' \sim S$? That is, is similarity symmetric? Keep in mind that there is a very specific sequence of a dilation followed by a congruence that would map S to S'.
  - *Expect students to say yes, they would expect similarity to be symmetric.*
- If we say that figure S is similar to another figure T, i.e., $S \sim T$, and figure T is similar to yet another figure U, i.e., $T \sim U$, is it true that $S \sim U$? That is, is similarity transitive?
  - *Expect students to say yes, they would expect similarity to be transitive.*

The Exploratory Challenges to follow are for students to get an intuitive sense that in fact these two statements are true.

Exploratory Challenge 1 (10 minutes)

Students work in pairs to complete Exploratory Challenge 1.

Exploratory Challenge 1

The goal is to show that if $\triangle ABC$ is similar to $\triangle A'B'C'$, then $\triangle A'B'C'$ is similar to $\triangle ABC$. Symbolically, if $\triangle ABC \sim \triangle A'B'C'$, then $\triangle A'B'C' \sim \triangle ABC$.

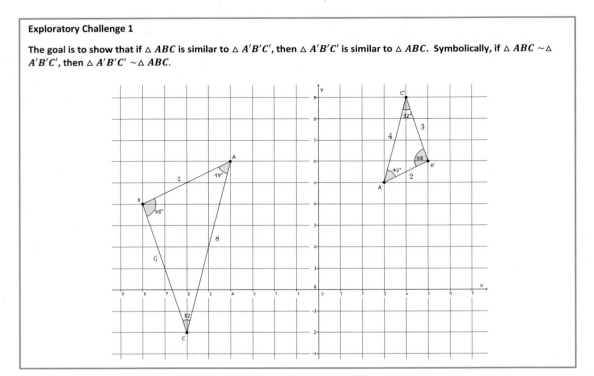

a.   First determine whether or not △ ABC is in fact similar to △ A'B'C'. (If it isn't, then there would is no further work to be done.) Use a protractor to verify that the corresponding angles are congruent and that the ratio of the corresponding sides are equal to some scale factor.

The corresponding angles are congruent: $\angle A \cong \angle A' = 49°$, $\angle B \cong \angle B' = 98°$, and $\angle C \cong \angle C' = 32°$.

The ratio of the corresponding sides are equal: $\dfrac{4}{8} = \dfrac{3}{6} = \dfrac{2}{4} = r$.

b.   Describe the sequence of dilation followed by a congruence that proves △ ABC ~ △ A'B'C'.

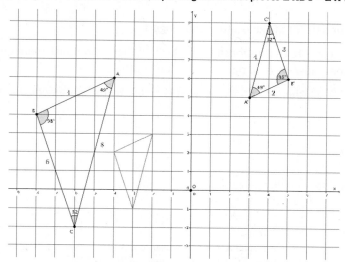

To map △ ABC onto △ A'B'C', dilate △ ABC from center O by scale factor $r = \dfrac{1}{2}$ *noted in the figure above by the red triangle. Then translate the red triangle up two units and five units to the right. Next, rotate the red triangle d degrees around point A' until AC coincides with A'C'.*

c.   Describe the sequence of dilation followed by a congruence that proves △ A'B'C' ~ △ ABC.

Note that in the diagram below the y-axis has been compressed.

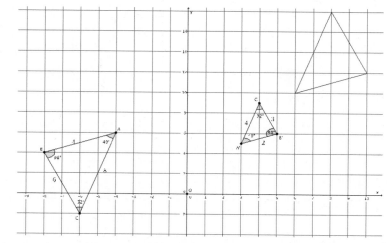

To map △ A'B'C' onto △ ABC, dilate △ A'B'C' from center O by scale factor $r = 2$, *noted by the blue triangle in the diagram. Then, translate the blue triangle ten units to the left and four units down. Next, rotate the blue triangle 180 degrees around point A until A'C' coincides with AC.*

> **d.** Is it true that △ *ABC* ~△ *A'B'C'* and △ *A'B'C'* ~△ *ABC*? Why do you think this is so?
>
> *Yes, it is true that △ ABC ~△ A'B'C' and △ A'B'C' ~△ ABC. I think it is true because when we say figures are similar, it means that they are the same figure, just a different size because one has been dilated by a scale factor. For that reason, if one figure, like △ ABC, is similar to another, like △ A'B'C', it must mean that △ A'B'C' ~△ ABC. However, the sequence you would use to map one of the figures onto the other will be different.*

Concept Development (3 minutes)

Ask students to share what they wrote for part (d) of Exploratory Challenge 1.

Expect students to respond in a similar manner to the response for part (d). If they do not, ask them questions about what similarity means, what a dilation does, how we map figures onto one another.

- For any two figures S and S', if $S \sim S'$, then $S' \sim S$. This is what is meant by the statement that **similarity is a symmetric relation**.

Exploratory Challenge 2 (15 minutes)

Students work in pairs to complete Exploratory Challenge 2.

> **Exploratory Challenge 2**
>
> The goal is to show that if △ *ABC* is similar to △ *A'B'C'*, and △ *A'B'C'* is similar to △ *A''B''C''*, then △ *ABC* is similar to △ *A''B''C''*. Symbolically, if △ *ABC* ~△ *A'B'C'* and △ *A'B'C'* ~△ *A''B''C''*, then △ *ABC* ~△ *A''B''C''*.
>
>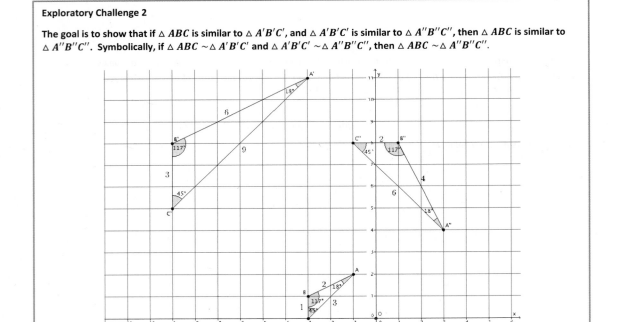

a.   **Describe the similarity that proves △ ABC ~ △ A'B'C'.**

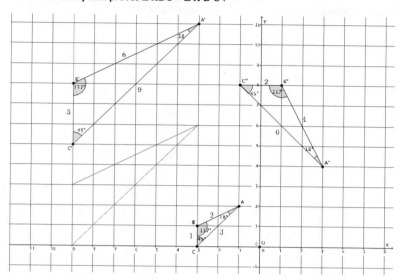

To map △ ABC onto △ A'B'C', we need to first determine the scale factor that will make △ ABC the same size as △ A'B'C'. Then $\frac{3}{1} = \frac{6}{2} = \frac{9}{3} = r$. Dilate △ ABC from center O by scale factor $r = 3$, shown in red in the diagram. Then, translate the red triangle 5 units up.

b.   **Describe the similarity that proves △ A'B'C' ~ △ A''B''C''.**

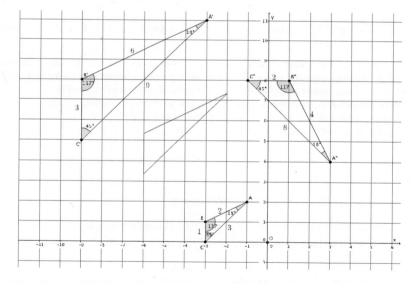

To map △ A'B'C' onto △ A''B''C'', we need to first determine the scale factor that will make △ A'B'C' the same size as △ A''B''C''. Then $\frac{4}{6} = \frac{6}{9} = \frac{2}{3} = r$. Dilate △ A'B'C' from center O by scale factor $r = \frac{2}{3}$, shown in blue in the diagram. Then, translate the blue triangle 3.5 units down and 5 units to the right. Next, rotate the blue triangle 90 degrees around point A'' until the blue triangle coincides with △ A''B''C''.

c.   **Verify that, in fact, $\triangle ABC \sim \triangle A''B''C''$ by checking corresponding angles and corresponding side lengths. Then describe the sequence that would prove the similarity $\triangle ABC \sim \triangle A''B''C''$.**

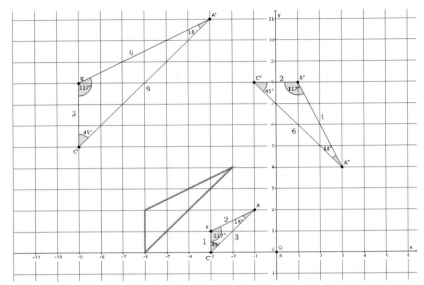

The corresponding angles are congruent: $\angle A \cong \angle A'' = 18°$, $\angle B \cong \angle B'' = 117°$, and $\angle C \cong \angle C'' = 45°$. The ratio of the corresponding sides are equal: $\frac{4}{2} = \frac{6}{3} = \frac{2}{1} = r$. Dilate $\triangle ABC$ from center O by scale factor $r = 2$, shown as the pink triangle in the diagram. Then translate the pink triangle 5 units to the right. Finally, rotate the pink triangle 90 degrees around point A'' until the pink triangle coincides with $\triangle A''B''C''$.

d.   **Is it true that if $\triangle ABC \sim \triangle A'B'C'$ and $\triangle A'B'C' \sim \triangle A''B''C''$, then $\triangle ABC \sim \triangle A''B''C''$? Why do you think this is so?**

Yes, it is true that if $\triangle ABC \sim \triangle A'B'C'$ and $\triangle A'B'C' \sim \triangle A''B''C''$, then $\triangle ABC \sim \triangle A''B''C''$. Again, because these figures are similar it means that they have equal angles and are made different sizes based on a specific scale factor. Since dilations map angles to angles of the same degree, it makes sense that all three figures would have the "same shape." Also, using the idea that similarity is a symmetric relation, the statement that $\triangle ABC \sim \triangle A'B'C'$ implies that $\triangle A'B'C' \sim \triangle ABC$. Since we know that $\triangle A'B'C' \sim \triangle A''B''C''$, it is reasonable to conclude that $\triangle ABC \sim \triangle A''B''C''$.

Concept Development (3 minutes)

Ask students to share what they wrote for part (d) of Exploratory Challenge 2.

Expect students to respond in a similar manner to the response for part (d). If they do not, ask them questions about what similarity means, what a dilation does, and how they might use what they just learned about similarity being a symmetric relation.

- For any three figures S, T, and U, if $S \sim T$, and $T \sim U$, then $S \sim U$. This is what is meant by the statement that **similarity is a transitive relation**.

Closing (5 minutes)

Summarize, or ask students to summarize, the main points from the lesson:

- We know that similarity is a symmetric relation. That means that if one figure is similar to another, $S \sim S'$, then we can be sure that $S' \sim S$. The sequence that maps one onto the other will be different, but we know that it is true.

- We know that similarity is a transitive relation. That means that if we are given two similar figures, $S \sim T$, and another statement about $T \sim U$, then we also know that $S \sim U$. Again, the sequence and scale factor will be different to prove the similarity, but we know it is true.

Lesson Summary

Similarity is a symmetric relation. That means that if one figure is similar to another, $S \sim S'$, then we can be sure that $S' \sim S$.

Similarity is a transitive relation. That means that if we are given two similar figures, $S \sim T$, and another statement about $T \sim U$, then we also know that $S \sim U$.

Exit Ticket (5 minutes)

Name _____   Date_____

Lesson 9: Basic Properties of Similarity

Exit Ticket

Use the diagram below to answer questions 1 and 2.

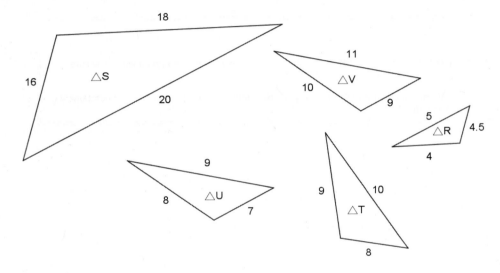

1.   Which triangles, if any, have similarity that is symmetric?

2.   Which triangles, if any, have similarity that is transitive?

Exit Ticket Sample Solutions

Use the diagram below to answer questions 1 and 2.

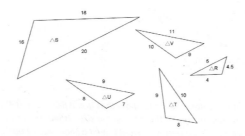

1. **Which triangles, if any, have similarity that is symmetric?**

   △ S ~ △ R and △ R ~ △ S.

   △ S ~ △ T and △ T ~ △ S.

   △ T ~ △ R and △ R ~ △ T.

2. **Which triangles, if any, have similarity that is transitive?**

   One possible solution: Since △ S ~ △ R and △ R~ △ T, then △ S~ △ T.

   Note that △ U and △ V are not similar to each other or any other triangles. Therefore, they should not be in any solution.

Problem Set Sample Solutions

1. **Would a dilation alone be enough to show that similarity is symmetric? That is, would a dilation alone prove that if △ ABC ~△ A'B'C', then △ A'B'C' ~△ ABC? Consider the two examples below.**

   a. **Given △ ABC ~△ A'B'C'. Is a dilation enough to show that △ A'B'C' ~△ ABC? Explain.**

   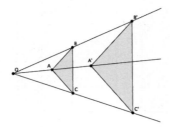

   For these two triangles, a dilation alone is enough to show that if △ ABC ~△ A'B'C', then △ A'B'C' ~△ ABC. The reason that dilation alone is enough is because both of the triangles have been dilated from the same center. Therefore, to map one onto the other, all that would be required is a dilation.

b.   Given $\triangle ABC \sim \triangle A'B'C'$. Is a dilation enough to show that $\triangle A'B'C' \sim \triangle ABC$? Explain.

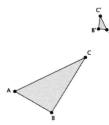

For these two triangles, a dilation alone is not enough to show that if $\triangle ABC \sim \triangle A'B'C'$, then $\triangle A'B'C' \sim \triangle ABC$. The reason is that a dilation would just make them the same size. It would not show that you could map one of the triangles onto the other. To do that, you would need a sequence of basic rigid motions to demonstrate the congruence.

c.   In general, is dilation enough to prove that similarity is a symmetric relation? Explain.

No, in general a dilation alone does not prove that similarity is a symmetric relation. In some cases, like part (a) it would be enough, but because we are talking about general cases, we must consider figures that require a sequence of basic rigid motions to map one onto the other. Therefore, in general, to show that there is a symmetric relationship, we must use what we know about similar figures, a dilation followed by a congruence, as opposed to dilation alone.

2.   Would a dilation alone be enough to show that similarity is transitive? That is, would a dilation alone prove that if $\triangle ABC \sim \triangle A'B'C'$, and $\triangle A'B'C' \sim \triangle A''B''C''$, then $\triangle ABC \sim \triangle A''B''C''$? Consider the two examples below.

a.   Given $\triangle ABC \sim \triangle A'B'C'$ and $\triangle A'B'C' \sim \triangle A''B''C''$. Is a dilation enough to show that $\triangle ABC \sim \triangle A''B''C''$? Explain.

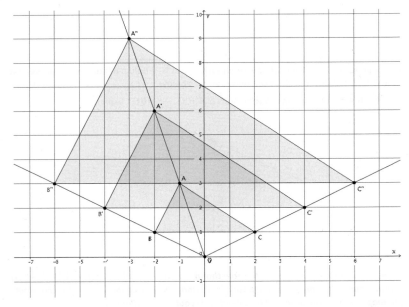

Yes, in this case, we could dilate by different scale factors to show that all three triangles are similar to each other.

b.   Given $\triangle ABC \sim \triangle A'B'C'$ and $\triangle A'B'C' \sim \triangle A''B''C''$. Is a dilation enough to show that $\triangle ABC \sim \triangle A''B''C''$? Explain.

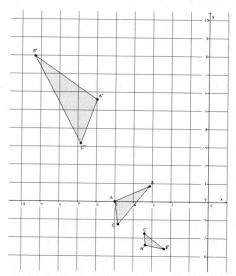

In this case, it would take more than just a dilation to show that all three triangles were similar to one another. Specifically, it would take a dilation followed by a congruence to prove the similarity among the three.

c.   In general, is dilation enough to prove that similarity is a transitive relation? Explain.

No, in some cases it might be enough, but the general case requires the use of dilation and a congruence. Therefore, to prove that similarity is a transitive relation you must use both a dilation and a congruence.

3.   In the diagram below, $\triangle ABC \sim \triangle A'B'C'$ and $\triangle A'B'C' \sim \triangle A''B''C''$. Is $\triangle ABC \sim \triangle A''B''C''$? If so, describe the dilation followed by the congruence that demonstrates the similarity.

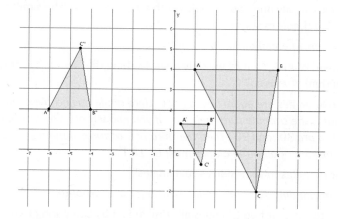

Yes, $\triangle ABC \sim \triangle A''B''C''$ because similarity is transitive. Since $r|AB| = |A'B'|$, then $r \times 4 = 2$, which means $r = \frac{1}{2}$. Then a dilation from the origin by scale factor $r = \frac{1}{2}$ will make $\triangle ABC$ the same size as $\triangle A''B''C''$. Translate the dilated image of $\triangle ABC$ $6\frac{1}{2}$ units to the left, then reflect across line $A''B''$. The sequence of the dilation and the congruence will map $\triangle ABC$ onto $\triangle A''B''C''$ demonstrating the similarity.

Lesson 10: Informal Proof of AA Criterion for Similarity

Student Outcomes

- Students know an informal proof of the Angle-Angle (AA) criterion for similar triangles.
- Students present informal arguments as to whether or not triangles are similar based on Angle-Angle criterion.

Classwork

Concept Development (5 minutes)

- Recall the exercise we did using lined paper to verify experimentally the properties of the Fundamental Theorem of Similarity (FTS). In that example, it was easy for us to see that that the triangles were similar because one was a dilation of the other by some scale factor. It was also easy for us to compare the size of corresponding angles because we could use what we knew about parallel lines cut by a transversal.

> **Scaffolding:**
> Consider having students review their work of the activity by talking to a partner about what they did and what they proved with respect to FTS.

- Our goal today is to show that we can say any two triangles with equal angles will be similar. It is what we call the AA criterion for similarity. The theorem states:

  □ *Two triangles with two pairs of equal angles are similar.*

- Notice that we only use AA instead of AAA, that is, we only need to show that two of the three angles are equal in measure. Why do you think that is so?

  □ *We only have to show two angles are equal because the third angle has no choice but to be equal as well. The reason for that is the triangle sum theorem. If you know that two pairs of corresponding angles are equal, say they are 30° and 90°, then the third pair of corresponding angles has no choice but to be 60° because the sum of all three angles must be 180°.*

- What other property do similar triangles have besides equal angles?

  □ *The lengths of their corresponding sides are equal in ratio (or proportional).*

- Do you believe that it is enough to say that two triangles are similar just by comparing two pairs of corresponding angles?

  □ *Some students may say yes, others no. Encourage students to justify their claim. Either way, they can verify the validity of the theorem by completing Exercises 1 and 2.*

Exercises 1–2 (8 minutes)

Students complete Exercises 1 and 2 independently.

Exercises

1. Use a protractor to draw a pair of triangles with two pairs of equal angles. Then measure the lengths of sides, and verify that the lengths of their corresponding sides are equal in ratio.

    Sample student work shown below.

    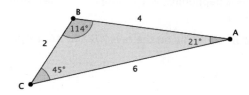

    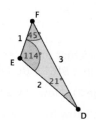

    > **Scaffolding:**
    >
    > If students hesitate to begin, suggest specific side lengths for them to use.

    $$\frac{4}{2} = \frac{6}{3} = \frac{2}{1}$$

2. Draw a new pair of triangles with two pairs of equal angles. Then measure the lengths of sides, and verify that the lengths of their corresponding sides are equal in ratio.

    Sample student work shown below.

    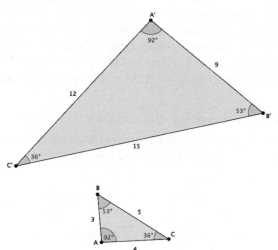

    $$\frac{3}{9} = \frac{5}{15} = \frac{4}{12}$$

Discussion (10 minutes)

- Did everyone notice that they had similar triangles in Exercises 1 and 2?

  □ *Yes.* (If they respond no, ask them how close the ratios were with respect to being equal. In some cases, human error either in measuring the angles or side lengths can cause the discrepancy. Another way around this is by selecting ahead of time one student to share their work on a document camera for all to see.)

To develop conceptual understanding, students may continue to generate triangles with two pairs of equal angles and then generalize to develop the AA criterion for similarity. A more formal proof follows, which may also be used.

- What we need to do now is informally prove why this is happening, even though we all drew different triangles with different angle measures and different side lengths.

- We begin with a special case. Suppose $A = A'$, and B' and C' lie on the rays $\overrightarrow{AB}$ and $\overrightarrow{AC}$, respectively.

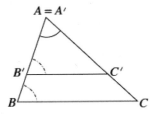

- In this case, we are given that $|\angle A'B'C'| = |\angle ABC|$ and $|\angle B'A'C'| = |\angle BAC|$ (notice that the latter is simply saying that an angle is equal to itself). The fact that $|\angle A'B'C'| = |\angle ABC|$ implies that $B'C' \parallel BC$ because if corresponding angles are equal, then we know we have parallel lines (from Module 2). Now, if we let $r = \frac{|AB'|}{|AB|}$, then the dilation from center A with scale factor r means that $|AB'| = r|AB|$. We know from our work in Lessons 4 and 5 that the location of C' is in a fixed location because $|AC'| = r|AC|$. Therefore, the dilation of $\triangle ABC$ is exactly $\triangle A'B'C'$.

Ask students to paraphrase the proof, or offer them this version: We are given that the corresponding angles $|\angle A'B'C'|$ and $|\angle ABC|$ are equal. The only way that corresponding angles can be equal is if we have parallel lines. That means that $B'C' \parallel BC$. If we say that the length of $|AB'|$ is equal to the length of $|AB|$ multiplied by some scale factor, then we are looking at a dilation from center A. Based on our work in previous lessons with dilated points in the coordinate plane, we know that C' has no choice as to its location and that the length of $|AC'|$ must be equal to the length of $|AC|$ multiplied by the same scale factor r. For those reasons, when we dilate $\triangle ABC$ by scale factor r, we get $\triangle A'B'C'$.

- This shows that given two pairs of equal corresponding angles that $\triangle ABC \sim \triangle A'B'C'$.

- In general, if $\triangle A'B'C'$ did not share a common point, i.e., A, with $\triangle ABC$, we would simply perform a sequence of rigid motions (a congruence), so that we would be in the situation just described.

The following are instructions as to how to prepare manipulatives to serve as a physical demonstration of the AA criterion for similarity when the triangles do not share a common angle. Prepare ahead of time cardboard or cardstock versions of triangles $A'B'C'$ and ABC (including a triangle $\triangle AB_0C_0$ drawn within $\triangle ABC$). Demonstrate the congruence $\triangle A'B'C' \cong \triangle AB_0C_0$ by moving the cardboard between these two triangles.

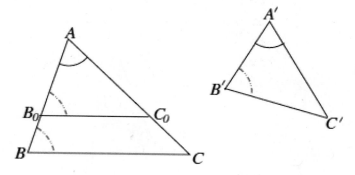

Example 1 (2 minutes)

- Are the triangles shown below similar? Present an informal argument as to why they are or why they are not.

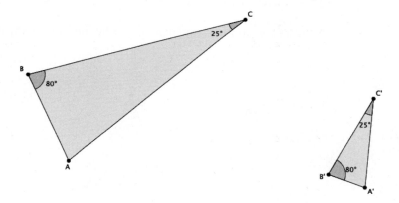

- *Yes, $\triangle ABC \sim \triangle A'B'C'$. They are similar because they have two pairs of corresponding angles that are equal. Namely, $|\angle B| = |\angle B'| = 80°$, and $|\angle C| = |\angle C'| = 25°$.*

Example 2 (2 minutes)

- Are the triangles shown below similar? Present an informal argument as to why they are or why they are not.

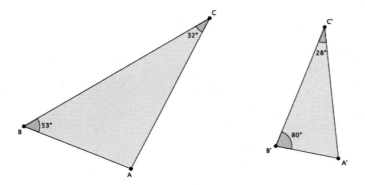

- No, △ ABC is not similar to △ A'B'C'. They are not similar because they do not have two pairs of corresponding angles that are equal. Namely, |∠B| ≠ |∠B'|, and |∠C| ≠ |∠C'|.

Example 3 (2 minutes)

- Are the triangles shown below similar? Present an informal argument as to why they are or why they are not.

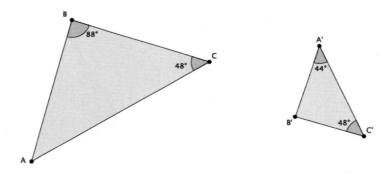

- Yes, △ ABC~ △ A'B'C'. They are similar because they have two pairs of corresponding angles that are equal. You have to use the triangle sum theorem to find out that |∠A| = 44° or |∠B'| = 88°. Then you can see that, |∠A| = |∠A'| = 44°, |∠B| = |∠B'| = 88°, and |∠C| = |∠C'| = 48°.

Exercises 3–5 (8 minutes)

3. Are the triangles shown below similar? Present an informal argument as to why they are or why they are not.

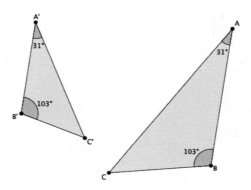

Yes, △ ABC∼ △ A′B′C′. They are similar because they have two pairs of corresponding angles that are equal. Namely, |∠B| = |∠B′| = 103°, and |∠A| = |∠A′| = 31°.

4. Are the triangles shown below similar? Present an informal argument as to why they are or why they are not.

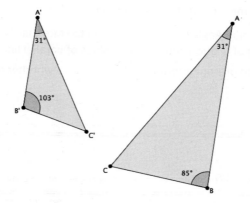

No, △ ABC is not similar to △ A′B′C′. They are not similar because they do not have two pairs of corresponding angles that are equal, just one. Namely, |∠B| ≠ |∠B′|, but |∠A| = |∠A′|.

5. Are the triangles shown below similar? Present an informal argument as to why they are or why they are not.

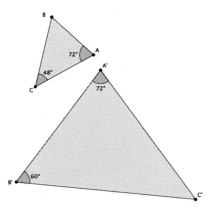

Yes, △ ABC∼ △ A′B′C′. They are similar because they have two pairs of corresponding angles that are equal. You have to use the triangle sum theorem to find out that $|\angle B| = 60°$ *or* $|\angle C'| = 48°$. *Then you can see that* $|\angle A| = |\angle A'| = 72°$, $|\angle B| = |\angle B'| = 60°$, *and* $|\angle C| = |\angle C'| = 48°$.

Closing (3 minutes)

Summarize, or ask students to summarize, the main points from the lesson:

- We understand a proof of why the Angle-Angle criterion is enough to state that two triangles are similar. The proof depends on our understanding of dilation, angle relationships of parallel lines, and congruence.

- We practiced using the AA criterion to present informal arguments as to whether or not two triangles were similar.

Lesson Summary

Two triangles are said to be similar if they have two pairs of corresponding angles that are equal.

Exit Ticket (5 minutes)

Lesson 10: Informal Proof of AA Criterion for Similarity
Date: 10/16/13

142

Name _____   Date_____

Lesson 10: Informal Proof of AA Criterion for Similarity

Exit Ticket

1.   Are the triangles shown below similar? Present an informal argument as to why they are or why they are not.

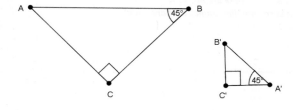

2.   Are the triangles shown below similar? Present an informal argument as to why they are or why they are not.

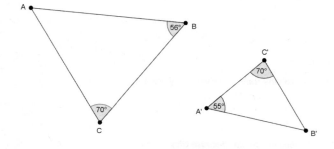

Exit Ticket Sample Solutions

1. Are the triangles shown below similar? Present an informal argument as to why they are or why they are not.

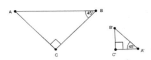

Yes, △ ABC~ △ A′B′C′. They are similar because they have two pairs of corresponding angles that are equal. You have to use the triangle sum theorem to find out that |∠B′| = 45°or |∠A| = 45°. Then you can see that |∠A| = |∠A′| = 45°, and |∠B| = |∠B′| = 45°, and |∠C| = |∠C′| = 90°.

2. Are the triangles shown below similar? Present an informal argument as to why they are or why they are not.

No, △ ABC is not similar to △ A′B′C′. They are not similar because they do not have two pairs of corresponding angles that are equal. Namely, |∠A| ≠ |∠A′| and |∠B| ≠ |∠B′|.

Problem Set Sample Solutions

Students practice presenting informal arguments to prove whether or not two triangles are similar.

1. Are the triangles shown below similar? Present an informal argument as to why they are or why they are not.

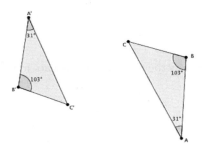

Yes, △ ABC~ △ A′B′C′. They are similar because they have two pairs of corresponding angles that are equal. Namely, |∠B| = |∠B′| = 103°, and |∠A| = |∠A′| = 31°.

2. Are the triangles shown below similar? Present an informal argument as to why they are or why they are not.

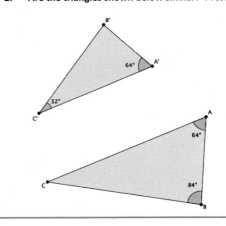

Yes, △ ABC ~ △ A′B′C′. They are similar because they have two pairs of corresponding angles that are equal. You have to use the triangle sum theorem to find out that |∠B′| = 84° or |∠C| = 32°. Then you can see that |∠A| = |∠A′| = 64°, |∠B| = |∠B′| = 84°, and |∠C| = |∠C′| =32°.

3. Are the triangles shown below similar? Present an informal argument as to why they are or why they are not.

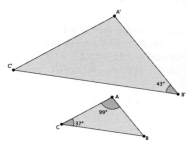

No, △ ABC is not similar to △ A'B'C'. We can use the triangle sum theorem to find out that |∠B| = 44°, but we do not have any information about |∠A'| or |∠C'|. To be considered similar, the two triangles must have two pairs of corresponding angles that are equal. In this problem, we only know of one pair.

4. Are the triangles shown below similar? Present an informal argument as to why they are or why they are not.

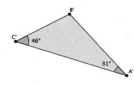

Yes, △ ABC ~ △ A'B'C'. They are similar because they have two pairs of corresponding angles that are equal. Namely, |∠C| = |∠C'| = 46°, and |∠A| = |∠A'| = 31°.

5. Are the triangles shown below similar? Present an informal argument as to why they are or why they are not.

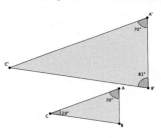

Yes, △ ABC ~ △ A'B'C'. They are similar because they have two pairs of corresponding angles that are equal. You have to use the triangle sum theorem to find out that |∠B| = 81° or |∠C'| = 29°. Then you can see that |∠A| = |∠A'| = 70°, |∠B| = |∠B'| = 81°, and |∠C| = |∠C'| = 29°.

6. Are the triangles shown below similar? Present an informal argument as to why they are or why they are not.

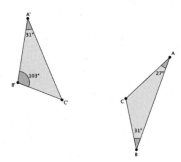

No, △ ABC is not similar to △ A'B'C'. By the given information, |∠B| ≠ |∠B'|, and |∠A| ≠ |∠A'|.

7. Are the triangles shown below similar? Present an informal argument as to why they are or why they are not.

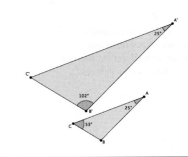

Yes, △ ABC ~ △ $A'B'C'$. They are similar because they have two pairs of corresponding angles that are equal. You have to use the triangle sum theorem to find out that $|\angle B| = 102°$ or $|\angle C'| = 53°$. Then you can see that $|\angle A| = |\angle A'| = 25°$, $|\angle B| = |\angle B'| = 102°$, and $|\angle C| = |\angle C'| = 53°$.

Lesson 11: More About Similar Triangles

Student Outcomes

- Students present informal arguments as to whether or not two triangles are similar.
- Students practice finding lengths of corresponding sides of similar triangles.

Lesson Notes

This lesson synthesizes the knowledge gained thus far in Module 3. Students use what they know about dilation, congruence, the Fundamental Theorem of Similarity (FTS), and the AA criterion to determine if two triangles are similar. In the first two examples, students use informal arguments to decide if a pair of triangles are similar. To do so, they look for pairs of corresponding angles that are equal (wanting to use the AA criterion). When they realize that information is not given, they compare lengths of corresponding sides to see if the sides could be dilations with the same scale factor. After a dilation and congruence is performed, students see that a pair of triangles are similar (or not) and then continue to give more proof as to why they must be, e.g., by FTS, a specific pair of lines are parallel, and the corresponding angles cut by a transversal must be equal; therefore, we can use AA criterion to state that two triangles are similar. Once students know how to determine if two triangles are similar or not, they apply this knowledge to finding lengths of segments of triangles that are unknown in Examples 3–5.

Classwork

Example 1 (6 minutes)

- Given the information provided, is $\triangle ABC \sim \triangle DEF$? (Give students a minute or two to discuss with a partner.)

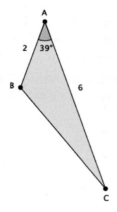
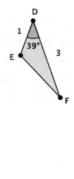

  - *Students will likely say that they cannot tell if the triangles are similar because there is only information for one angle provided. In the previous lesson, students could determine if two triangles were similar using Angle-Angle criterion.*

- What if we combined our knowledge of dilation and similarity? That is, we know we can translate $\triangle ABC$ so that $\angle A = \angle D$. Then our picture would look like this:

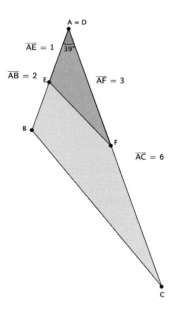

- Can we tell if the triangles are similar now?
  - *We still do not have information about the angles, but we can use what we know about dilation and the Fundamental Theorem of Similarity to find out if EF is parallel to BC. If they are, then $\triangle ABC \sim \triangle DEF$ because the corresponding angles of parallel lines are equal.*
- We do not have the information we need about corresponding angles. So let's examine the information we are provided. Compare the given side lengths to see if the ratios of corresponding sides are equal:

  Is $\frac{|AE|}{|AB|} = \frac{|AF|}{|AC|}$? That's the same as asking if $\frac{1}{2} = \frac{3}{6}$? Since the ratios of corresponding sides are equal, then there exists a dilation from center A with scale factor $r = \frac{1}{2}$ that maps $\triangle ABC \sim \triangle DEF$. Since the ratios of corresponding sides are equal, then by the Fundamental Theorem of Similarity, we know EF is parallel to BC and the corresponding angles of the parallel lines are also equal in measure.
- This example illustrates another way for us to determine if two triangles are similar. That is, if they have one pair of equal corresponding angles, and the ratio of corresponding sides (along each side of the given angle) are equal, then the triangles are similar.

Example 2 (4 minutes)

- Given the information provided, is △ $ABC \sim$ △ $AB'C'$? Explain. (Give students a minute or two to discuss with a partner.)

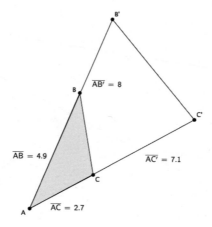

- If students say that the triangles are not similar because lines BC and $B'C'$ are not parallel, ask them how they know this. If they say "They don't look parallel", tell students that the way they look is not good enough. They must prove mathematically that the lines are not parallel. For that reason, the following response is more legitimate.

  □ *We do not have information about two pairs of corresponding angles, so we will need to examine the ratios of corresponding side lengths. If the ratios are equal, then the triangles are similar.*

- If the ratios of the corresponding sides are equal, it means that the lengths were dilated by the same scale factor. Write the ratios of the corresponding sides.

  □ *The ratios of corresponding sides are* $\dfrac{|AC'|}{|AC|} = \dfrac{|AB'|}{|AB|}$.

- Does $\dfrac{|AC'|}{|AC|} = \dfrac{|AB'|}{|AB|}$? That is the same as asking if $\dfrac{7.1}{2.7}$ and $\dfrac{8}{4.9}$ are equivalent fractions. One possible way of verifying if the fractions are equal is by multiplying the numerator of each fraction by the denominator of the other. If the products are equal, then we know the fractions are equivalent.

  □ *The products are 34.79 and 21.6. Since 34.79 ≠ 21.6, the fractions are not equivalent, and the triangles are not similar.*

Example 3 (4 minutes)

- Given that $\triangle ABC \sim \triangle AB'C'$, could we determine the length of AB'? What does it mean to say that $\triangle ABC \sim \triangle AB'C'$? (Give students a minute or two to discuss with a partner.)

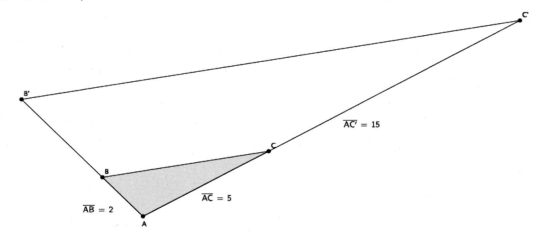

$\overline{AC'} = 15$

$\overline{AB} = 2$ $\overline{AC} = 5$

- □ It means that corresponding angles are equal, the ratio of corresponding sides are equal, i.e.,
  $$\frac{|AC'|}{|AC|} = \frac{|AB'|}{|AB|} = \frac{|B'C'|}{|BC|},$$ and lines BC and $B'C'$ are parallel.

- How can we use what we know about similar triangles to determine the length of AB'?

  - □ The corresponding sides are supposed to be equal in ratio: $\dfrac{|AC'|}{|AC|} = \dfrac{|AB'|}{|AB|}$ is the same as $\dfrac{15}{5} = \dfrac{|AB'|}{2}$.

- Since we know that for equivalent fractions, when we multiply the numerator of each fraction by the denominator of the other fraction, the products are equal, we can use that fact to find the length of AB'. Let x represent the length of AB'; then $\dfrac{15}{5} = \dfrac{|AB'|}{2}$ is the same as $\dfrac{15}{5} = \dfrac{x}{2}$. Equivalently, we get $30 = 5x$. The value of x that makes the statement true is $x = 6$. Therefore, the length of AB' is 6.

Example 4 (4 minutes)

- If we suppose XY is parallel to $X'Y'$, can we use the information provided to determine if $\triangle OXY \sim \triangle OX'Y'$? Explain. (Give students a minute or two to discuss with a partner.)

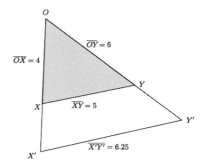

O

$\overline{OY} = 6$

$\overline{OX} = 4$

Y

X $\overline{XY} = 5$

Y'

$\overline{X'Y'} = 6.25$

X'

- ▫ *Since we assume $XY \| X'Y'$, then we know we have similar triangles because each triangle shares $\angle O$ and the corresponding angles are congruent: $\angle OXY \cong \angle OX'Y'$, and $\angle OYX \cong \angle OY'X'$. By the AA criterion, we can conclude that $\triangle OXY \sim \triangle OX'Y'$.*

- ▪ Now that we know the triangles are similar, can we determine the length of OX'? Explain.

  - ▫ *By the converse of the Fundamental Theorem of Similarity, since we are given parallel lines and the lengths of the corresponding sides XY and $X'Y'$, we can write the ratio that represents the scale factor and compute using the fact that cross products must be equal to determine the length of OX'.*

- ▪ Write the ratio for the known side lengths XY and $X'Y'$ and the ratio that would contain the side length we are looking for. Then use the cross products to find the length of OX'.

  - ▫ $\dfrac{|X'Y'|}{|XY|} = \dfrac{|OX'|}{|OX|}$ *is the same as* $\dfrac{6.25}{5} = \dfrac{|OX'|}{4}$. *Let z represent the length of OX', then we have* $\dfrac{6.25}{5} = \dfrac{z}{4}$ *or equivalently, $5z = 25$ and $z = 5$. Therefore, the length of OX' is 5.*

- ▪ Now find the length of OY'.

  - ▫ $\dfrac{|X'Y'|}{|XY|} = \dfrac{|OY'|}{|OY|}$ *is the same as* $\dfrac{6.25}{5} = \dfrac{|OY'|}{6}$. *Let z represent the length of OY', then we have* $\dfrac{6.25}{5} = \dfrac{z}{6}$ *or equivalently, $5z = 37.5$ and $z = 7.5$. Therefore, the length of OY' is 7.5.*

Example 5 (3 minutes)

- ▪ Given the information provided, can you determine if $\triangle OPQ \sim \triangle OP'Q'$? Explain. (Give students a minute or two to discuss with a partner.)

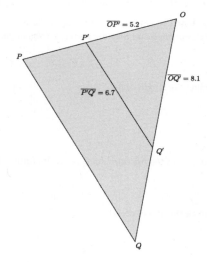

- ▫ *No, in order to determine if $\triangle OPQ \sim \triangle OP'Q'$ we need information about two pairs of corresponding angles. As is, we only know that the two triangles have one equal angle, the common angle at O. We would have corresponding angles that were equal if we knew that $PQ \parallel P'Q'$. Our other option is to compare the ratio of the sides that comprise the common angle. However, we do not have information about the lengths OP or OQ. For that reason, we cannot determine whether or not $\triangle OPQ \sim \triangle OP'Q'$.*

Exercises 1–3 (14 minutes)

Students can work independently or in pairs to complete Exercises 1–3.

Exercises

1. In the diagram below, you have $\triangle ABC$ and $\triangle AB'C'$. Use this information to answer parts (a)–(d).

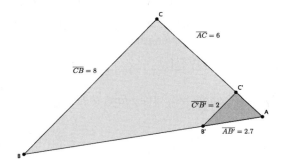

$\overline{AC} = 6$

$\overline{CB} = 8$

$\overline{C'B'} = 2$

$\overline{AB'} = 2.7$

    a. Based on the information given, is $\triangle ABC \sim \triangle AB'C'$? Explain.

    There is not enough information provided to determine if the triangles are similar. We would need information about a pair of corresponding angles or more information about the side lengths of each of the triangles.

    b. Assume line BC is parallel to line $B'C'$. With this information, can you say that $\triangle ABC \sim \triangle AB'C'$? Explain.

    If line BC is parallel to line $B'C'$, then $\triangle ABC \sim \triangle AB'C'$. Both triangles share $\angle A$. Another pair of equal angles is $\angle AB'C'$ and $\angle ABC$. They are equal because they are corresponding angles of parallel lines. By the AA criterion, $\triangle ABC \sim \triangle AB'C'$.

    c. Given that $\triangle ABC \sim \triangle AB'C'$, determine the length of AC'.

    Let x represent the length of AC'.

    $$\frac{x}{6} = \frac{2}{8}$$

    We are looking for the value of x that makes the fractions equivalent. Therefore, $8x = 12$, and $x = 1.5$. The length of AC' is 1.5.

    d. Given that $\triangle ABC \sim \triangle AB'C'$, determine the length of AB.

    Let x represent the length of AB.

    $$\frac{2.7}{x} = \frac{2}{8}$$

    We are looking for the value of x that makes the fractions equivalent. Therefore, $2x = 21.6$ and $x = 10.8$. The length of AB is 10.8.

---

2. In the diagram below, you have △ ABC and △ A'B'C'. Use this information to answer parts (a)–(c).

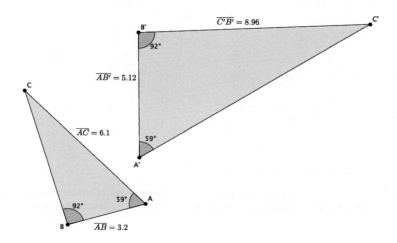

a. Based on the information given, is △ ABC~ △ A'B'C'? Explain.

Yes, △ ABC~ △ A'B'C'. There are two pairs of corresponding angles that are equal in measure. Namely, ∠A = ∠A' = 59°, and ∠B = ∠B' = 92°. By the AA criterion, these triangles are similar.

b. Given that △ ABC~ △ A'B'C', determine the length of A'C'.

Let x represent the length of A'C'.

$$\frac{x}{6.1} = \frac{5.12}{3.2}$$

We are looking for the value of x that makes the fractions equivalent. Therefore, 3.2x = 31.232, and x = 9.76. The length of A'C' is 9.76.

c. Given that △ ABC~ △ A'B'C', determine the length of BC.

Let x represent the length of BC.

$$\frac{8.96}{x} = \frac{5.12}{3.2}$$

We are looking for the value of x that makes the fractions equivalent. Therefore, 5.12x = 28.672, and x = 5.6. The length of BC is 5.6.

3. In the diagram below you have △ *ABC* and △ *A′B′C′*. Use this information to answer the question below.

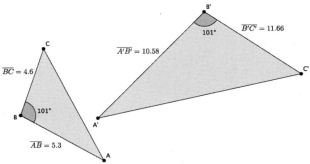

Based on the information given, is △ *ABC*∼ △ *A′B′C′*? Explain.

No, △ ABC is not similar to △ A′B′C′. Since there is only information about one pair of corresponding angles, then we must check to see that the corresponding sides have equal ratios. That is, the following must be true:

$$\frac{10.58}{5.3} = \frac{11.66}{4.6}$$

When we compare products of each numerator with the denominator of the other fraction, we see that 48.668 ≠ 61.798. Since the corresponding sides do not have equal ratios, then the fractions are not equivalent, and the triangles are not similar.

Closing (5 minutes)

Summarize, or ask students to summarize, the main points from the lesson:

- We know that if we are given just one pair of corresponding angles as equal, we can use the side lengths along the given angle to determine if triangles are in fact similar.

- If we know that we are given similar triangles, then we can use the fact that ratios of corresponding sides are equal to find any missing measurements.

Lesson Summary

Given just one pair of corresponding angles of a triangle as equal, use the side lengths along the given angle to determine if triangles are in fact similar.

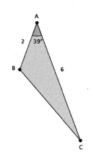

$|\angle A| = |\angle D|$ and $\frac{1}{2} = \frac{3}{6} = r$; therefore,

△ *ABC*∼ △ *DEF*.

Given similar triangles, use the fact that ratios of corresponding sides are equal to find any missing measurements.

Exit Ticket (5 minutes)

Name _____   Date_____

Lesson 11: More About Similar Triangles

Exit Ticket

1. In the diagram below, you have △ ABC and △ $A'B'C'$. Based on the information given, is △ $ABC \sim$ △ $A'B'C'$?
    Explain.

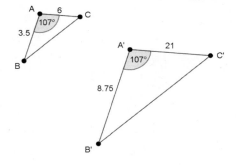

2. In the diagram below, △ $ABC \sim$ △ DEF. Use the information to answer parts (a)–(b).

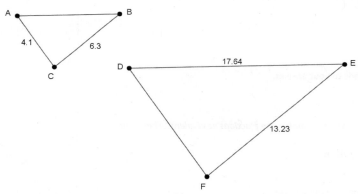

a. Determine the length of AB. Show work that leads to your answer.

b. Determine the length of DF. Show work that leads to your answer.

Exit Ticket Sample Solutions

1.   **In the diagram below, you have** $\triangle ABC$ **and** $\triangle A'B'C'$. **Based on the information given, is** $\triangle ABC \sim \triangle A'B'C'$?
     Explain.

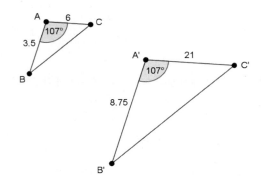

Since there is only information about one pair of corresponding angles, we need to check to see if corresponding sides have equal ratios. That is, does $\frac{|AB|}{|A'B'|} = \frac{|AC|}{|A'C'|}$, *or does* $\frac{3.5}{8.75} = \frac{6}{21}$? *The products are not equal:* $73.5 \neq 52.5$. *Since the corresponding sides do not have equal ratios, the triangles are not similar.*

2.   **In the diagram below,** $\triangle ABC \sim \triangle DEF$. **Use the information to answer parts (a)–(b).**

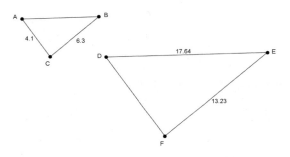

a.   **Determine the length of** AB. **Show work that leads to your answer.**

     Let x represent the length of AB.

     Then $\dfrac{x}{17.64} = \dfrac{6.3}{13.23}$. *We are looking for the value of x that makes the fractions equivalent. Therefore,*

     $111.132 = 13.23x$, *and* $x = 8.4$. *The length of AB is 8.4.*

b.   **Determine the length of** DF. **Show work that leads to your answer.**

     Let y represent the length of DF.

     Then $\dfrac{4.1}{y} = \dfrac{6.3}{13.23}$. *We are looking for the value of y that makes the fractions equivalent. Therefore,*

     $54.243 = 6.3y$, *and* $8.61 = y$. *The length of DF is 8.61.*

Problem Set Sample Solutions

Students practice presenting informal arguments as to whether or not two given triangles are similar. Students practice finding measurements of similar triangles.

---

1. In the diagram below, you have △ ABC and △ A'B'C'. Use this information to answer parts (a)–(b).

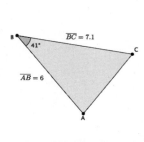 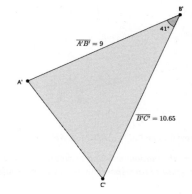

a. Based on the information given, is △ ABC~ △ A'B'C'? Explain.

Yes, △ ABC~ △ A'B'C'. Since there is only information about one pair of corresponding angles being equal, then the corresponding sides must be checked to see if their ratios are equal:

$$\frac{10.65}{7.1} = \frac{9}{6}$$

63.9 = 63.9. Since the cross products are equal, the triangles are similar.

b. Assume the length of AC is 4.3. What is the length of A'C'?

Let x represent the length of A'C'.

$$\frac{x}{4.3} = \frac{9}{6}$$

We are looking for the value of x that makes the fractions equivalent. Therefore, $6x = 38.7$, and $x = 6.45$. The length of A'C' is 6.45.

---

2. In the diagram below you have △ ABC and △ AB'C'. Use this information to answer parts (a)–(d).

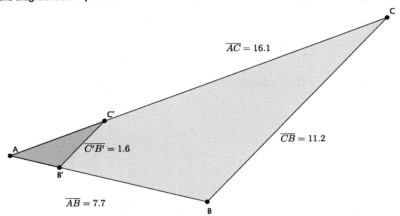

$\overline{AC} = 16.1$

$\overline{CB} = 11.2$

$\overline{C'B'} = 1.6$

$\overline{AB} = 7.7$

a. Based on the information given, is △ ABC~ △ AB'C'? Explain.

There is not enough information provided to determine if the triangles are similar. We would need information about a pair of corresponding angles or more information about the side lengths of each of the triangles.

b. Assume line BC is parallel to line B'C'. With this information, can you say that △ ABC~ △ AB'C'? Explain.

If line BC is parallel to line B'C', then △ ABC~ △ AB'C'. Both triangles share ∠A. Another pair of equal angles is ∠AB'C' and ∠ABC. They are equal because they are corresponding angles of parallel lines. By the AA criterion, △ ABC~ △ AB'C'.

c. Given that △ ABC~ △ AB'C', determine the length of AC'.

Let x represent the length of AC'.

$$\frac{x}{16.1} = \frac{1.6}{11.2}$$

We are looking for the value of x that makes the fractions equivalent. Therefore, $11.2x = 25.76$, and $x = 2.3$. The length of AC' is 2.3.

d. Given that △ ABC~ △ AB'C', determine the length of AB'.

Let x represent the length of AB'.

$$\frac{x}{7.7} = \frac{1.6}{11.2}$$

We are looking for the value of x that makes the fractions equivalent. Therefore, $11.2x = 12.32$, and $x = 1.1$. The length of AB' is 1.1.

3.   In the diagram below you have $\triangle ABC$ and $\triangle A'B'C'$. Use this information to answer parts (a)–(c).

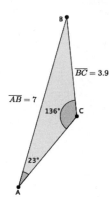
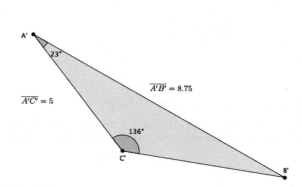

a.   Based on the information given, is $\triangle ABC \sim \triangle A'B'C'$? Explain.

Yes, $\triangle ABC \sim \triangle A'B'C'$. There are two pairs of corresponding angles that are equal in measure. Namely, $\angle A = \angle A' = 23°$, and $\angle C = \angle C' = 136°$. By the AA criterion, these triangles are similar.

b.   Given that $\triangle ABC \sim \triangle A'B'C'$, determine the length of $B'C'$.

Let x represent the length of $B'C'$.

$$\frac{x}{3.9} = \frac{8.75}{7}$$

We are looking for the value of x that makes the fractions equivalent. Therefore, $7x = 34.125$, and $x = 4.875$. The length of $B'C'$ is 4.875.

c.   Given that $\triangle ABC \sim \triangle A'B'C'$, determine the length of AC.

Let x represent the length of AC.

$$\frac{5}{x} = \frac{8.75}{7}$$

We are looking for the value of x that makes the fractions equivalent. Therefore, $8.75x = 35$, and $x = 4$. The length of AC is 4.

4. In the diagram below you have $\triangle ABC$ and $\triangle AB'C'$. Use this information to answer the question below.

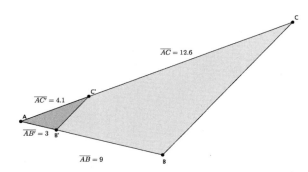

Based on the information given, is $\triangle ABC \sim \triangle AB'C'$? Explain.

No, $\triangle ABC$ is not similar to $\triangle AB'C'$. Since there is only information about one pair of corresponding angles, then we must check to see that the corresponding sides have equal ratios. That is, the following must be true:

$$\frac{9}{3} = \frac{12.6}{4.1}$$

When we compare products of each numerator with the denominator of the other fraction, we see that $36.9 \neq 37.8$. Since the corresponding sides do not have equal ratios, the fractions are not equivalent, and the triangles are not similar.

5. In the diagram below, you have $\triangle ABC$ and $\triangle A'B'C'$. Use this information to answer parts (a)–(b).

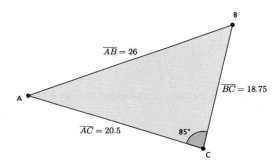

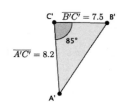

a. Based on the information given, is $\triangle ABC \sim \triangle A'B'C'$? Explain.

Yes, $\triangle ABC \sim \triangle A'B'C'$. Since there is only information about one pair of corresponding angles being equal, then the corresponding sides must be checked to see if their ratios are equal:

$$\frac{8.2}{20.5} = \frac{7.5}{18.75}$$

When we compare products of each numerator with the denominator of the other fraction, we see that $153.75 = 153.75$. Since the products are equal, the fractions are equivalent, and the triangles are similar.

b.   Given that $\triangle ABC \sim \triangle A'B'C'$, determine the length of $A'B'$.

Let x represent the length of $A'B'$.

$$\frac{x}{26} = \frac{7.5}{18.75}$$

We are looking for the value of x that makes the fractions equivalent. Therefore, $18.75x = 195$, and $x = 10.4$. The length of $A'B'$ is 10.4.

Lesson 12: Modeling Using Similarity

Student Outcomes

- Students use properties of similar triangles to solve real-world problems.

Lesson Notes

This lesson is the first opportunity for students to see how the mathematics they have learned in this module relate to real-world problems. Each example, exercise, and item in the problem set is in a real-world context, e.g., height of tree, distance across a lake, length needed for a skateboard ramp. Many of the problems begin by asking students if they have enough information to determine if the situation described lends itself to the use of similar triangles. Once that criterion is satisfied, students use what they know about dilation and scale factor to solve the problem and explain the real-world situation.

Classwork

Example 1 (7 minutes)

Consider offering this first task without any scaffolding in order to build students' persistence and stamina in solving problems. Allow students time to make sense of the situation, offering scaffolding only as necessary.

Example 1

Not all flagpoles are perfectly *upright* (i.e., perpendicular to the ground). Some are oblique (neither parallel nor at a right angle, slanted). Imagine an oblique flagpole in front of an abandoned building. The question is, can we use sunlight and shadows to determine the length of the flagpole?

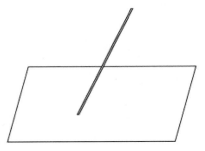

- Assume the length of the shadow that the flagpole casts is 15 feet long. Also assume that the portion of the flagpole that is 3 feet above the ground casts a shadow with a length of 1.7 feet.

Students may say that they would like to directly measure the length of the pole. Remind them a direct measurement may not always be possible.

- Where would the shadow of the flagpole be?
  - *On the ground, some distance from the base of the flagpole.*

- In the picture below, OA is the length of the flagpole. OB is the length of the shadow cast by the flagpole. OC represents the 3 feet mark up the flagpole, and OD is the shadow cast by OC that is 1.7 feet in length. (Note: the picture is not drawn to scale.)

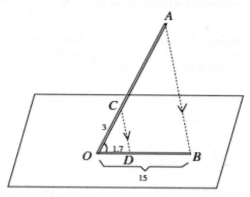

- If we assume that all sunbeams are parallel to each other, i.e., $CD \parallel AB$, do we have a pair of similar triangles? Explain.

  □ *If $CD \parallel AB$, then $\triangle COD \sim \triangle AOB$, by the AA criterion. Corresponding angles of parallel lines are equal, so we know that $\angle CDO = \angle ABO$, and $\angle COD$ is equal to itself.*

- Now that we know $\triangle COD \sim \triangle AOB$, how can we find the length of the flagpole?

  □ *Since the triangles are similar, then we know that the ratios of their corresponding sides must be equal. Therefore, if we let x represent the length of the flagpole, i.e., OA, then*

$$\frac{x}{3} = \frac{15}{1.7}$$

- We are looking for the value of x that makes the fractions equivalent.

  □ *Therefore, $1.7x = 45$, and $x \approx 26.47$. The length of the flagpole is approximately 26.47 feet.*

Exercises 1–3 (28 minutes)

Students work in small groups to model the use of similar triangles in real-world problems.

Exercises

1. You want to determine the approximate height of one of the tallest buildings in the city. You are told that if you place a mirror some distance from yourself so that you can see the top of the building in the mirror, then you can indirectly measure the height using similar triangles. Let O be the location of the mirror so that the figure shown can see the top of the building.

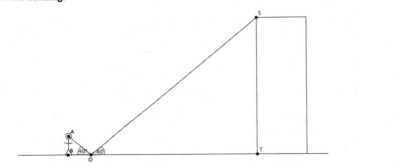

a.   **Explain why** $\triangle ABO \sim \triangle STO$.

The triangles are similar by the AA criterion. The angle that is formed by the figure standing is $90°$ with the ground. The building also makes a $90°$ angle with the ground. The angle formed with the mirror at $\angle AOB$ is equal to $\angle SOT$. Since there are two pairs of corresponding angles that are equal, then $\triangle ABO \sim \triangle STO$.

b.   **Label the diagram with the following information: The distance from eye-level to the ground is 5.3 feet. The distance from the figure to the mirror is 7.2 feet. The distance from the figure to the base of the building is $1,750$ feet. The height of the building will be represented by x.**

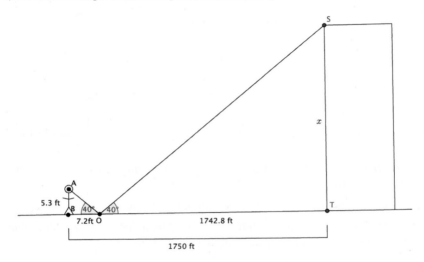

c.   **What is the distance from the mirror to the building?**

$1,750 - 7.2 = 1,742.8\ ft.$

d.   **Do you have enough information to determine the approximate height of the building? If yes, determine the approximate height of the building. If not, what additional information is needed?**

Yes, there is enough information about the similar triangles to determine the height of the building. Since x represents the height of the building, then

$$\frac{x}{5.3} = \frac{1,742.8}{7.2}$$

We are looking for the value of x that makes the fractions equivalent. Then $7.2x = 9,236.84$, and $x \approx 1,282.9$. The height of the building is approximately $1,282.9$ feet.

2.   A geologist wants to determine the distance across the widest part of a nearby lake. The geologist marked off specific points around the lake so that line DE would be parallel to line BC. The segment BC is selected specifically because it is the widest part of the lake. The segment DE is selected specifically because it was a short enough distance to easily measure. The geologist sketched the situation as shown below:

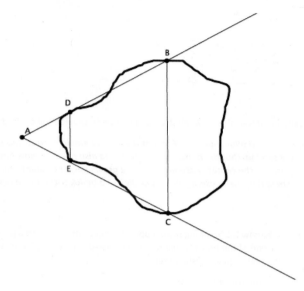

a.   Has the geologist done enough work so far to use similar triangles to help measure the widest part of the lake? Explain.

Yes. Based on the sketch, the geologist found a center of dilation, point A. The geologist marked points around the lake that, when connected, would make parallel lines. So the triangles are similar by the AA criterion. Corresponding angles of parallel lines are equal in measure, and $\angle DAE$ is equal to itself. Since there are two pairs of corresponding angles that are equal, then $\triangle DAE \sim \triangle BAC$.

b.   The geologist has made the following measurements: $|DE| = 5$ feet, $|AE| = 7$ feet, and $|EC| = 15$ feet. Does she have enough information to complete the task? If so, determine the length across the widest part of the lake. If not, state what additional information is needed.

Yes, there is enough information about the similar triangles to determine the distance across the widest part of the lake.

Let x represents the length of BC, then

$$\frac{x}{5} = \frac{22}{7}$$

We are looking for the value of x that makes the fractions equivalent. Therefore, $7x = 110$, and $x \approx 15.7$. The distance across the widest part of the lake is approximately 15.7 feet.

c.   Assume the geologist could only measure a maximum distance of 12 feet. Could she still find the distance across the widest part of the lake? What would need to be done differently?

The geologist could still find the distance across the widest part of the lake. However, she would have to select different points D and E at least 3 feet closer to points B and C, respectively. That would decrease the distance of EC to at most 12 feet. The segment DE, in its new position, would still have to make a line that was parallel to BC in order to calculate the desired distance.

                       Date: 10/16/13

---

3. A tree is planted in the backyard of a house with the hope that one day it will be tall enough to provide shade to cool the house. A sketch of the house, tree, and sun is shown below.

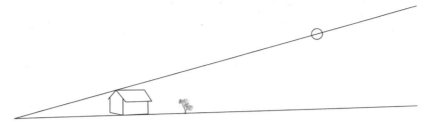

a. What information is needed to determine how tall the tree must be to provide the desired shade?

We need to ensure that we have similar triangles. For that reason, we would need to know the height of the house and the length of the shadow that the house casts. We would also need to know how far away the tree was planted from that point, i.e., the center. Assuming the tree grows perpendicular to the ground, then the height of the tree and the height of the house would be parallel, and by AA criterion we would have similar triangles.

b. Assume that the sun casts a shadow 32 feet long from a point on top of the house to a point in front of the house. The distance from the end of the house's shadow to the base of the tree is 53 feet. If the house is 16 feet tall, how tall must the tree get to provide shade for the house?

If we let x represent the height the tree must be, then

$$\frac{16}{x} = \frac{32}{53}$$

We are looking for the value of x that makes the fractions equivalent. Therefore, $32x = 848$, and $x = 26.5$. The tree must grow to a height of 26.5 feet to provide the desired shade for the house.

c. Assume that the tree grows at a rate of 2.5 feet per year. If the tree is now 7 feet tall, about how many years will it take for the tree to reach the desired height?

The tree needs to grow an additional 19.5 feet to reach the desired height. If the tree grows 2.5 feet per year, then it will take the tree 7.8 years or about 8 years to reach a height of 26.5 feet.

Closing (5 minutes)

Summarize, or ask students to summarize, the main points from the lesson:

- We can use similar triangles to determine the height or distance of objects in everyday life that we cannot directly measure.
- We have to determine whether or not we actually have enough information to use properties of similar triangles to solve problems.

Exit Ticket (5 minutes)

Name _____ Date_____

Lesson 12: Modeling Using Similarity

Exit Ticket

1. Henry thinks he can figure out how high his kite is while flying it in the park. First, he lets out 150 feet of string and ties the string to a rock on the ground. Then he moves from the rock until the string touches the top of his head. He stands up straight, forming a right angle with the ground. He wants to find out the distance from the ground to his kite. He draws the following diagram to illustrate what he has done.

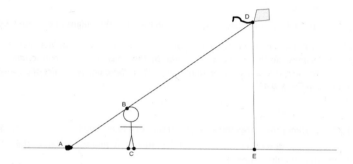

a. Has Henry done enough work so far to use similar triangles to help measure the height of the kite? Explain.

b. Henry knows he is $5\frac{1}{2}$ feet tall. Henry measures the string from the rock to his head and found it to be 8 feet. Does he have enough information to determine the height of the kite? If so, find the height of the kite. If not, state what other information would be needed.

Exit Ticket Sample Solutions

1. Henry thinks he can figure out how high his kite is while flying it in the park. First, he lets out 150 feet of string and ties the string to a rock on the ground. Then he moves from the rock until the string touches the top of his head. He stands up straight, forming a right angle with the ground. He wants to find out the distance from the ground to his kite. He draws the following diagram to illustrate what he has done.

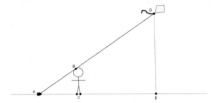

a. Has Henry done enough work so far to use similar triangles to help measure the height of the kite? Explain.

Yes, based on the sketch, Henry found a center of dilation, point A. Henry has marked points so that when connected would make parallel lines. So the triangles are similar by the AA criterion. Corresponding angles of parallel lines are equal in measure, and $\angle BAC$ is equal to itself. Since there are two pairs of corresponding angles that are equal, then $\triangle BAC \sim \triangle DAE$.

b. Henry knows he is $5\frac{1}{2}$ feet tall. Henry measures the string from the rock to his head and found it to be 8 feet. Does he have enough information to determine the height of the kite? If so, find the height of the kite. If not, state what other information would be needed.

Yes, there is enough information. Let x represent the height DE. Then,

$$\frac{8}{150} = \frac{5.5}{x}$$

We are looking for the value of x that makes the fractions equivalent. Therefore, $8x = 825$, and $x = 103.125$ feet. The height of the kite is approximately 103 feet high in the air.

Problem Set Sample Solutions

Students practice solving real-world problems using properties of similar triangles.

1. The world's tallest living tree is a redwood in California. It's about 370 feet tall. In a local park is a very tall tree. You want to find out if the tree in the local park is anywhere near the height of the famous redwood.

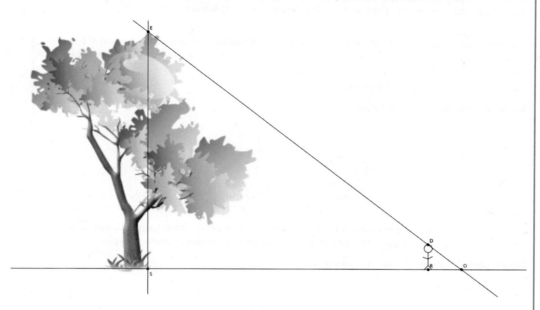

a. Describe the triangles in the diagram, and explain how you know they are similar or not.

    There are two triangles in the diagram, one formed by the tree and the shadow it casts, $\triangle ESO$, and another formed by the person and his shadow, $\triangle DRO$. The triangles are similar if the height of the tree is measured at a $90°$ angle with the ground and if the person standing forms a $90°$ angle with the ground. We know that $\angle DOR$ is an angle common to both triangles. If $\angle ESO = \angle DRO = 90°$, then $\triangle ESO \sim \triangle DRO$ by the AA criterion.

b. Assume $\triangle ESO \sim \triangle DRO$. A friend stands in the shadow of the tree. He is exactly 5.5 feet tall and casts a shadow of 12 feet. Is there enough information to determine the height of the tree? If so, determine the height, if not, state what additional information is needed.

    No, there is not enough information to determine the height of the tree. I need either the total length of the shadow that the tree casts or the distance between the base of the tree and the friend.

c. Your friend stands exactly 477 feet from the base of the tree. Given this new information, determine about how many feet taller the world's tallest tree is compared to the one in the local park.

    Let x represent the height of the tree, then

    $$\frac{x}{5.5} = \frac{489}{12}$$

    We are looking for the value of x that makes the fractions equivalent. Therefore, $12x = 2,689.5$, and $x = 224.125$. The world's tallest tree is about 146 feet taller than the tree in the park.

d. Assume that your friend stands in the shadow of the world's tallest redwood and the length of his shadow is just 8 feet long. How long is the shadow cast by the tree?

Let x represent the length of the shadow cast by the tree, then

$$\frac{x}{8} = \frac{370}{5.5}$$

We are looking for the value of x that makes the fractions equivalent. Therefore, $5.5x = 2,960$, and $x \approx 538.2$. The shadow cast by the world's tallest tree is about 538 feet in length.

2. A reasonable skateboard ramp makes a $25°$ angle with the ground. A two feet tall ramp requires about 4.3 feet of wood along the base and about 4.7 feet of wood from the ground to the top of the two-foot height to make the ramp.

a. Sketch a diagram to represent the situation.

Sample student drawing shown below.

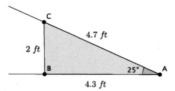

b. Your friend is a daredevil and has decided to build a ramp that is 5 feet tall. What length of wood will be needed to make the base of the ramp? Explain your answer using properties of similar triangles.

Sample student drawing and work shown below.

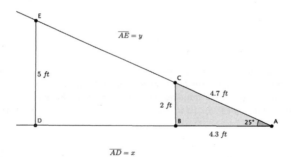

△ EDA~ △ CBA, by the AA criterion because ∠A is common to both triangles, and ∠EDA = ∠CBA = 90°.

If we let x represent the base of the 5 foot ramp, then

$$\frac{4.3}{x} = \frac{2}{5}$$

We are looking for the value of x that makes the fractions equivalent. Therefore, $2x = 21.5$, and $x = 10.75$. The base of the 5 foot ramp must be 10.75 feet in length.

c. What length of wood is required to go from the ground to the top of the 5 feet height to make the ramp? Explain your answer using properties of similar triangles.

If we let y represent the length of the wood needed to make the ramp, then

$$\frac{4.7}{y} = \frac{2}{5}$$

We are looking for the value of y that makes the fractions equivalent. Therefore, $2y = 23.5$, and $y = 11.75$. The length of wood needed to make the ramp is 11.75 feet.

Name _____   Date _____

1. Use the diagram below to answer the questions that follow.

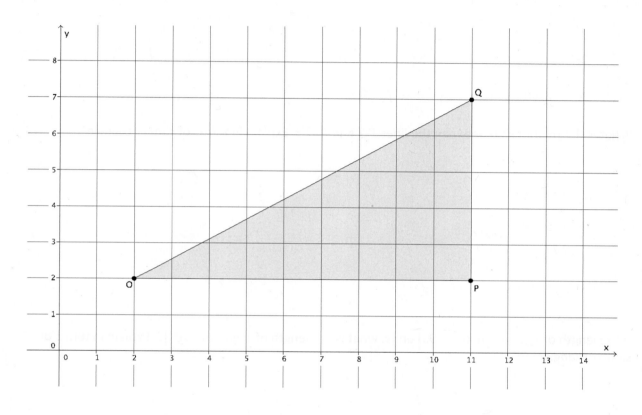

a. Dilate triangle $\triangle OPQ$ from center O and scale factor $r = \frac{4}{9}$. Label the image $\triangle OP'Q'$.

b. Find the coordinates of P' and Q'.

c. Are $\angle OQP$ and $\angle OQ'P'$ equal in measure? Explain.

d. What is the relationship between the lines PQ and $P'Q'$? Explain in terms of similar triangles.

e. If the length of segment $|OQ| = 9.8$ units, what is the length of segment $|OQ'|$? Explain in terms of similar triangles.

2. Use the diagram below to answer the questions that follow. The length of each segment is as shown: segment OX is 5 units, segment OY is 7 units, segment XY is 3 units, and segment $X'Y'$ is 12.6 units.

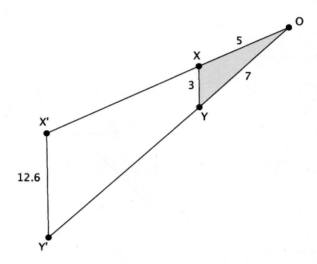

a. Suppose XY is parallel to $X'Y'$. Is triangle $\triangle OXY$ similar to triangle $\triangle OX'Y'$? Explain.

b. What is the length of segment OX'? Show your work.

c. What is the length of segment OY'? Show your work.

3. Given $\triangle ABC \sim \triangle A'B'C'$ and $\triangle ABC \sim \triangle A''B''C''$ in the diagram below, answer parts (a)–(c).

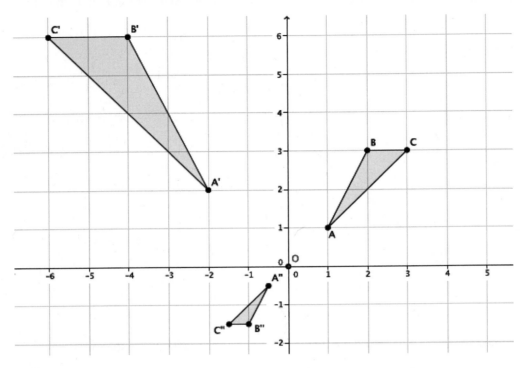

a. Describe the sequence that shows the similarity for $\triangle ABC$ and $\triangle A'B'C'$.

b. Describe the sequence that shows the similarity for $\triangle ABC$ and $\triangle A''B''C''$.

c. Is $\triangle A'B'C'$ similar to $\triangle A''B''C''$? How do you know?

A Progression Toward Mastery

Assessment Task Item		STEP 1 Missing or incorrect answer and little evidence of reasoning or application of mathematics to solve the problem.	STEP 2 Missing or incorrect answer but evidence of some reasoning or application of mathematics to solve the problem.	STEP 3 A correct answer with some evidence of reasoning or application of mathematics to solve the problem, or an incorrect answer with substantial evidence of solid reasoning or application of mathematics to solve the problem.	STEP 4 A correct answer supported by substantial evidence of solid reasoning or application of mathematics to solve the problem.
1	**a** 8.G.A.4	Student does not mark any points on the drawing.	Student drew an arbitrary triangle that is not a dilation according to the scale factor and is not labeled.	Student drew a triangle $\Delta OQ'P'$ and labeled the points, but it was not a dilation according to the scale factor.	Student drew a triangle $\Delta OQ'P'$ according to the scale factor and labeled the points.
	b 8.G.A.4	Student does not attempt the problem or leaves the problem blank.	Student identifies both of the coordinates of P' or Q' incorrectly <u>OR</u> student may have transposed the coordinates of P' as $(2, 6)$.	Student identifies one of the coordinates of P' correctly and the x-coordinate of Q' correctly. A calculation error may have led to to an incorrect y-coordinate of Q'.	Student correctly identifies the coordinates of Q' as $\left(6, \frac{38}{9}\right)$. Student correctly identifies the coordinates of P' as $(6, 2)$.
	c 8.G.A.4	Student does not attempt the problem or leaves the problem blank. Student states that $\angle OQP \neq \angle OQ'P'$.	Student states that $\angle OQP = \angle OQ'P'$. Student does not attempt any explanation or reasoning. Explanation or reasoning is not mathematically based. For example, student may write: "it looks like they are the same."	Student states that $\angle OQP = \angle OQ'P'$. Student explanation includes mathematical language. Student explanation may not be complete, e.g., stating dilations are degree persevering without explaining $D(\angle OQP) = \angle OQ'P'$.	Student states that $\angle OQP = \angle OQ'P'$. Student explanation includes mathematical language. Reasoning includes that $D(\angle OQP) = \angle OQ'P'$, and dilations are degree preserving.

	d 8.G.A.5	Student does not attempt the problem or leaves the problem blank. Student may state that $PQ \parallel P'Q'$. Student does not attempt any explanation or reasoning.	Student may state that $PQ \parallel P'Q'$. Student may not use mathematical language in explanation or reasoning. For example, student may write: "they look like they won't touch," or "the angles are the same." Reasoning may include some facts. Reasoning may not be complete. There are significant gaps in explanation.	Student states that $PQ \parallel P'Q'$. Student uses some mathematical language in explanation or reasoning. Reasoning includes some of the following facts: $\angle O = \angle O$, $\angle OQP = \angle OQ'P'$ and $\angle OPQ = \angle OP'Q'$, then by AA criterion for similarity, $\triangle OPQ \sim \triangle OP'Q'$. Then, by FTS $PQ \parallel P'Q'$. Reasoning may not be complete.	Student states that $PQ \parallel P'Q'$. Student uses mathematical language in explanation or reasoning. Reasoning includes the following facts: At least two pairs of corresponding angles are equal, e.g., $\angle O = \angle O$ and/or $\angle OQP = \angle OQ'P'$ and/or $\angle OPQ = \angle OP'Q'$, then by AA criterion for similarity, $\triangle OPQ \sim \triangle OP'Q'$. Then, by FTS $PQ \parallel P'Q'$. Reasoning is thorough and complete.
	e 8.G.A.5	Student does not attempt the problem or leaves the problem blank.	Student answers incorrectly. Student may not use mathematical language in explanation or reasoning. Student reasoning does not include a reference to similar triangles. Student reasoning may or may not include that the ratio of lengths are equal to scale factor. There are significant gaps in explanation.	Student answers correctly that $OQ' \approx 4.4$ units. Student uses some mathematical language in explanation or reasoning. Student may or may not have referenced similar triangles in reasoning. Student reasoning includes that the ratio of lengths are equal to scale factor. Explanation or reasoning may not be complete.	Student answers correctly that $OQ' \approx 4.4$ units. Student uses mathematical language in explanation or reasoning. Student referenced similar triangles in reasoning. Student reasoning includes that the ratio of lengths are equal to scale factor. Reasoning is thorough and complete.
2	**a** 8.G.A.5	Student does not attempt the problem or leaves the problem blank. Student answers yes or no only. Student does not attempt to explain reasoning.	Student may or may not answer correctly. Student may use some mathematical language in explanation or reasoning. Explanation or reasoning is not mathematically based, e.g., "they look like they are." There are significant gaps in explanation.	Student answers yes correctly. Student uses some mathematical language in explanation or reasoning. Explanation includes some of the following facts: Since $XY \parallel X'Y'$, then corresponding angles of parallel lines are congruent by AA criterion for similar triangles; therefore,	Student answers yes correctly. Student uses mathematical language in explanation or reasoning. Explanation includes the following facts: Since $XY \parallel X'Y'$, then corresponding angles of parallel lines are congruent by AA criterion for similar triangles; therefore, $\triangle OXY \sim \triangle OX'Y'$. Reasoning is thorough

				$\Delta OXY \sim \Delta OX'Y'$. Reasoning may not be complete.	and complete.
b 8.G.A.5	Student does not attempt the problem or leaves the problem blank.	Student may or may not have answered correctly. Student uses some method other than proportion to solve problems, e.g., guessing. Student may have made calculation errors.	Student may or may not have answered correctly. Student uses a proportion to solve problem. Student may have set up proportion incorrectly. Student may have made calculation errors.	Student answers correctly with length of $OX' = 21$ units. Student uses a proportion to solve problem.
c 8.G.A.5	Student does not attempt the problem or leaves the problem blank.	Student may or may not have answered correctly. Student uses some method other than proportion to solve problems, e.g., guessing. Student may have made calculation errors.	Student may or may not have answered correctly. Student uses a proportion to solve problem. Student may have set up proportion incorrectly. Student may have made calculation errors.	Student answers correctly with length of $OY' = 29.4$ units. Student uses a proportion to solve problem.
3 **a** 8.G.A.5	Student does not attempt the problem or leaves the problem blank.	Student does not attempt any explanation or reasoning. Student may or may not have stated dilation and does not give any center or scale factor. Student may or may not have stated the congruence. Student may have stated the incorrect congruence. Explanation or reasoning is not mathematically based, e.g., "one looks about three times bigger than the other."	Student states dilation. Student states dilation is centered at origin, but does not give scale factor, $r > 1$, or states scale factor of $r > 1$, but does not give center. Student may or may not have stated the congruence. Student may have stated the incorrect congruence. Student uses some mathematical language in explanation or reasoning.	Student states correctly there is a dilation with center at the origin and has a scale factor, $r = 2$. Student states correctly there is a congruence of reflection across the y-axis. Student uses mathematical language in explanation or reasoning such as $\Lambda(D(\Delta ABC)) = \Delta A'B'C'$ and $\Delta ABC \sim \Delta A'B'C'$. Reasoning is thorough and complete.
b 8.G.A.5	Student does not attempt the problem or leaves the problem blank.	Student does not attempt any explanation or reasoning. Student may or may not have stated dilation and does not give any center or scale factor. Student may or may not have stated the congruence. Student may have stated the incorrect	Student states dilation. Student states dilation is centered at origin, but does not give scale factor, $0 < r < 1$ or states scale factor of $0 < r < 1$, but does not give center. Student may or may not have stated the congruence. Student may have stated	Student states correctly there is a dilation with center at the origin and has a scale factor, $0 < r < 1$. Student states correctly there is a congruence of rotation of 180° centered at the origin. Student uses mathematical language in explanation or

			congruence. Explanation or reasoning is not mathematically based, e.g., "one looks about half the size of the other."	the incorrect congruence. Student uses some mathematical language in explanation or reasoning.	reasoning, such as: $R(D(\Delta ABC)) = \Delta A''B''C''$ and $\Delta ABC \sim \Delta A''B''C''$. Reasoning is thorough and complete.
c **8.G.5**	Student does not attempt the problem or leaves the problem blank.	Student may or may not have answered correctly. Student does not attempt any explanation or reasoning. Student does not reference the AA Criterion for similarity. Explanation or reasoning is not mathematically based, e.g., "They don't look like they are the same."	Student may or may not have answered correctly. Student states that only one set of angles is congruent. Student uses some mathematical language in explanation or reasoning. Student may or may not reference the AA Criterion for similarity.	Student answers correctly that yes, $\Delta A'B'C' \sim \Delta A''B''C''$. Student states that dilations are angle preserving. Student shows that since $\Delta ABC \sim \Delta A'B'C'$ and $\Delta ABC \sim \Delta A''B''C''$, at least two corresponding angles are congruent (i.e., $\angle A \cong \angle A' \cong \angle A''$). Student references the AA Criterion for similarity. Student uses mathematical language in explanation or reasoning. Reasoning is thorough and complete.

Name _____   Date _____

1. Use the diagram below to answer the questions that follow.

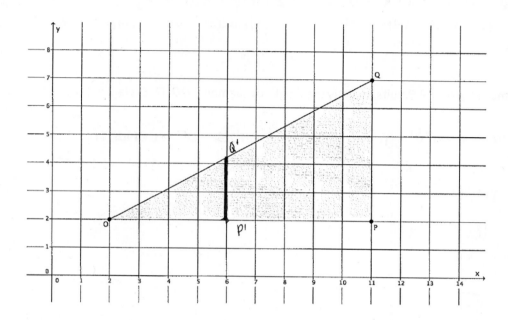

a. Dilate triangle $\triangle OPQ$ from center O and scale factor $r = \frac{4}{9}$. Label the image $\triangle OP'Q'$.

b. Find the coordinates of P' and Q'.

$$P' = (6, 2)$$

$$Q' = \left(6, \frac{30}{9}\right)$$

$$\frac{|P'Q'|}{|PQ|} = \frac{4}{9}$$

$$\frac{|P'Q'|}{5} = \frac{4}{9}$$

$$|P'Q'| = \frac{20}{9}$$

$$\frac{20}{9} + 2 = \frac{20}{9} + \frac{18}{9}$$

$$= \frac{38}{9}$$

c. Are $\angle OQP$ and $\angle OQ'P'$ equal in measure? Explain.

YES $\angle OQP = \angle OQ'P'$.   SINCE $D(\triangle OQP) = \triangle OQ'P'$ AND DILATIONS ARE DEGREE PRESERVING, THEN $\angle OQP = \angle OQ'P'$.

$\angle OQP$ & $\angle OQ'P'$ ARE CORRESPONDING ANGLES OF PARALLEL LINES PQ & P'Q', THEREFORE $\angle OQP = \angle OQ'P'$.

d. What is the relationship between the lines PQ and $P'Q'$? Explain in terms of similar triangles.

> THE LINES PQ AND P'Q' ARE PARALLEL.   △OPQ ~ △OP'Q'
> BY THE AA CRITERION (∠O=∠O, ∠OPQ = ∠OP'Q'),
> THEREFORE BY THE FUNDAMENTAL THEOREM OF SIMILARITY
> PQ || P'Q'.

e. If the length of segment $|OQ| = 9.8$ units, what is the length of segment $|OQ'|$? Explain in terms of similar triangles.

> SINCE △OPQ ~ △OP'Q', THEN THE RATIOS OF LENGTHS OF
> CORRESPONDING SIDES WILL BE EQUAL TO THE SCALE
> FACTOR.   THEN
>
> $$\frac{|OP'|}{|OP|} = \frac{|OQ'|}{|OQ|} = \frac{4}{9}$$
>
> $$\frac{4}{9} = \frac{|OQ'|}{9.8}$$
>
> $$39.2 = 9\left(|OQ'|\right)$$
>
> $$4.36 = |OQ'|$$
>
> THE LENGTH OF |OQ'| IS APPROXIMATELY 4.4 UNITS.

2. Use the diagram below to answer the questions that follow. The length of each segment is as shown: segment OX is 5 units, segment OY is 7 units, segment XY is 3 units, and segment $X'Y'$ is 12.6 units.

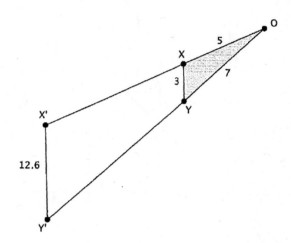

a. Suppose XY is parallel to $X'Y'$. Is triangle $\triangle OXY$ similar to triangle $\triangle OX'Y'$? Explain.

YES, $\triangle OXY \sim OX'Y'$. SINCE $XY \parallel X'Y'$ THEN $\angle OXY = \angle OX'Y'$ AND $\angle OYX = \angle OY'X'$ BECAUSE CORRESPONDING ANGLES OF PARALLEL LINES ARE EQUAL, BY AA $\triangle OXY \sim \triangle OX'Y'$.

b. What is the length of segment OX'? Show your work.

$\dfrac{12.6}{3} = \dfrac{|OX'|}{5}$ $5(12.6) = 3(|OX'|)$
$63 = 3(|OX'|)$
$21 = |OX'|$

THE LENGTH OF $|OX'|$ IS 21 UNITS.

c. What is the length of segment OY'? Show your work.

$\dfrac{12.6}{3} = \dfrac{|OY'|}{7}$ $12.6(7) = 3(|OY'|)$
$88.2 = 3(|OY'|)$
$29.4 = |OY'|$

THE LENGTH OF $|OY'|$ IS 29.4 UNITS.

3. Given $\triangle ABC \sim \triangle A'B'C'$ and $\triangle ABC \sim \triangle A''B''C''$ in the diagram below, answer parts (a)-(c).

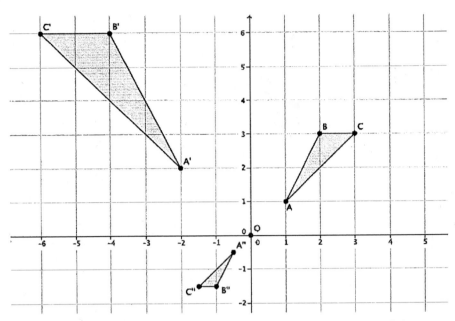

a. Describe the sequence that shows the similarity for $\triangle ABC$ and $\triangle A'B'C'$. $\dfrac{B'C'}{BC} = \dfrac{2}{1} = 2 = r$

    LET D BE THE DILATION FROM CENTER O AND SCALE FACTOR r=2.
    LET THERE BE A REFLECTION ACROSS THE Y-AXIS. THEN THE
    DILATION FOLLOWED BY THE REFLECTION MAPS △ABC ONTO
    △A'B'C'.

b. Describe the sequence that shows the similarity for $\triangle ABC$ and $\triangle A''B''C''$.

    LET D BE THE DILATION FROM CENTER O AND SCALE FACTOR
    0<r<1. LET THERE BE A ROTATION OF 180° AROUND CENTER O.
    THEN THE DILATION FOLLOWED BY THE ROTATION MAPS
    △ABC ONTO △A''B''C''.

c. Is $\triangle A'B'C'$ similar to $\triangle A''B''C''$? How do you know?

    YES. △A'B'C' ~ △A''B''C''. DILATIONS PRESERVE ANGLE MEASURES
    AND SINCE △ABC ~ △A'B'C' AND △ABC ~ △A''B''C'', WE KNOW
    ∠A = ∠A' = ∠A'', ∠B = ∠B' = ∠B''. BY AA CRITERION FOR
    SIMILARITY △A'B'C' ~ △A''B''C''. ALSO, SIMILARITY IS
    TRANSITIVE.

Mathematics Curriculum

Topic C:

The Pythagorean Theorem

8.G.B.6, 8.G.B.7

Focus Standard:	8.G.B.6	Explain a proof of the Pythagorean Theorem and its converse.
	8.G.B.7	Apply the Pythagorean Theorem to determine unknown side lengths in right triangles in real-world and mathematical problems in two and three dimensions.
Instructional Days:	2	
Lesson 13:	Proof of the Pythagorean Theorem (S)[1]	
Lesson 14:	Converse of the Pythagorean Theorem (P)	

It is recommended that students have some experience with the lessons in Topic D from Module 2 before beginning these lessons. In Lesson 13 of Topic C, students are presented with a general proof that uses the Angle-Angle criterion. In Lesson 14, students are presented with a proof of the converse of the Pythagorean Theorem. Also in Lesson 14, students apply their knowledge of the Pythagorean Theorem (i.e., given a right triangle with sides a, b, c, where c is the hypotenuse, then $a^2 + b^2 = c^2$) to determine unknown side lengths in right triangles. Students also use the converse of the theorem (i.e., given a triangle with lengths a, b, c, so that $a^2 + b^2 = c^2$, then the triangle is a right triangle with hypotenuse c) to determine if a given triangle is in fact a right triangle.

---

[1] Lesson Structure Key: **P**-Problem Set Lesson, **M**-Modeling Cycle Lesson, **E**-Exploration Lesson, **S**-Socratic Lesson

Lesson 13: Proof of the Pythagorean Theorem

Student Outcomes

- Students practice applying the Pythagorean Theorem to find lengths of right triangles in two dimensions.

Lesson Notes

Since 8.G.6 and 8.G.7 are post-test standards, this lesson is designated as an extension lesson for this module.   However, the content within this lesson is prerequisite knowledge for Module 7.   If this lesson is not used with students as part of the work within Module 3, it must be used with students prior to beginning work on Module 7.   Please realize that many mathematicians agree that the Pythagorean Theorem is the most important theorem in geometry and has immense implications in much of high school mathematics in general (e.g., learning of quadratics, trigonometry, etc.).   It is crucial that students see the teacher explain several proofs of the Pythagorean Theorem and practice using it before being expected to produce a proof on their own.

Classwork

Discussion (20 minutes)

The following proof of the Pythagorean Theorem is based on the fact that similarity is transitive. It begins with the right triangle, shown on the next page, split into two other right triangles. The three triangles are placed in the same orientation, and students verify that one pair of triangles are similar using the AA criterion, then a second pair of triangles are shown to be similar using the AA criterion, and then finally all three triangles are shown to be similar by the fact that similarity is transitive. Once it is shown that all three triangles are in fact similar, the theorem is proved by comparing the ratios of corresponding side lengths. Because some of the triangles share side lengths that are the same (or sums of lengths), then the formula $a^2 + b^2 = c^2$ is derived. Symbolic notation is used explicitly for the lengths of sides. For that reason, it may be beneficial to do this proof simultaneously with triangles that have concrete numbers for side lengths. Another option to prepare students for the proof is showing the video presentation first, then working through this Socratic discussion.

- The concept of similarity can be used to prove one of the great theorems in mathematics, the Pythagorean Theorem. What do you recall about the Pythagorean Theorem from our previous work?

    □ *The Pythagorean Theorem is a theorem about the lengths of the legs and the hypotenuse of right triangles. Specifically, if a and b are the legs of a right triangle and c is the hypotenuse, then $a^2 + b^2 = c^2$. The hypotenuse is the longest side of the triangle, and it is opposite the right angle.*

- What we are going to do in this lesson is take a right triangle, $\triangle ABC$, and use what we know about similarity of triangles to prove $a^2 + b^2 = c^2$.

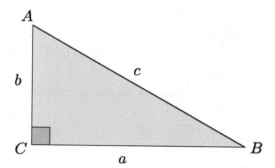

- For the proof, we will draw a line from vertex C to a point D so that the line is perpendicular to side AB.

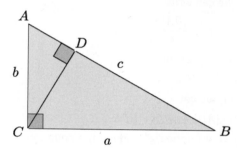

- We draw this particular line, line CD, because it divides the original triangle into three similar triangles. Before we move on, can you name the three triangles?

  □   *The three triangles are $\triangle ABC$, $\triangle ACD$, and $\triangle BCD$.*

- Let's look at the triangles in a different orientation in order to see why they are similar. We can use our basic rigid motions to separate the three triangles. Doing so ensures that the lengths of segments and degrees of angles are preserved.

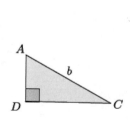 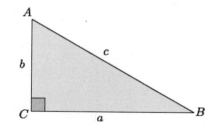 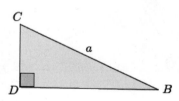

- In order to have similar triangles, they must have two common angles, by the AA criterion. Which angles prove that $\triangle ADC$ and $\triangle ACB$ similar?

  □   *It is true that $\triangle ADC \sim \triangle ACB$ because they each have a right angle, and they each share $\angle A$.*

- What must that mean about $\angle C$ from $\triangle ADC$ and $\angle B$ from $\triangle ACB$?

  □   *It means that the angles correspond and must be equal in measure because of the triangle sum theorem.*

 | **Lesson 13:**   Proof of the Pythagorean Theorem
Date: 10/16/13

185

- Which angles prove that △ ACB and △ CDB similar?

  □ *It is true that △ ACB ∽ △ CDB because they each have a right angle and they each share ∠B.*

- What must that mean about ∠A from △ ACB and ∠C from △ CDB?

  □ *The angles correspond and must be equal in measure because of the triangle sum theorem.*

- If △ ADC ∽ △ ACB and △ ACB ∽ △ CDB, is it true that △ ADC ∽ △ CDB? How do you know?

  □ *Yes, because similarity is a transitive relation.*

- When we have similar triangles, we know that their side lengths are proportional. Therefore, if we consider △ ADC and △ ACB, we can write

$$\frac{|AC|}{|AB|} = \frac{|AD|}{|AC|}.$$

By the cross-multiplication algorithm,

$$|AC|^2 = |AB| \cdot |AD|.$$

By considering △ ACB and △ CDB, we can write

$$\frac{|BA|}{|BC|} = \frac{|BC|}{|BD|}.$$

Which again by the cross-multiplication algorithm,

$$|BC|^2 = |BA| \cdot |BD|.$$

If we add the two equations together, we get

$$|AC|^2 + |BC|^2 = |AB| \cdot |AD| + |BA| \cdot |BD|.$$

By the distributive property, we can rewrite the right side of the equation because there is a common factor of $|AB|$. Now we have

$$|AC|^2 + |BC|^2 = |AB|(|AD| + |BD|).$$

Keeping our goal in mind, we want to prove that $a^2 + b^2 = c^2$; let's see how close we are.

> *Scaffolding:*
>
> Use concrete numbers to quickly convince students that adding two equations together leads to another true equation. For example: $5 = 3 + 2$ and $8 = 4 + 4$, therefore, $5 + 8 = 3 + 2 + 4 + 4.$

- Using our diagram where three triangles are within one, (shown below), what side lengths are represented by $|AC|^2 + |BC|^2$?

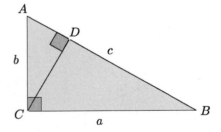

  □ *AC is side length b, and BC is side length a, so the left side of our equation represents $a^2 + b^2$.*

- Now let's examine the right side of our equation: $|AB|(|AD| + |BD|)$. We want this to be equal to c^2; does it?

  □ *If we add the lengths AD and BD we get the entire length of AB; therefore, we have $|AB|(|AD| + |BD|) = |AB| \cdot |AB| = |AB|^2 = c^2$.*

- We have just proven the Pythagorean Theorem using what we learned about similarity. At this point we have seen the proof of the theorem in terms of congruence and now similarity.

Video Presentation (7 minutes)

The video located at the following link is an animation[1] of the preceding proof using similar triangles:
http://www.youtube.com/watch?v=QCyvxYLFSfU

Exercises 1–3 (8 minutes)

Students work independently to complete Exercises 1–3.

Exercises

Use the Pythagorean Theorem to determine the unknown length of the right triangle.

1. Determine the length of side c in each of the triangles below.

   a.

   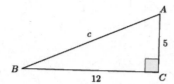

   $$5^2 + 12^2 = c^2$$

   $$25 + 144 = c^2$$

   $$169 = c^2$$

   $$13 = c$$

   b.

   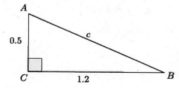

   $$0.5^2 + 1.2^2 = c^2$$

   $$0.25 + 1.44 = c^2$$

   $$1.69 = c^2$$

   $$1.3 = c$$

2. Determine the length of side b in each of the triangles below.

   a.

   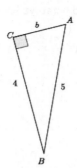

   $$4^2 + b^2 = 5^2$$

   $$16 + b^2 = 25$$

   $$16 - 16 + b^2 = 25 - 16$$

   $$b^2 = 9$$

   $$b = 3$$

---

[1] Animation developed by Larry Francis.

b.

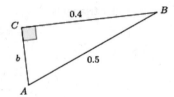

$0.4^2 + b^2 = 0.5^2$

$1.6 + b^2 = 2.5$

$1.6 - 1.6 + b^2 = 2.5 - 1.6$

$b^2 = 0.9$

$b = 0.3$

3. Determine the length of QS. (Hint: Use the Pythagorean Theorem twice.)

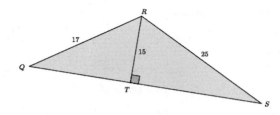

$15^2 + |QT|^2 = 17^2$

$225 + |QT|^2 = 289$

$225 - 225 + |QT|^2 = 289 - 225$

$|QT|^2 = 64$

$|QT| = 8$

$15^2 + |TS|^2 = 25^2$

$225 + |TS|^2 = 625$

$225 - 225 + |TS|^2 = 625 - 225$

$|TS|^2 = 400$

$|TS| = 20$

Since $|QT| + |TS| = |QS|$, then the length of QS is $8 + 20$, which is 28.

Closing (5 minutes)

Summarize, or ask students to summarize, the main points from the lesson:

- We have now seen another proof of the Pythagorean Theorem, but this time we used what we knew about similarity, specifically similar triangles.
- We practiced using the Pythagorean Theorem to find unknown lengths of right triangles.

Exit Ticket (5 minutes)

Name _____   Date_____

Lesson 13: Proof of the Pythagorean Theorem

Exit Ticket

Determine the length of side BD in the triangle below.

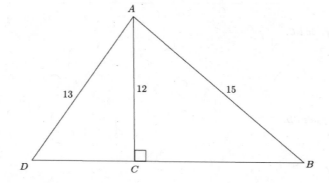

Exit Ticket Sample Solutions

Determine the length of BD in the triangle below.

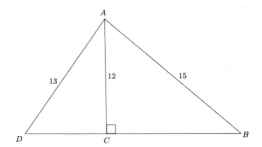

First determine the length of side BC.

$12^2 + BC^2 = 15^2$

$144 + BC^2 = 225$

$\qquad BC^2 = 225 - 144$

$\qquad BC^2 = 81$

$\qquad BC = 9$

Then determine the length of side CD.

$12^2 + CD^2 = 13^2$

$144 + CD^2 = 169$

$\qquad CD^2 = 169 - 144$

$\qquad CD^2 = 25$

$\qquad CD = 5$

Adding the length of BC and CD will determine the length of BD; therefore, $5 + 9 = 14$. BD has a length of 14.

Problem Set Sample Solutions

Students practice using the Pythagorean Theorem to find unknown lengths of right triangles.

Use the Pythagorean theorem to determine the unknown length of the right triangle.

1. Determine the length of side c in each of the triangles below.

   a.

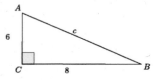

$6^2 + 8^2 = c^2$

$36 + 64 = c^2$

$100 = c^2$

$10 = c$

b.

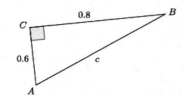

$$0.6^2 + 0.8^2 = c^2$$

$$0.36 + 0.64 = c^2$$

$$1 = c^2$$

$$1 = c$$

2. Determine the length of side a in each of the triangles below.

a.

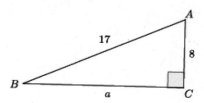

$$a^2 + 8^2 = 17^2$$

$$a^2 + 64 = 289$$

$$a^2 + 64 - 64 = 289 - 64$$

$$a^2 = 225$$

$$a = 15$$

b.

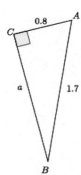

$$a^2 + 0.8^2 = 1.7^2$$

$$a^2 + 0.64 = 2.89$$

$$a^2 + 0.64 - 0.64 = 2.89 - 0.64$$

$$a^2 = 2.25$$

$$a = 1.5$$

3. Determine the length of side b in each of the triangles below.

a.

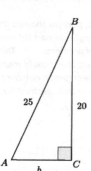

$$20^2 + b^2 = 25^2$$

$$400 + b^2 = 625$$

$$400 - 400 + b^2 = 625 - 400$$

$$b^2 = 225$$

$$b = 15$$

b.

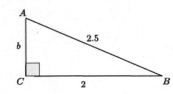

$$2^2 + b^2 = 2.5^2$$

$$4 + b^2 = 6.25$$

$$4 - 4 + b^2 = 6.25 - 4$$

$$b^2 = 2.25$$

$$b = 1.5$$

4. Determine the length of side a in each of the triangles below.

a.

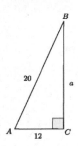

$$a^2 + 12^2 = 20^2$$

$$a^2 + 144 = 400$$

$$a^2 + 144 - 144 = 400 - 144$$

$$a^2 = 256$$

$$a = 16$$

b.

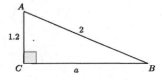

$$a^2 + 1.2^2 = 2^2$$

$$a^2 + 1.44 = 4$$

$$a^2 + 1.44 - 1.44 = 4 - 1.44$$

$$a^2 = 2.56$$

$$a = 1.6$$

5. What did you notice in each of the pairs of problems 1–4? How might what you noticed be helpful in solving problems like these?

In each pair of problems, the problems and solutions were similar. For example, in problem 1, part (a) showed the sides of the triangle were $6, 8,$ and $10,$ and in part (b) they were $0.6, 0.8,$ and $1.$ The side lengths in part (b) were a tenth of the value of the lengths in part (a). The same could be said about parts (a) and (b) of problems 2–4. This might be helpful for solving problems in the future. If I'm given sides lengths that are decimals, then I could multiply them by a factor of 10 to make whole numbers, which are easier to work with. Also, if I know common numbers of Pythagorean Theorem, like side lengths of $3, 4,$ and $5,$ then I will recognize them more easily in their decimal forms, i.e., $0.3, 0.4,$ and $0.5.$

Lesson 14: The Converse of the Pythagorean Theorem

Student Outcomes

- Students illuminate the converse of the Pythagorean Theorem through computation of examples and counterexamples.
- Students apply the theorem and its converse to solve problems.

Lesson Notes

Since 8.G.6 and 8.G.7 are post-test standards, this lesson is designated as an extension lesson for this module. However, the content within this lesson is prerequisite knowledge for Module 7. If this lesson is not used with students as part of the work within Module 3, it must be used with students prior to beginning work on Module 7. Please realize that many mathematicians agree that the Pythagorean Theorem is the most important theorem in geometry and has immense implications in much of high school mathematics in general (e.g., learning of quadratics, trigonometry, etc.). It is crucial that students see the teacher explain several proofs of the Pythagorean Theorem and practice using it before being expected to produce a proof on their own.

Classwork

Concept Development (8 minutes)

- So far, you have seen two different proofs of the Pythagorean Theorem:

  If the lengths of the legs of a right triangle are a and b, and the length of the hypotenuse is c, then $a^2 + b^2 = c^2$.

- This theorem has a converse:

  If the lengths of three sides of a triangle, a, b, and c, satisfy $c^2 = a^2 + b^2$, then the triangle is a right triangle, and furthermore, the side of length c is opposite the right angle.

Consider an activity in which students attempt to draw a triangle on graph paper that satisfies $c^2 = a^2 + b^2$ but is not a right triangle. Students should have access to rulers for this. Activities of this type may be sufficient to develop conceptual understanding of the converse; a formal proof by contradiction follows that may also be used.

- The following is a proof of the converse. Assume we are given a triangle ABC with sides a, b, and c. We want to show that $\angle ACB$ is a right angle. To do so, we will assume that $\angle ACB$ is not a right angle. Then $|\angle ACB| > 90°$ or $|\angle ACB| < 90°$. For brevity, we will only show the case for when $|\angle ACB| > 90°$ (the proof of the other case is similar). In the diagram below, we extend BC to a ray BC and let the perpendicular from A meet the ray at point D.

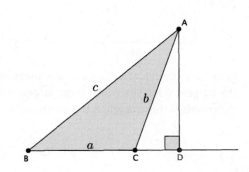

- Let $m = |CD|$ and $n = |AD|$.

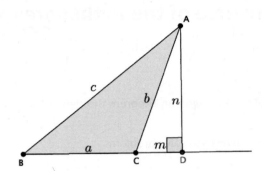

- Then by the Pythagorean Theorem applied to $\triangle ACD$ and $\triangle ABD$ results in

$$b^2 = m^2 + n^2 \text{ and } c^2 = (a + m)^2 + n^2.$$

Since we know what b^2 and c^2 are from the above equations, we can substitute those values into $c^2 = a^2 + b^2$ to get

$$(a + m)^2 + n^2 = a^2 + m^2 + n^2.$$

Since $(a + m)^2 = (a + m)(a + m) = a^2 + am + am + m^2 = a^2 + 2am + m^2$, then we have

$$a^2 + 2am + m^2 + n^2 = a^2 + m^2 + n^2.$$

We can subtract the terms $a^2, m^2,$ and n^2 from both sides of the equal sign. Then we have

$$2am = 0.$$

- But this cannot be true because $2am$ is a length; therefore, it cannot be equal to zero. Which means our assumption that $|\angle ACB| > 90°$ cannot be true. We can write a similar proof to show that $|\angle ACB| < 90°$ cannot be true either. Therefore, $|\angle ACB| = 90°$.

Example 1 (7 minutes)

To maintain the focus of the lesson, allow the use of calculators in order to check the validity of the right angle using the Pythagorean Theorem.

- The numbers in the diagram below indicate the units of length of each side of the triangle. Is the triangle shown below a right triangle?

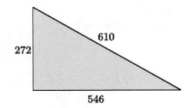

> *Scaffolding:*
> You may need to demonstrate how to use the squared button on a calculator.

- In order to find out, we need to put these numbers into the Pythagorean Theorem. Recall that side c is always the longest side. Since 610 is the largest number, it is representing the c in the Pythagorean Theorem. To determine if this triangle is a right triangle, then we need to verify the computation:

$$272^2 + 546^2 \overset{?}{=} 610^2$$

Lesson 14:   The Converse of the Pythagorean Theorem
Date: 10/16/13

194

- Find the value of the left side of the equation: $272^2 + 546^2 = 372,100$. Then, find the value of the right side of the equation: $610^2 = 372,100$. Since the left side of the equation is equal to the right side of the equation, then we have a true statement, i.e., $272^2 + 546^2 = 610^2$. What does that mean about the triangle?

  □ *It means that the triangle with side lengths of $272, 546,$ and 610 is a right triangle.*

Example 2 (5 minutes)

- The numbers in the diagram below indicate the units of length of each side of the triangle. Is the triangle shown below a right triangle?

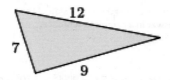

- What do we need to do to find out if this is a right triangle?

  □ *We need to see if it makes a true statement when we replace a, b, and c with the numbers using the Pythagorean Theorem.*

- Which number is c? How do you know?

  □ *The longest side is 12; therefore, $c = 12$.*

- Use your calculator to see if it makes a true statement. (Give students a minute to calculate.) Is it a right triangle? Explain.

  □ *No, it is not a right triangle. If it were a right triangle the equation $7^2 + 9^2 = 12^2$ would be true. But the left side of the equation is equal to 130, and the right side of the equation is equal to 144. Since $130 \neq 144$, then these lengths do not form a right triangle.*

Exercises 1–7 (15 minutes)

Students complete Exercises 1–4 independently. Use of calculators is recommended.

Exercises

1. The numbers in the diagram below indicate the units of length of each side of the triangle. Is the triangle shown below a right triangle? Show your work, and answer in a complete sentence.

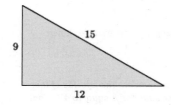

We need to check if $9^2 + 12^2 = 15^2$ is a true statement. The left side of the equation is equal to 225. The right side of the equation is equal to 225. That means $9^2 + 12^2 = 15^2$ is true, and the triangle shown is a right triangle.

---

2.   The numbers in the diagram below indicate the units of length of each side of the triangle. Is the triangle shown below a right triangle? Show your work, and answer in a complete sentence.

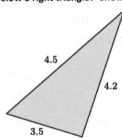

We need to check if $3.5^2 + 4.2^2 = 4.5^2$ is a true statement. The left side of the equation is equal to 29.89. The right side of the equation is equal to 20.25. That means $3.5^2 + 4.2^2 = 4.5^2$ is not true, and the triangle shown is not a right triangle.

3.   The numbers in the diagram below indicate the units of length of each side of the triangle. Is the triangle shown below a right triangle? Show your work, and answer in a complete sentence.

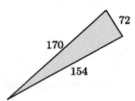

We need to check if $72^2 + 154^2 = 170^2$ is a true statement. The left side of the equation is equal to 28,900. The right side of the equation is equal to 28,900. That means $72^2 + 154^2 = 170^2$ is true, and the triangle shown is a right triangle.

4.   The numbers in the diagram below indicate the units of length of each side of the triangle. Is the triangle shown below a right triangle? Show your work, and answer in a complete sentence.

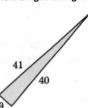

We need to check if $9^2 + 40^2 = 41^2$ is a true statement. The left side of the equation is equal to 1,681. The right side of the equation is equal to 1,681. That means $9^2 + 40^2 = 41^2$ is true, and the triangle shown is a right triangle.

5.   The numbers in the diagram below indicate the units of length of each side of the triangle. Is the triangle shown below a right triangle? Show your work, and answer in a complete sentence.

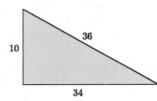

We need to check if $10^2 + 34^2 = 36^2$ is a true statement. The left side of the equation is equal to 1,256. The right side of the equation is equal to 1,296. That means $10^2 + 34^2 = 36^2$ is not true, and the triangle shown is not a right triangle.

6.   The numbers in the diagram below indicate the units of length of each side of the triangle. Is the triangle shown below a right triangle? Show your work, and answer in a complete sentence.

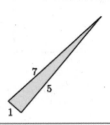

We need to check if $1^2 + 5^2 = 7^2$ is a true statement. The left side of the equation is equal to 26. The right side of the equation is equal to 49. That means $1^2 + 5^2 = 7^2$ is not true, and the triangle shown is not a right triangle.

7. The numbers in the diagram below indicate the units of length of each side of the triangle. Is the triangle shown below a right triangle? Show your work, and answer in a complete sentence.

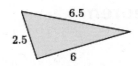

6.5

2.5

6

We need to check if $2.5^2 + 6^2 = 6.5^2$ is a true statement. The left side of the equation is equal to 42.25. The right side of the equation is equal to 42.25. That means $2.5^2 + 6^2 = 6.5^2$ is true, and the triangle shown is a right triangle.

Closing (5 minutes)

Summarize, or ask students to summarize, the main points from the lesson:

- We know the converse of the Pythagorean Theorem states that if side lengths of a triangle a, b, c, satisfy $a^2 + b^2 = c^2$, then the triangle is a right triangle.

- We know that if the side lengths of a triangle a, b, c, do not satisfy $a^2 + b^2 = c^2$, then the triangle is not a right triangle.

Lesson Summary

The converse of the Pythagorean Theorem states that if side lengths of a triangle a, b, c, satisfy $a^2 + b^2 = c^2$, then the triangle is a right triangle.

If the side lengths of a triangle a, b, c, do not satisfy $a^2 + b^2 = c^2$, then the triangle is not a right triangle.

Exit Ticket (5 minutes)

Name _____   Date_____

Lesson 14: The Converse of the Pythagorean Theorem

Exit Ticket

1. The numbers in the diagram below indicate the lengths of the sides of the triangle. Bernadette drew the following triangle and claims it a right triangle. How can she be sure?

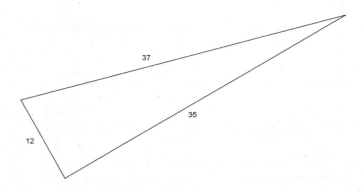

2. Will the lengths 5, 9, and 14 form a right triangle? Explain.

Exit Ticket Sample Solutions

1. The numbers in the diagram below indicate the units of length of each side of the triangle. Bernadette drew the following triangle and claims it a right triangle. How can she be sure?

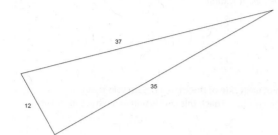

Since 37 is the longest side, if this triangle was a right triangle 37 would have to be the hypotenuse (or c). Now she needs to check to see if $12^2 + 35^2 = 37^2$ is a true statement. The left side is $1,369$, and the right side is $1,369$. That means $12^2 + 35^2 = 37^2$ is true, and this is a right triangle.

2. Will the lengths $5, 9$, and 14 form a right triangle? Explain.

    No, lengths of $5, 9$, and 14 will not form a right triangle. If they did, then the equation $5^2 + 9^2 = 14^2$ would be a true statement. However, the left side equals 106, and the right side equals 196. Therefore, these lengths do not form a right triangle.

Problem Set Sample Solutions

Students practice using the converse of the Pythagorean Theorem and identifying common errors in computations.

1. The numbers in the diagram below indicate the units of length of each side of the triangle. Is the triangle shown below a right triangle? Show your work, and answer in a complete sentence.

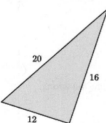

We need to check if $12^2 + 16^2 = 20^2$ is a true statement. The left side of the equation is equal to 400. The right side of the equation is equal to 400. That means $12^2 + 16^2 = 20^2$ is true, and the triangle shown is a right triangle.

2. The numbers in the diagram below indicate the units of length of each side of the triangle. Is the triangle shown below a right triangle? Show your work, and answer in a complete sentence.

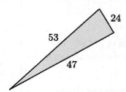

We need to check if $47^2 + 24^2 = 53^2$ is a true statement. The left side of the equation is equal to $2,785$. The right side of the equation is equal to $2,809$. That means $47^2 + 24^2 = 53^2$ is not true, and the triangle shown is not a right triangle.

3. The numbers in the diagram below indicate the units of length of each side of the triangle. Is the triangle shown below a right triangle? Show your work, and answer in a complete sentence.

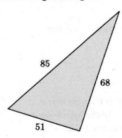

We need to check if $51^2 + 68^2 = 85^2$ is a true statement. The left side of the equation is equal to $7,225$. The right side of the equation is equal to $7,225$. That means $51^2 + 68^2 = 85^2$ is true, and the triangle shown is a right triangle.

4. The numbers in the diagram below indicate the units of length of each side of the triangle. Sam said that the following triangle is a right triangle. Explain to Sam what he did wrong to reach this conclusion and what the correct solution is.

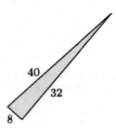

Sam forgot to square each of the side lengths. In other words, he said $8 + 32 = 40$, which is a true statement. However, to show that a triangle is a right triangle, you have to use the Pythagorean Theorem, which is $a^2 + b^2 = c^2$. Using the Pythagorean Theorem, the left side of the equation is equal to $1,088$, and the right side is equal to $1,600$. Since $1,088 \neq 1,600$, then the triangle is not a right triangle.

5. The numbers in the diagram below indicate the units of length of each side of the triangle. Is the triangle shown below a right triangle? Show your work, and answer in a complete sentence.

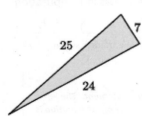

We need to check if $24^2 + 7^2 = 25^2$ is a true statement. The left side of the equation is equal to 625. The right side of the equation is equal to 625. That means $24^2 + 7^2 = 25^2$ is true, and the triangle shown is a right triangle.

6. Jocelyn said that the triangle below is not a right triangle. Her work is shown below. Explain what she did wrong, and show Jocelyn the correct solution.

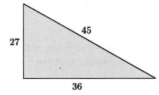

We need to check if $27^2 + 45^2 = 36^2$ is a true statement. The left side of the equation is equal to $2,754$. The right side of the equation is equal to $1,296$. That means $27^2 + 45^2 = 36^2$ is not true, and the triangle shown is not a right triangle.

Jocelyn made the mistake of not putting the longest side of the triangle in place of c in the Pythagorean Theorem, $a^2 + b^2 = c^2$. Specifically, she should have used 45 for c, but instead she used 36 for c. If she had done that part correctly, she would have seen that, in fact, $27^2 + 36^2 = 45^2$ is a true statement because both sides of the equation equal $2,025$. That means that the triangle is a right triangle.

Mathematics Curriculum

Student Materials

Lesson 1: What Lies Behind "Same Shape"?

Exploratory Challenge

Two geometric figures are said to be similar if they have the same shape but not necessarily the same size. Using that informal definition, are the following pairs of figures similar to one another? Explain.

Pair A:

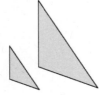

Pair B:

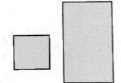

Pair C:

Pair D:

Pair E:

Pair F: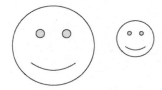

Pair G: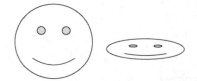

Pair H:

Exercises

1. Given $|OP| = 5$ in.

    a. If segment OP is dilated by a scale factor $r = 4$, what is the length of segment OP'?

    b. If segment OP is dilated by a scale factor $= \frac{1}{2}$, what is the length of segment OP'?

Use the diagram below to answer Exercises 2–6. Let there be a dilation from center O. Then $dilation(P) = P'$ and $dilaton(Q) = Q'$. In the diagram below, $|OP| = 3$ cm and $|OQ| = 4$ cm as shown.

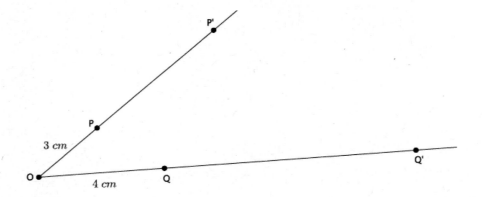

2. If the scale factor is $r = 3$, what is the length of segment OP'?

3. Use the definition of dilation to show that your answer to Exercise 2 is correct.

4. If the scale factor is $r = 3$, what is the length of segment OQ'?

5. Use the definition of dilation to show that your answer to Exercise 4 is correct.

6. If you know that $|OP| = 3, |OP'| = 9$, how could you use that information to determine the scale factor?

Lesson Summary

Definition: A dilation is a transformation of the plane with center O, while scale factor r ($r > 0$) is a rule that assigns to each point P of the plane a point $dilation(P)$ so that:

1. $Dilation(O) = O$, (i.e., a dilation does not move the center of dilation.)

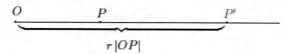

$$r|OP|$$

2. If $P \neq O$, then the point $dilation(P)$, (to be denoted more simply by P') is the point on the ray $\overrightarrow{OP}$ so that $|OP'| = r|OP|$.

In other words, a dilation is a rule that moves points in the plane a specific distance, determined by the scale factor r, from a center O. When the scale factor $r > 1$, the dilation magnifies a figure. When the scale factor $0 < r < 1$, the dilation shrinks a figure. When the scale factor $r = 1$, there is no change in the size of the figure, that is, the figure and its image are congruent.

Problem Set

1. Let there be a dilation from center O. Then $dilation(P) = P'$ and $dilation(Q) = Q'$. Examine the drawing below. What can you determine about the scale factor of the dilation?

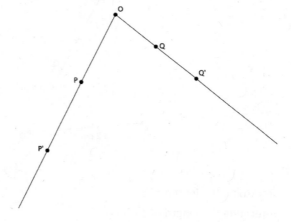

2. Let there be a dilation from center O. Then $dilation(P) = P'$, and $dilation(Q) = Q'$. Examine the drawing below. What can you determine about the scale factor of the dilation?

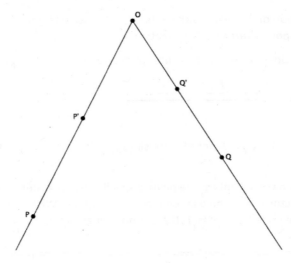

3. Let there be a dilation from center O with a scale factor $r = 4$. Then $dilation(P) = P'$ and $dilation(Q) = Q'$. $|OP| = 3.2$ cm, and $|OQ| = 2.7$ cm as shown. Use the drawing below to answer parts (a) and (b).

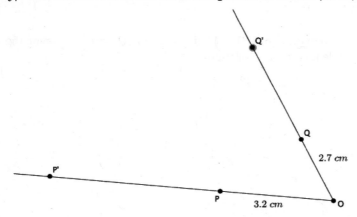

a. Use the definition of dilation to determine the length of OP'.

b. Use the definition of dilation to determine the length of OQ'.

4. Let there be a dilation from center O with a scale factor r. Then $dilation(A) = A'$, $dilation(B) = B'$, and $dilation(C) = C'$. $|OA| = 3$, $|OB| = 15$, $|OC| = 6$, and $|OB'| = 5$ as shown. Use the drawing below to answer parts (a)–(c).

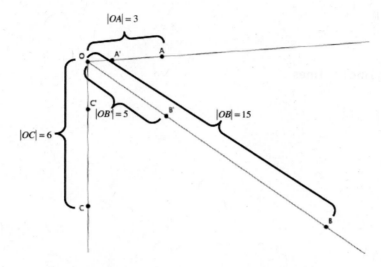

a. Using the definition of dilation with lengths OB and OB', determine the scale factor of the dilation.

b. Use the definition of dilation to determine the length of OA'.

c. Use the definition of dilation to determine the length of OC'.

Lesson 2: Properties of Dilations

Classwork

Examples 1–2: Dilations Map Lines to Lines

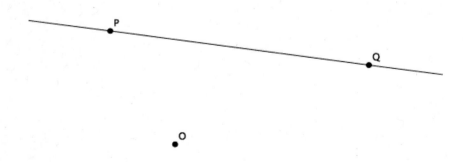

Example 3: Dilations Map Lines to Lines

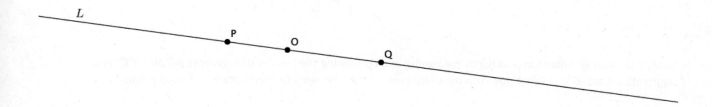

Exercise

Given center O and triangle ABC, dilate the triangle from center O with a scale factor $r = 3$.

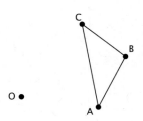

a.   Note that the triangle ABC is made up of segments AB, BC, and CA. Were the dilated images of these segments still segments?

b. Measure the length of the segments AB and $A'B'$. What do you notice? (Think about the definition of dilation.)

c. Verify the claim you made in part (b) by measuring and comparing the lengths of segments BC and $B'C'$ and segments CA and $C'A'$. What does this mean in terms of the segments formed between dilated points?

d. Measure $\angle ABC$ and $\angle A'B'C'$. What do you notice?

e. Verify the claim you made in part (d) by measuring and comparing angles $\angle BCA$ and $\angle B'C'A'$ and angles $\angle CAB$ and $\angle C'A'B'$. What does that mean in terms of dilations with respect to angles and their degrees?

Lesson Summary

Dilations map lines to lines, rays to rays, and segments to segments. Dilations map angles to angles of the same degree.

Problem Set

1. Use a ruler to dilate the following figure from center O, with scale factor $r = \frac{1}{2}$.

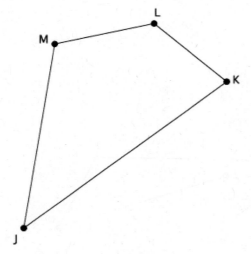

2.   Use a compass to dilate the figure $ABCDE$ from center O, with scale factor $r = 2$.

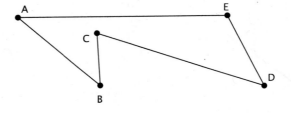

    a.   Dilate the same figure, $ABCDE$, from a new center, O', with scale factor $r = 2$. Use double primes to distinguish this image from the original ($A''B''C''D''E''$).

    b.   What rigid motion, or sequence of rigid motions, would map $A''B''C''D''E''$ to $A'B'C'D'E'$?

3. Given center O and triangle ABC, dilate the figure from center O by a scale factor of $r = \frac{1}{4}$. Label the dilated triangle $A'B'C'$.

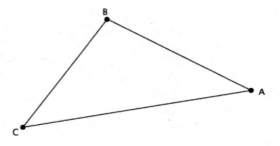

O

a. A line segment AB undergoes a dilation. Based on today's lesson, what will the image of the segment be?

b. Angle $\angle GHI$ measures 78°. After a dilation, what will the measure of $\angle G'H'I'$ be ? How do you know?

Lesson 3: Examples of Dilations

Classwork

Example 1

Dilate circle A, from center O at the origin by a scale factor $r = 3$.

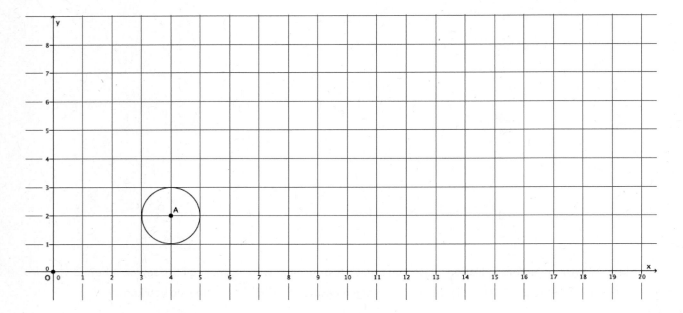

Exercises

1. Dilate ellipse E, from center O at the origin of the graph, with scale factor $r = 2$. Use as many points as necessary to develop the dilated image of ellipse E.

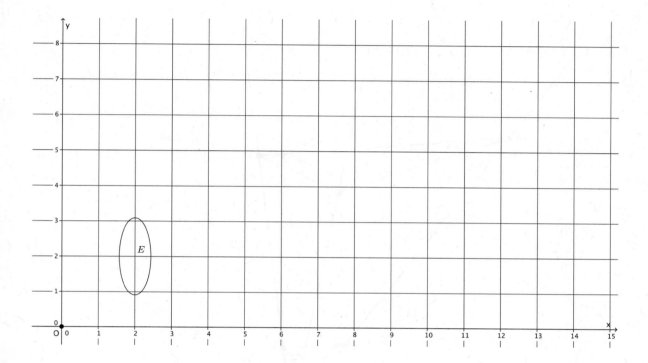

2. What shape was the dilated image?

3. Triangle ABC has been dilated from center O by a scale factor of $r = \frac{1}{4}$ denoted by triangle $A'B'C'$. Using a ruler, verify that it would take a scale factor of $r = 4$ from center O to map triangle $A'B'C'$ onto triangle ABC.

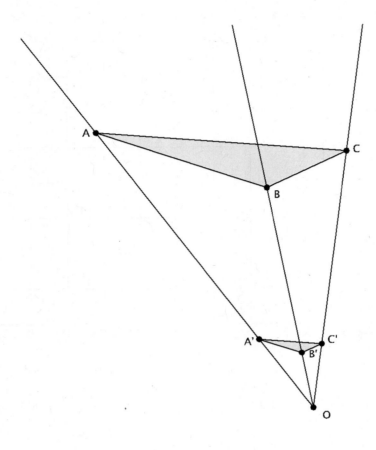

Problem Set

1. Dilate the figure from center O by a scale factor $r = 2$. Make sure to use enough points to make a good image of the original figure.

2. Describe the process for selecting points when dilating a curved figure.

3. A triangle ABC was dilated from center O by a scale factor of $r = 5$. What scale factor would shrink the dilated figure back to the original size?

4. A figure has been dilated from center O by a scale factor of $r = \frac{7}{6}$. What scale factor would shrink the dilated figure back to the original size?

5. A figure has been dilated from center O by a scale factor of $r = \frac{3}{10}$. What scale factor would magnify the dilated figure back to the original size?

Lesson 4: Fundamental Theorem of Similarity (FTS)

Exercises

1.   In the diagram below, points R and S have been dilated from center O, by a scale factor of $r = 3$.

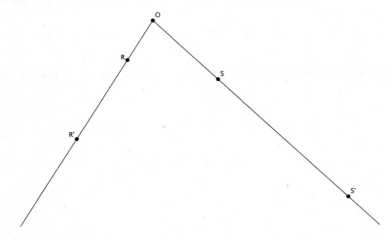

a.   If the length of $|OR| = 2.3$ cm, what is the length of $|OR'|$?

b.   If the length of $|OS| = 3.5$ cm, what is the length of $|OS'|$?

c.   Connect the point R to the point S and the point R' to the point S'. What do you know about lines RS and $R'S'$?

d.   What is the relationship between the length of RS and the length of $R'S'$?

e.   Identify pairs of angles that are equal in measure. How do you know they are equal?

Problem Set

1. Use a piece of notebook paper to verify the Fundamental Theorem of Similarity for a scale factor r that is $0 < r < 1$.

   ✓ Mark a point O on the first line of notebook paper.

   ✓ Draw a ray, $\overrightarrow{OP}$. Mark the point P on a line, several lines down from the center. Mark the point P' on the ray, and on a line of the notebook paper, closer to O than you placed point P. This ensures that you have a scale factor that is $0 < r < 1$. Write your scale factor at the top of the notebook paper.

   ✓ Draw another ray, $\overrightarrow{OQ}$, and mark the points Q and Q' according to your scale factor.

   ✓ Connect points P and Q. Then, connect points P' and Q'.

   ✓ Place a point A on line PQ between points P and Q. Draw ray $\overrightarrow{OA}$. Mark the point A' at the intersection of line $P'Q'$ and ray $\overrightarrow{OA}$.

   a. Are lines PQ and $P'Q'$ parallel lines? How do you know?

   b. Which, if any, of the following pairs of angles are equal? Explain.
      i. $\angle OPQ$ and $\angle OP'Q'$
      ii. $\angle OAQ$ and $\angle OA'Q'$
      iii. $\angle OAP$ and $\angle OA'P'$
      iv. $\angle OQP$ and $\angle OQ'P'$

   c. Which, if any, of the following statements are true? Show your work to verify or dispute each statement.
      i. $|OP'| = r|OP|$
      ii. $|OQ'| = r|OQ|$
      iii. $|P'A'| = r|PA|$
      iv. $|A'Q'| = r|AQ|$

   d. Do you believe that the Fundamental Theorem of Similarity (FTS) is true even when the scale factor is $0 < r < 1$? Explain.

2. Caleb sketched the following diagram on graph paper. He dilated points B and C from center O.

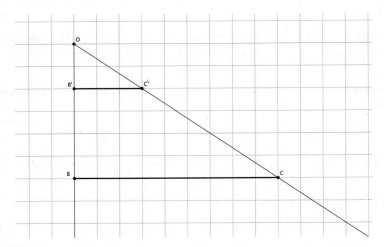

a. What is the scale factor r? Show your work.

b. Verify the scale factor with a different set of segments.

c. Which segments are parallel? How do you know?

d. Which angles are equal in measure? How do you know?

3. Points B and C were dilated from center O.

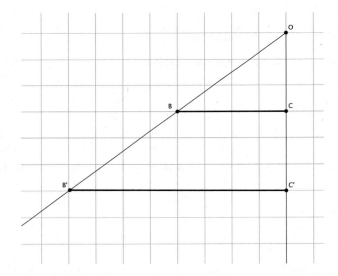

a. What is the scale factor r? Show your work.

b. If the length of $|OB| = 5$, what is the length of $|OB'|$?

c. How does the perimeter of $\triangle OBC$ compare to the perimeter of triangle $OB'C'$?

d. Did the perimeter of triangle $OB'C' = r \times$ (perimeter of triangle OBC)? Explain.

Lesson 5: First Consequences of FTS

Classwork

Exercises

1. In the diagram below, points P and Q have been dilated from center O by scale factor r. $PQ \parallel P'Q'$, $|PQ| = 5$ cm, and $|P'Q'| = 10$ cm.

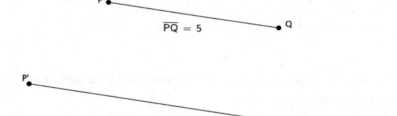

a. Determine the scale factor r.

b. Locate the center O of dilation. Measure the segments to verify that $|OP'| = r|OP|$ and $|OQ'| = r|OQ|$. Show your work below.

2. In the diagram below, you are given center O and ray $\overrightarrow{OA}$. Point A is dilated by a scale factor $r = 4$. Use what you know about FTS to find the location of point A'.

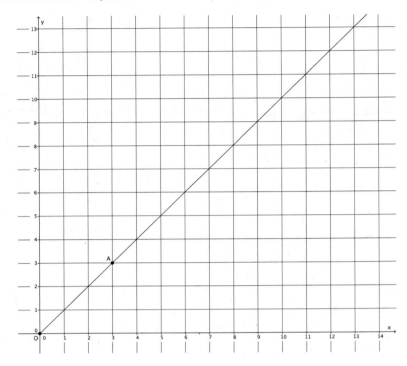

3. In the diagram below, you are given center O and ray $\overrightarrow{OA}$. Point A is dilated by a scale factor $r = \frac{5}{12}$. Use what you know about FTS to find the location of point A'.

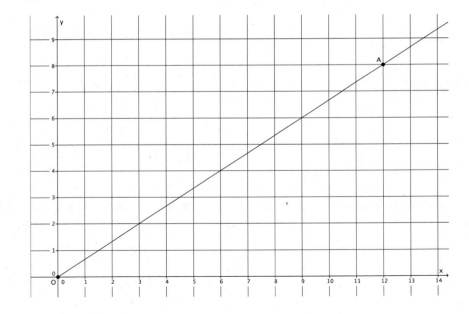

Lesson Summary

Converse of the Fundamental Theorem of Similarity:

If lines PQ and $P'Q'$ are parallel, and $|P'Q'| = r|PQ|$, then from a center O, $P' = dilation(P)$, $Q' = dilation(Q)$, and $|OP'| = r|OP|$ and $|OQ'| = r|OQ|$.

To find the coordinates of a dilated point, we must use what we know about FTS, dilation, and scale factor.

Problem Set

1. Dilate point A, located at $(3, 4)$ from center O, by a scale factor $r = \dfrac{5}{3}$.

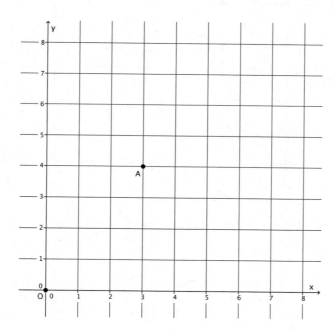

What is the precise location of point A'?

2. Dilate point A, located at $(9, 7)$ from center O, by a scale factor $r = \frac{4}{9}$. Then dilate point B, located at $(9, 5)$ from center O, by a scale factor of $r = \frac{4}{9}$. What are the coordinates of A' and B'? Explain.

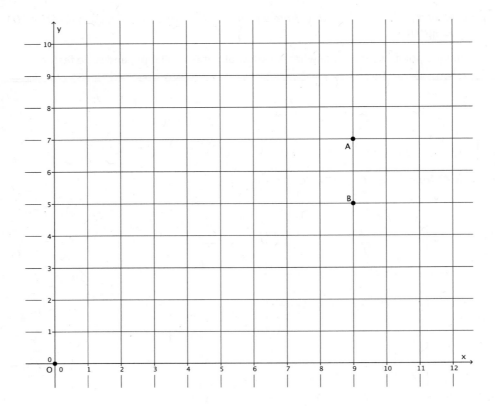

3. Explain how you used the Fundamental Theorem of Similarity in problems 1 and 2.

Lesson 6: Dilations on the Coordinate Plane

Classwork

Exercises

1. Point $A = (7, 9)$ is dilated from the origin by scale factor $r = 6$. What are the coordinates of point A'?

2. Point $B = (-8, 5)$ is dilated from the origin by scale factor $r = \frac{1}{2}$. What are the coordinates of point B'?

3. Point $C = (6, -2)$ is dilated from the origin by scale factor $r = \frac{3}{4}$. What are the coordinates of point C'?

4. Point $D = (0, \ 11)$ is dilated from the origin by scale factor $r = 4$. What are the coordinates of point D'?

5. Point $E = (-2, -5)$ is dilated from the origin by scale factor $r = \frac{3}{2}$. What are the coordinates of point E'?

6. The coordinates of triangle ABC are shown on the coordinate plane below. The triangle is dilated from the origin by scale factor $r = 12$. Identify the coordinates of the dilated triangle $A'B'C'$.

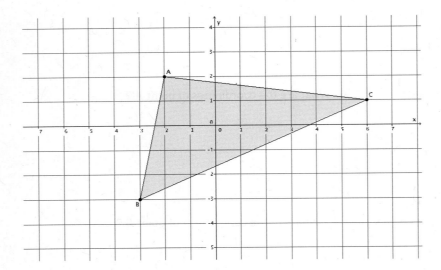

7. Figure $DEFG$ is shown on the coordinate plane below. The figure is dilated from the origin by scale factor $r = \frac{2}{3}$. Identify the coordinates of the dilated figure $D'E'F'G'$, then draw and label figure $D'E'F'G'$ on the coordinate plane.

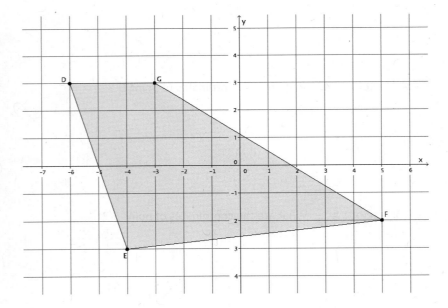

8. The triangle ABC has coordinates $A = (3, 2)$, $B = (12, 3)$, and $C = (9, 12)$. Draw and label triangle ABC on the coordinate plane. The triangle is dilated from the origin by scale factor $r = \frac{1}{3}$. Identify the coordinates of the dilated triangle $A'B'C'$, then draw and label triangle $A'B'C'$ on the coordinate plane.

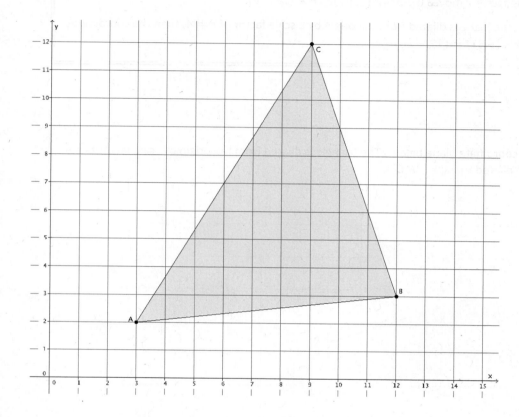

Lesson Summary

Dilation has a multiplicative effect on the coordinates of a point in the plane. Given a point (x, y) in the plane, a dilation from the origin with scale factor r moves the point (x, y) to $(r \times x, r \times y)$.

For example, if a point $(3, -5)$ in the plane is dilated from the origin by a scale factor of $r = 4$, then the coordinates of the dilated point are $\left(4 \times 3, 4 \times (-5)\right) = (12, -20)$.

Problem Set

1.   Triangle ABC is shown on the coordinate plane below. The triangle is dilated from the origin by scale factor $r = 4$. Identify the coordinates of the dilated triangle $A'B'C'$.

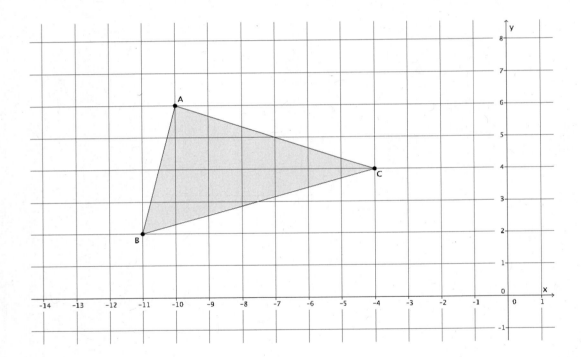

2. Triangle ABC is shown on the coordinate plane below. The triangle is dilated from the origin by scale factor $r = \frac{5}{4}$.
    Identify the coordinates of the dilated triangle $A'B'C'$.

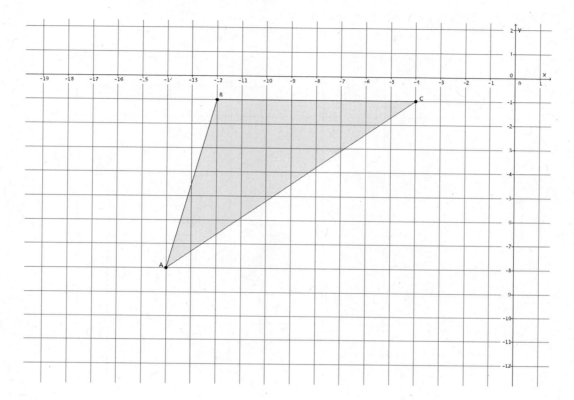

3. The triangle ABC has coordinates $A = (6, 1), B = (12, 4)$, and $C = (-6, 2)$. The triangle is dilated from the origin
    by a scale factor $r = \frac{1}{2}$. Identify the coordinates of the dilated triangle $A'B'C'$.

4. Figure $DEFG$ is shown on the coordinate plane below. The figure is dilated from the origin by scale factor $r = \frac{3}{2}$. Identify the coordinates of the dilated figure $D'E'F'G'$, then draw and label figure $D'E'F'G'$ on the coordinate plane.

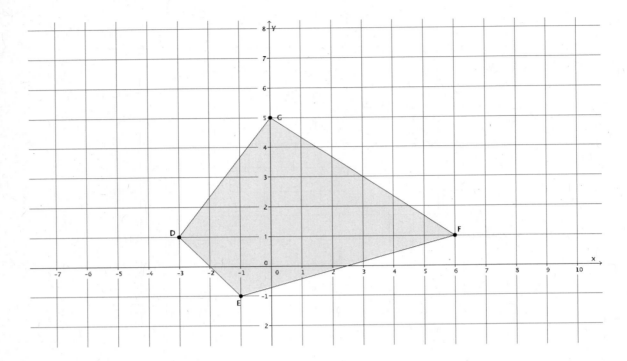

5. Figure $DEFG$ has coordinates $D = (1,1), E = (7,3), F = (5,-4)$ and $G = (-1,-4)$. The figure is dilated from the origin by scale factor $r = 7$. Identify the coordinates of the dilated figure $D'E'F'G'$.

Lesson 7: Informal Proofs of Properties of Dilation

Exercise

Use the diagram below to prove the theorem: *Dilations preserve the degrees of angles.*

Let there be a dilation from center O with scale factor r. Given $\angle PQR$, show that since $P' = dilation(P)$, $Q' = dilation(Q)$, and $R' = dilation(R)$, then $|\angle PQR| = |\angle P'Q'R'|$. That is, show that the image of the angle after a dilation has the same measure, in degrees, as the original.

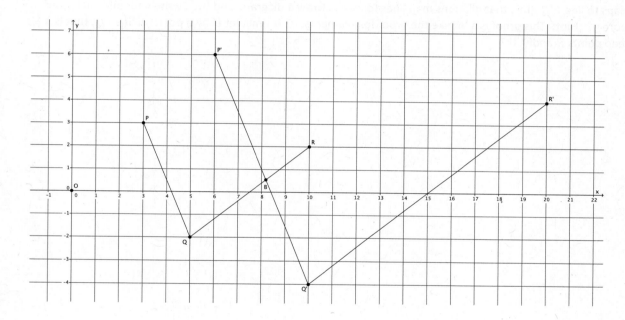

Problem Set

1. A dilation from center O by scale factor r of a line maps to what? Verify your claim on the coordinate plane.

2. A dilation from center O by scale factor r of a segment maps to what? Verify your claim on the coordinate plane.

3. A dilation from center O by scale factor r of a ray maps to what? Verify your claim on the coordinate plane.

4. Challenge Problem:

   Prove the theorem: *A dilation maps lines to lines.*

   Let there be a dilation from center O with scale factor r so that $P' = dilation(P)$ and $Q' = dilation(Q)$. Show that line PQ maps to line $P'Q'$ (i.e., that dilations map lines to lines). Draw a diagram, and then write your informal proof of the theorem. (Hint: This proof is a lot like the proof for segments. This time, let U be a point on line PQ, that is not between points P and Q.)

Lesson 7:	Informal Proofs of Properties of Dilations
Date:	10/16/13

S.31

© 2013 Common Core, Inc. All rights reserved. **commoncore.org**

Lesson 8: Similarity

Classwork

Example 1

In the picture below we have a triangle ABC, that has been dilated from center O, by a scale factor of $r = \frac{1}{2}$. It is noted by $A'B'C'$. We also have triangle $A''B''C''$, which is congruent to triangle $A'B'C'$ (i.e., $\Delta A'B'C' \cong \Delta A''B''C''$).

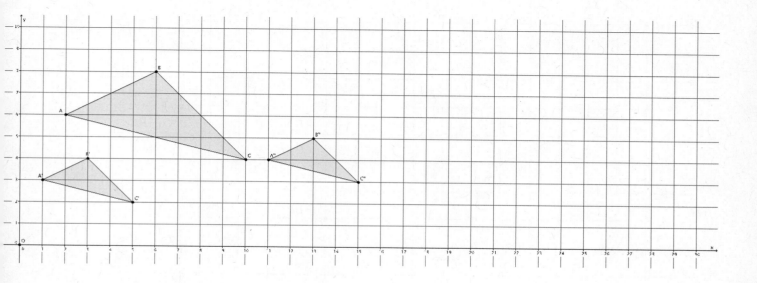

Describe the sequence that would map triangle $A''B''C''$ onto triangle ABC.

Exercises

1. Triangle ABC was dilated from center O by scale factor $r = \frac{1}{2}$. The dilated triangle is noted by $A'B'C'$. Another triangle $A''B''C''$ is congruent to triangle $A'B'C'$ (i.e., $\triangle A''B''C'' \cong \triangle A'B'C'$). Describe the dilation followed by the basic rigid motion that would map triangle $A''B''C''$ onto triangle ABC.

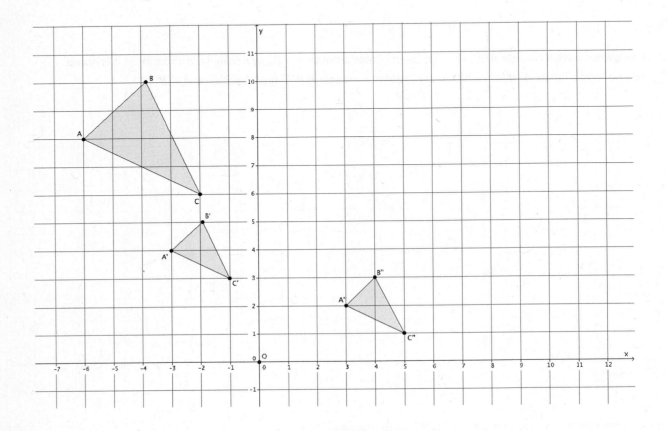

2. Describe the sequence that would show $\triangle ABC \sim \triangle A'B'C'$.

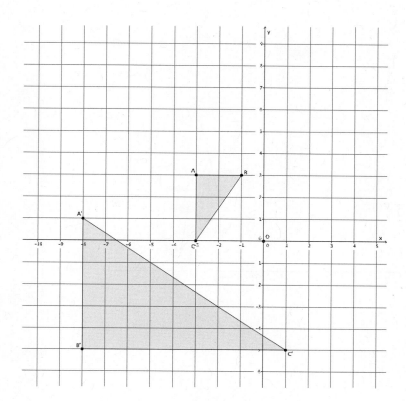

3. Are the two triangles shown below similar? If so, describe the sequence that would prove $\triangle ABC \sim \triangle A'B'C'$. If not, state how you know they are not similar.

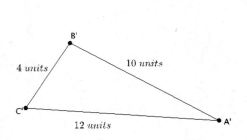

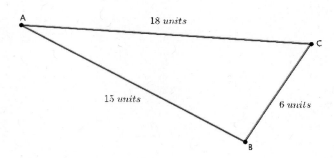

4. Are the two triangles shown below similar? If so, describe the sequence that would prove $\triangle ABC \sim \triangle A'B'C'$. If not, state how you know they are not similar.

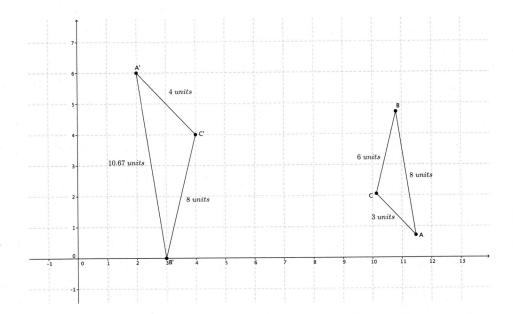

Lesson Summary

Similarity is defined as mapping one figure onto another as a sequence of a dilation followed by a congruence (a sequence of rigid motions).

The notation, $\triangle ABC \sim \triangle A'B'C'$, means that $\triangle ABC$ is similar to $\triangle A'B'C'$.

Problem Set

1. In the picture below, we have a triangle DEF, that has been dilated from center O, by scale factor $r = 4$. It is noted by $D'E'F'$. We also have a triangle $D''E''F''$, which is congruent to triangle $D'E'F'$ (i.e., $\triangle D'E'F' \cong \triangle D''E''F''$). Describe the sequence of a dilation, followed by a congruence (a sequence of one or more rigid motions), that would map triangle $D''E''F''$ onto triangle DEF.

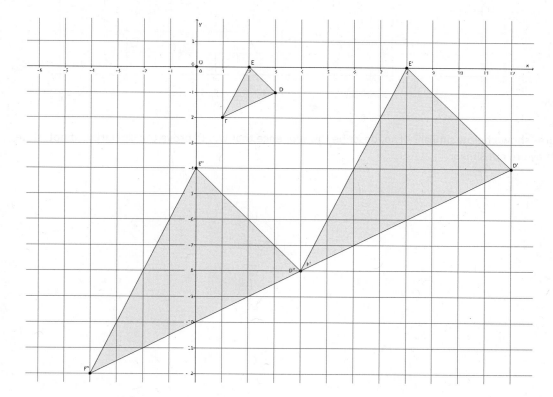

2. Triangle ABC was dilated from center O by scale factor $r = \frac{1}{2}$. The dilated triangle is noted by $A'B'C'$. Another triangle $A''B''C''$ is congruent to triangle $A'B'C'$ (i.e., $\Delta A''B''C'' \cong \Delta A'B'C'$). Describe the dilation followed by the basic rigid motion that would map triangle $A''B''C''$ onto triangle ABC.

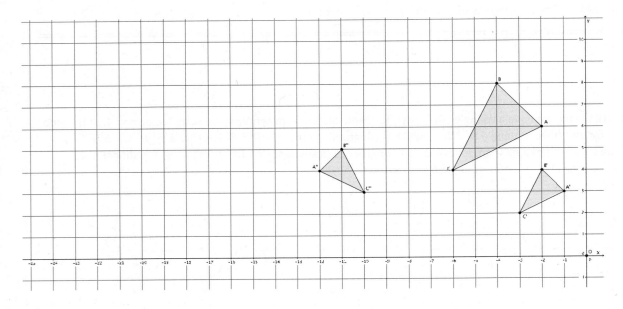

3. Are the two figures shown below similar? If so, describe the sequence that would prove the similarity. If not, state how you know they are not similar.

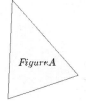

4. Triangle ABC is similar to triangle $A'B'C'$, (i.e, $\triangle ABC \sim \triangle A'B'C'$). Prove the similarity by describing the sequence that would map triangle $A'B'C'$ onto triangle ABC.

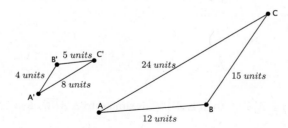

5. Are the two figures shown below similar? If so, describe the sequence that would prove $\triangle ABC \sim \triangle A'B'C'$. If not, state how you know they are not similar.

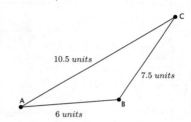

6. Describe the sequence that would show $\triangle ABC \sim \triangle A'B'C'$.

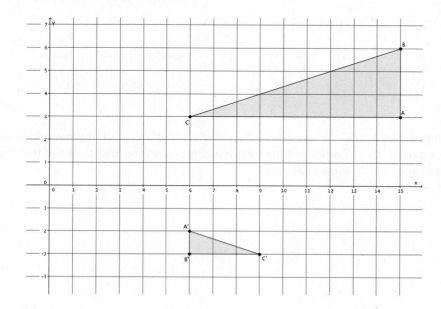

Lesson 9: Basic Properties of Similarity

Exploratory Challenge 1

The goal is to show that if △ ABC is similar to △ $A'B'C'$, then △ $A'B'C'$ is similar to △ ABC. Symbolically, if △ ABC ~△ $A'B'C'$, then △ $A'B'C'$ ~△ ABC.

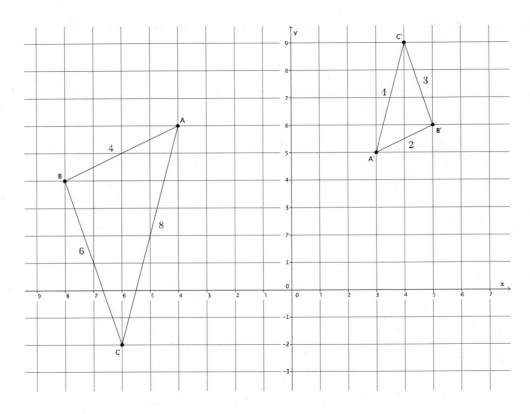

a.   First determine whether or not △ ABC is in fact similar to △ $A'B'C'$. (If it isn't, then there would is no further work to be done.) Use a protractor to verify that the corresponding angles are congruent and that the ratio of the corresponding sides are equal to some scale factor.

b.   Describe the sequence of dilation followed by a congruence that proves $\triangle ABC \sim \triangle A'B'C'$.

c.   Describe the sequence of dilation followed by a congruence that proves $\triangle A'B'C' \sim \triangle ABC$.

d.   Is it true that $\triangle ABC \sim \triangle A'B'C'$ and $\triangle A'B'C' \sim \triangle ABC$? Why do you think this is so?

Exploratory Challenge 2

The goal is to show that if △ ABC is similar to △ $A'B'C'$, and △ $A'B'C'$ is similar to △ $A''B''C''$, then △ ABC is similar to △ $A''B''C''$. Symbolically, if △ $ABC \sim$ △ $A'B'C'$ and △ $A'B'C' \sim$ △ $A''B''C''$, then △ $ABC \sim$ △ $A''B''C''$.

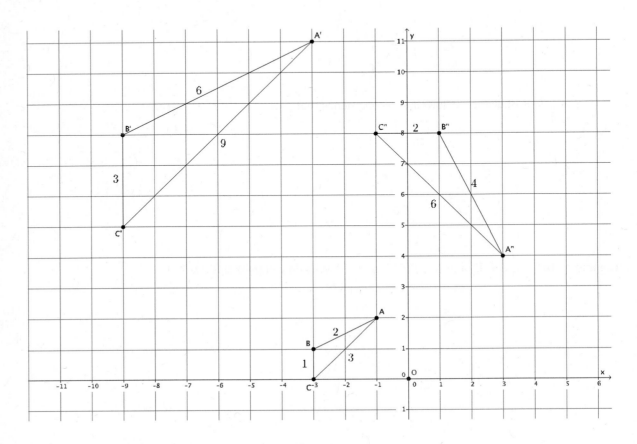

a.   Describe the similarity that proves △ $ABC \sim$ △ $A'B'C'$.

b.   Describe the similarity that proves △ $A'B'C' \sim$ △ $A''B''C''$.

c. Verify that, in fact, $\triangle ABC \sim \triangle A''B''C''$ by checking corresponding angles and corresponding side lengths. Then describe the sequence that would prove the similarity $\triangle ABC \sim \triangle A''B''C''$.

d. Is it true that if $\triangle ABC \sim \triangle A'B'C'$ and $\triangle A'B'C' \sim \triangle A''B''C''$, then $\triangle ABC \sim \triangle A''B''C''$? Why do you think this is so?

> **Lesson Summary**
>
> Similarity is a symmetric relation. That means that if one figure is similar to another, $S \sim S'$, then we can be sure that $S' \sim S$.
>
> Similarity is a transitive relation. That means that if we are given two similar figures, $S \sim T$, and another statement about $T \sim U$, then we also know that $S \sim U$.

Problem Set

1. Would a dilation alone be enough to show that similarity is symmetric? That is, would a dilation alone prove that if $\triangle ABC \sim \triangle A'B'C'$, then $\triangle A'B'C' \sim \triangle ABC$? Consider the two examples below.

    a. Given $\triangle ABC \sim \triangle A'B'C'$. Is a dilation enough to show that $\triangle A'B'C' \sim \triangle ABC$? Explain.

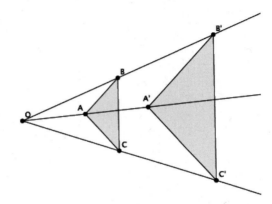

    b. Given $\triangle ABC \sim \triangle A'B'C'$. Is a dilation enough to show that $\triangle A'B'C' \sim \triangle ABC$? Explain.

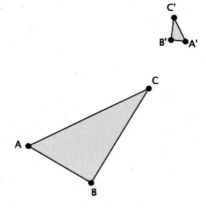

    c. In general, is dilation enough to prove that similarity is a symmetric relation? Explain.

2. Would a dilation alone be enough to show that similarity is transitive? That is, would a dilation alone prove that if
    $\triangle ABC \sim \triangle A'B'C'$, and $\triangle A'B'C' \sim \triangle A''B''C''$, then $\triangle ABC \sim \triangle A''B''C''$? Consider the two examples below.

    a.   Given $\triangle ABC \sim \triangle A'B'C'$ and $\triangle A'B'C' \sim \triangle A''B''C''$. Is a dilation enough to show that $\triangle ABC \sim \triangle A''B''C''$?
         Explain.

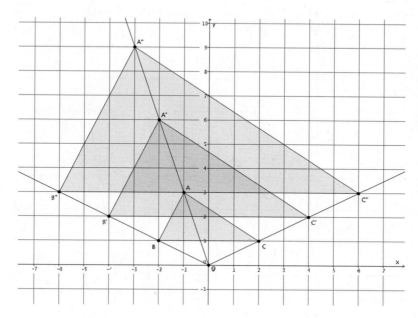

    b.   Given $\triangle ABC \sim \triangle A'B'C'$ and $\triangle A'B'C' \sim \triangle A''B''C''$. Is a dilation enough to show that $\triangle ABC \sim \triangle A''B''C''$?
         Explain.

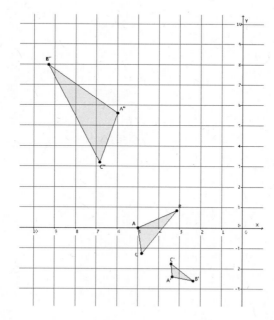

    c.   In general, is dilation enough to prove that similarity is a transitive relation? Explain.

3. In the diagram below, $\triangle ABC \sim \triangle A'B'C'$ and $\triangle A'B'C' \sim \triangle A''B''C''$. Is $\triangle ABC \sim \triangle A''B''C''$? If so, describe the dilation followed by the congruence that demonstrates the similarity.

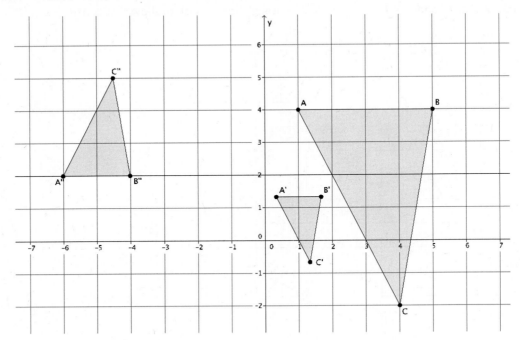

Lesson 10: Informal Proof of AA Criterion for Similarity

Classwork

Exercises

1. Use a protractor to draw a pair of triangles with two pairs of equal angles. Then measure the lengths of sides, and verify that the lengths of their corresponding sides are equal in ratio.

2. Draw a new pair of triangles with two pairs of equal angles. Then measure the lengths of sides, and verify that the lengths of their corresponding sides are equal in ratio.

3. Are the triangles shown below similar? Present an informal argument as to why they are or why they are not.

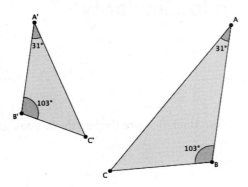

4. Are the triangles shown below similar? Present an informal argument as to why they are or why they are not.

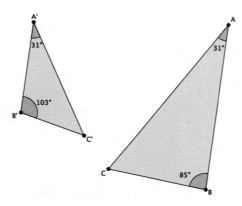

5. Are the triangles shown below similar? Present an informal argument as to why they are or why they are not.

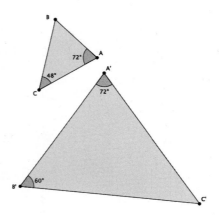

Problem Set

1. Are the triangles shown below similar? Present an informal argument as to why they are or why they are not.

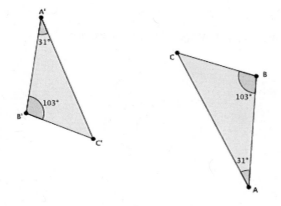

2. Are the triangles shown below similar? Present an informal argument as to why they are or why they are not.

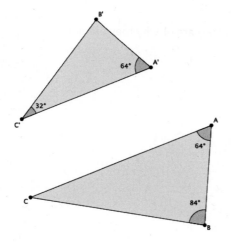

3. Are the triangles shown below similar? Present an informal argument as to why they are or why they are not.

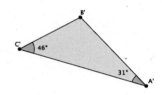

4. Are the triangles shown below similar? Present an informal argument as to why they are or why they are not.

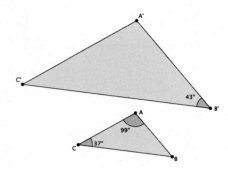

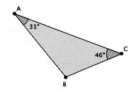

5. Are the triangles shown below similar? Present an informal argument as to why they are or why they are not.

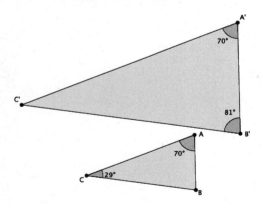

| | Lesson 10: | Informal Proofs of AA Criterion for Similarity |
| | Date: | 10/16/13 |

6. Are the triangles shown below similar? Present an informal argument as to why they are or why they are not.

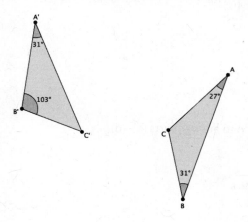

7. Are the triangles shown below similar? Present an informal argument as to why they are or why they are not.

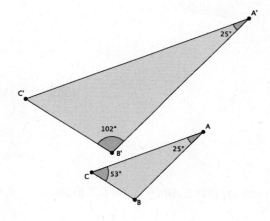

Lesson 11: More About Similar Triangles

Classwork

Exercises

1. In the diagram below, you have $\triangle ABC$ and $\triangle AB'C'$. Use this information to answer parts (a)–(d).

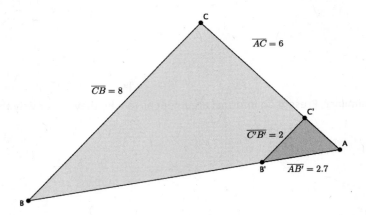

a. Based on the information given, is $\triangle ABC \sim \triangle AB'C'$? Explain.

b. Assume line BC is parallel to line $B'C'$. With this information, can you say that $\triangle ABC \sim \triangle AB'C'$? Explain.

c. Given that $\triangle ABC \sim \triangle AB'C'$, determine the length of AC'.

d. Given that $\triangle ABC \sim \triangle AB'C'$, determine the length of AB.

2. In the diagram below, you have △ ABC and △ $A'B'C'$. Use this information to answer parts (a)–(c).

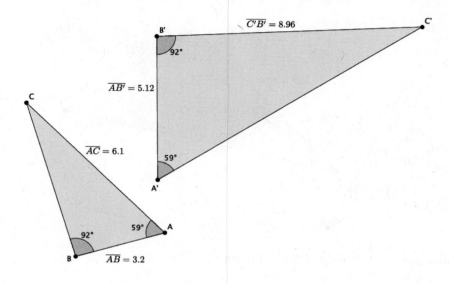

a. Based on the information given, is △ $ABC \sim$ △ $A'B'C'$? Explain.

b. Given that △ $ABC \sim$ △ $A'B'C'$, determine the length of $A'C'$.

c. Given that △ $ABC \sim$ △ $A'B'C'$, determine the length of BC.

3. In the diagram below you have △ ABC and △ $A'B'C'$. Use this information to answer the question below.

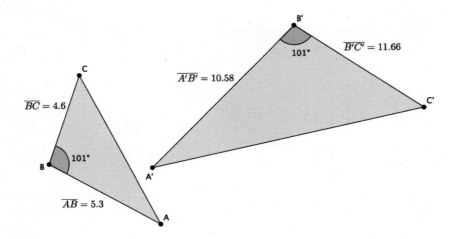

Based on the information given, is △ $ABC \sim$ △ $A'B'C'$? Explain.

Lesson Summary

Given just one pair of corresponding angles of a triangle as equal, use the side lengths along the given angle to determine if triangles are in fact similar.

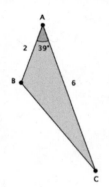

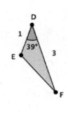

$|\angle A| = |\angle D|$ and $\dfrac{1}{2} = \dfrac{3}{6} = r$; therefore,

$\triangle ABC \sim \triangle DEF$.

Given similar triangles, use the fact that ratios of corresponding sides are equal to find any missing measurements.

Problem Set

1. In the diagram below, you have $\triangle ABC$ and $\triangle A'B'C'$. Use this information to answer parts (a)–(b).

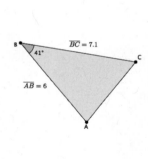

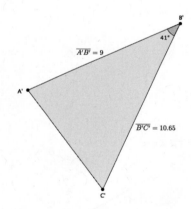

a. Based on the information given, is $\triangle ABC \sim \triangle A'B'C'$? Explain.

b. Assume the length of AC is 4.3. What is the length of $A'C'$?

2. In the diagram below you have △ ABC and △ $AB'C'$. Use this information to answer parts (a)–(d).

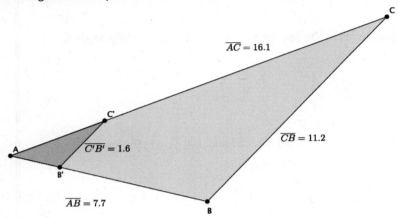

a. Based on the information given, is △ ABC ~ △ $AB'C'$? Explain.

b. Assume line BC is parallel to line $B'C'$. With this information, can you say that △ ABC ~ △ $AB'C'$? Explain.

c. Given that △ ABC ~ △ $AB'C'$, determine the length of AC'.

d. Given that △ ABC ~ △ $AB'C'$, determine the length of AB'.

3. In the diagram below you have △ ABC and △ $A'B'C'$. Use this information to answer parts (a)–(c).

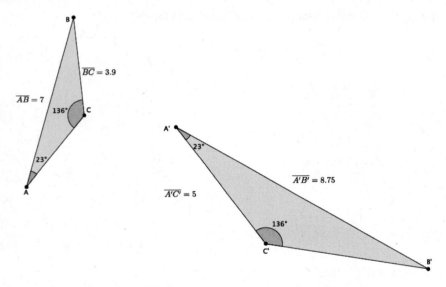

a. Based on the information given, is △ ABC ~ △ $A'B'C'$? Explain.

b. Given that △ ABC ~ △ $A'B'C'$, determine the length of $B'C'$.

c. Given that △ ABC ~ △ $A'B'C'$, determine the length of AC.

4. In the diagram below you have △ ABC and △ $AB'C'$. Use this information to answer the question below.

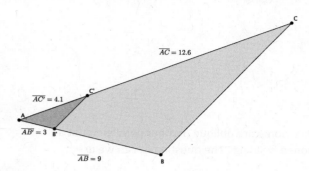

Based on the information given, is △ $ABC \sim$ △ $AB'C'$? Explain.

5. In the diagram below, you have △ ABC and △ $A'B'C'$. Use this information to answer parts (a)–(b).

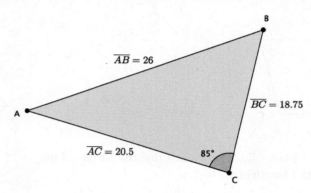

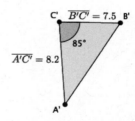

a. Based on the information given, is △ $ABC \sim$ △ $A'B'C'$? Explain.

b. Given that △ $ABC \sim$ △ $A'B'C'$, determine the length of $A'B'$.

Lesson 12: Modeling Using Similarity

Example 1

Not all flagpoles are perfectly *upright* (i.e., perpendicular to the ground). Some are oblique (neither parallel nor at a right angle, slanted). Imagine an oblique flagpole in front of an abandoned building. The question is, can we use sunlight and shadows to determine the length of the flagpole?

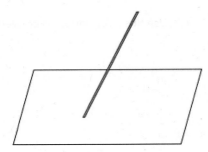

- Assume the length of the shadow that the flagpole casts is 15 feet long. Also assume that the portion of the flagpole that is 3 feet above the ground casts a shadow with a length of 1.7 feet.

Exercises

1. You want to determine the approximate height of one of the tallest buildings in the city. You are told that if you place a mirror some distance from yourself so that you can see the top of the building in the mirror, then you can indirectly measure the height using similar triangles. Let O be the location of the mirror so that the figure shown can see the top of the building.

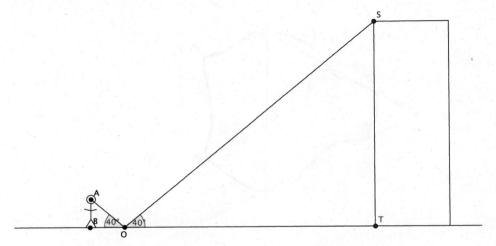

a. Explain why $\triangle ABO \sim \triangle STO$.

b. Label the diagram with the following information: The distance from eye-level to the ground is 5.3 feet. The distance from the figure to the mirror is 7.2 feet. The distance from the figure to the base of the building is 1,750 feet. The height of the building will be represented by x.

c. What is the distance from the mirror to the building?

d. Do you have enough information to determine the approximate height of the building? If yes, determine the approximate height of the building. If not, what additional information is needed?

2. A geologist wants to determine the distance across the widest part of a nearby lake. The geologist marked off specific points around the lake so that line DE would be parallel to line BC. The segment BC is selected specifically because it is the widest part of the lake. The segment DE is selected specifically because it was a short enough distance to easily measure. The geologist sketched the situation as shown below:

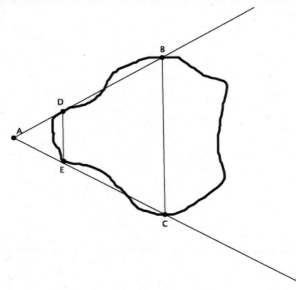

a. Has the geologist done enough work so far to use similar triangles to help measure the widest part of the lake? Explain.

b. The geologist has made the following measurements: $|DE| = 5$ feet, $|AE| = 7$ feet, and $|EC| = 15$ feet. Does she have enough information to complete the task? If so, determine the length across the widest part of the lake. If not, state what additional information is needed.

c. Assume the geologist could only measure a maximum distance of 12 feet. Could she still find the distance across the widest part of the lake? What would need to be done differently?

   | **Date:**   10/16/13

3. A tree is planted in the backyard of a house with the hope that one day it will be tall enough to provide shade to cool the house. A sketch of the house, tree, and sun is shown below.

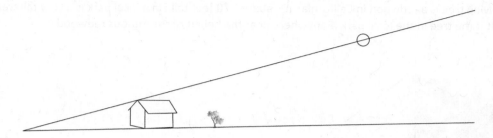

a. What information is needed to determine how tall the tree must be to provide the desired shade?

b. Assume that the sun casts a shadow 32 feet long from a point on top of the house to a point in front of the house. The distance from the end of the house's shadow to the base of the tree is 53 feet. If the house is 16 feet tall, how tall must the tree get to provide shade for the house?

c. Assume that the tree grows at a rate of 2.5 feet per year. If the tree is now 7 feet tall, about how many years will it take for the tree to reach the desired height?

Problem Set

1. The world's tallest living tree is a redwood in California. It's about 370 feet tall. In a local park is a very tall tree. You want to find out if the tree in the local park is anywhere near the height of the famous redwood.

    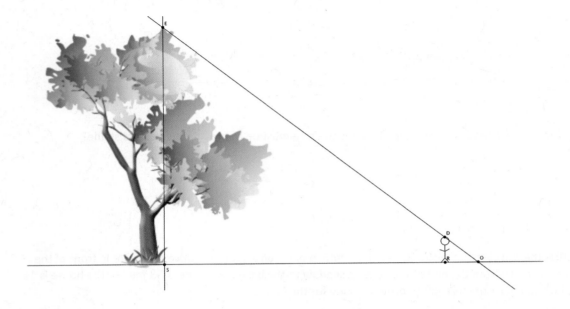

    a. Describe the triangles in the diagram, and explain how you know they are similar or not.

    b. Assume $\triangle ESO \sim \triangle DRO$. A friend stands in the shadow of the tree. He is exactly 5.5 feet tall and casts a shadow of 12 feet. Is there enough information to determine the height of the tree? If so, determine the height, if not, state what additional information is needed.

    c. Your friend stands exactly 477 feet from the base of the tree. Given this new information, determine about how many feet taller the world's tallest tree is compared to the one in the local park.

    d. Assume that your friend stands in the shadow of the world's tallest redwood and the length of his shadow is just 8 feet long. How long is the shadow cast by the tree?

2. A reasonable skateboard ramp makes a 25° angle with the ground. A two feet tall ramp requires about 4.3 feet of wood along the base and about 4.7 feet of wood from the ground to the top of the two-foot height to make the ramp.

    a. Sketch a diagram to represent the situation.

    b. Your friend is a daredevil and has decided to build a ramp that is 5 feet tall. What length of wood will be needed to make the base of the ramp? Explain your answer using properties of similar triangles.

    c. What length of wood is required to go from the ground to the top of the 5 feet height to make the ramp? Explain your answer using properties of similar triangles.

	Lesson 12:	Modeling Using Similarity	
	Date:	10/16/13	S.61

Lesson 13: Proof of the Pythagorean Theorem

Classwork

Exercises

Use the Pythagorean Theorem to determine the unknown length of the right triangle.

1. Determine the length of side c in each of the triangles below.

    a.

    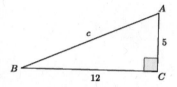

    b.

    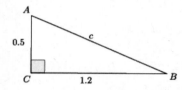

2. Determine the length of side b in each of the triangles below.

    a.

    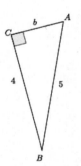

    b.

    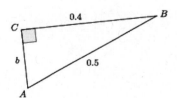

3. Determine the length of QS. (Hint: Use the Pythagorean Theorem twice.)

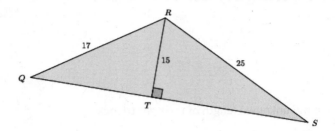

Problem Set

Use the Pythagorean Theorem to determine the unknown length of the right triangle.

1. Determine the length of side c in each of the triangles below.

   a.

   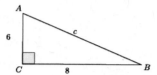

   b.

   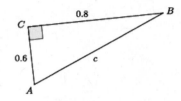

2. Determine the length of side a in each of the triangles below.

   a.

   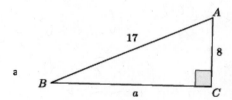

   b.

   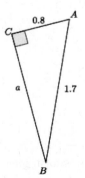

3. Determine the length of side b in each of the triangles below.

    a.

    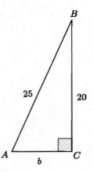

    b.

    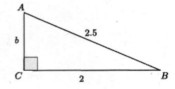

4. Determine the length of side a in each of the triangles below.

    a.

    b.

    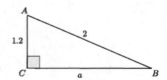

5. What did you notice in each of the pairs of problems 1–4? How might what you noticed be helpful in solving problems like these?

Lesson 14: The Converse of the Pythagorean Theorem

Classwork

Exercises

1. The numbers in the diagram below indicate the units of length of each side of the triangle. Is the triangle shown below a right triangle? Show your work, and answer in a complete sentence.

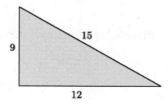

2. The numbers in the diagram below indicate the units of length of each side of the triangle. Is the triangle shown below a right triangle? Show your work, and answer in a complete sentence.

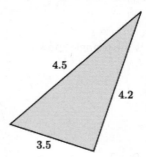

3. The numbers in the diagram below indicate the units of length of each side of the triangle. Is the triangle shown below a right triangle? Show your work, and answer in a complete sentence.

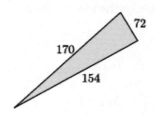

4. The numbers in the diagram below indicate the units of length of each side of the triangle. Is the triangle shown below a right triangle? Show your work, and answer in a complete sentence.

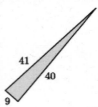

5. The numbers in the diagram below indicate the units of length of each side of the triangle. Is the triangle shown below a right triangle? Show your work, and answer in a complete sentence.

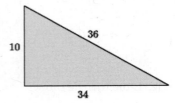

6. The numbers in the diagram below indicate the units of length of each side of the triangle. Is the triangle shown below a right triangle? Show your work, and answer in a complete sentence.

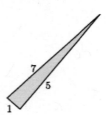

7. The numbers in the diagram below indicate the units of length of each side of the triangle. Is the triangle shown below a right triangle? Show your work, and answer in a complete sentence.

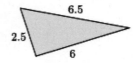

> **Lesson Summary**
>
> The converse of the Pythagorean Theorem states that if side lengths of a triangle a, b, c, satisfy $a^2 + b^2 = c^2$, then the triangle is a right triangle.
>
> If the side lengths of a triangle a, b, c, do not satisfy $a^2 + b^2 = c^2$, then the triangle is not a right triangle.

Problem Set

1. The numbers in the diagram below indicate the units of length of each side of the triangle. Is the triangle shown below a right triangle? Show your work, and answer in a complete sentence.

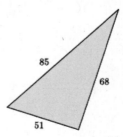

2. The numbers in the diagram below indicate the units of length of each side of the triangle. Is the triangle shown below a right triangle? Show your work, and answer in a complete sentence.

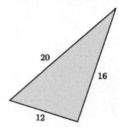

3. The numbers in the diagram below indicate the units of length of each side of the triangle. Is the triangle shown below a right triangle? Show your work, and answer in a complete sentence.

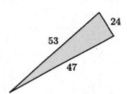

4. The numbers in the diagram below indicate the units of length of each side of the triangle. Sam said that the following triangle is a right triangle. Explain to Sam what he did wrong to reach this conclusion and what the correct solution is.

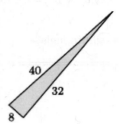

5. The numbers in the diagram below indicate the units of length of each side of the triangle. Is the triangle shown below a right triangle? Show your work, and answer in a complete sentence.

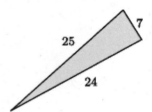

6. Jocelyn said that the triangle below is not a right triangle. Her work is shown below. Explain what she did wrong, and show Jocelyn the correct solution.

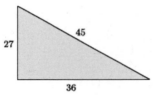

We need to check if $27^2 + 45^2 = 36^2$ is a true statement. The left side of the equation is equal to 2,754. The right side of the equation is equal to 1,296. That means $27^2 + 45^2 = 36^2$ is not true, and the triangle shown is not a right triangle.

Copy Ready Materials

Name _____   Date_____

Lesson 1: What Lies Behind "Same Shape"?

Exit Ticket

1. Why do we need a better definition for similarity than "same shape, not the same size"?

2. Use the diagram below. Let there be a dilation from center O with scale factor $r = 3$. Then $dilation(P) = P'$. In the diagram below, $|OP| = 5$ cm. What is $|OP'|$? Show your work.

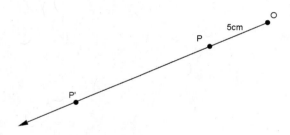

3. Use the diagram below. Let there be a dilation from center O. Then $dilation(P) = P'$. In the diagram below, $|OP| = 18$ cm and $|OP'| = 9$ cm. What is the scale factor r? Show your work.

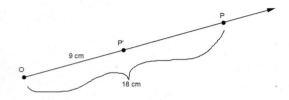

Name _____   Date_____

Lesson 2: Properties of Dilations

Exit Ticket

1.   Given center O and quadrilateral $ABCD$, dilate the figure from center O by a scale factor of $r = 2$. Label the dilated quadrilateral $A'B'C'D'$.

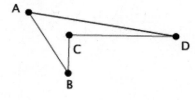

2.   Describe what you learned today about what happens to lines, segments, rays, and angles after a dilation.

Name _____   Date_____

Lesson 3: Examples of Dilations

Exit Ticket

1. Dilate circle A from center O by a scale factor $= \frac{1}{2}$. Make sure to use enough points to make a good image of the original figure.

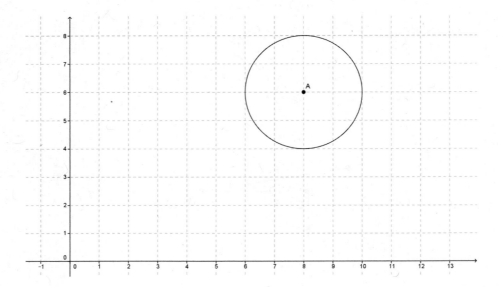

2. What scale factor would magnify the dilated circle back to the original size of circle A? How do you know?

Name _____   Date_____

Lesson 4: Fundamental Theorem of Similarity (FTS)

Exit Ticket

Steven sketched the following diagram on graph paper. He dilated points B and C from point O. Answer the following questions based on his drawing:

1. What is the scale factor r? Show your work.

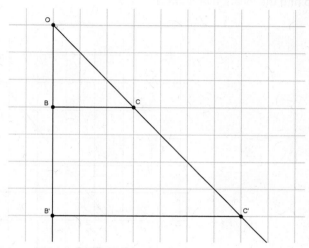

2. Verify the scale factor with a different set of segments.

3. Which segments are parallel? How do you know?

4. Are $\angle OBC = \angle OB'C'$ right angles? How do you know?

**COMMON
CORE**

Lesson 4:
Date:

Fundamental Theorem of Similarity (FTS)
10/16/13

Name _____   Date_____

Lesson 5: First Consequences of FTS

Exit Ticket

In the diagram below, you are given center O and ray $\overrightarrow{OA}$. Point A is dilated by a scale factor $r = \dfrac{6}{4}$. Use what you know about FTS to find the location of point A'.

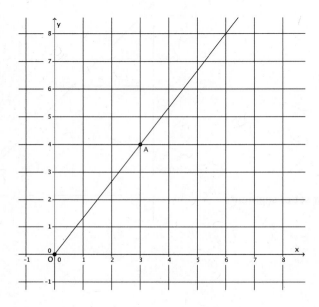

Name _____ Date _____

Lesson 6: Dilations on the Coordinate Plane

Exit Ticket

1. The point $A = (7, 4)$ is dilated from the origin by a scale factor $r = 3$. What are the coordinates of A'?

2. The triangle ABC, shown on the coordinate plane below, is dilated from the origin by scale factor $r = \frac{1}{2}$. What is the location of triangle $A'B'C'$? Draw and label it on the coordinate plane.

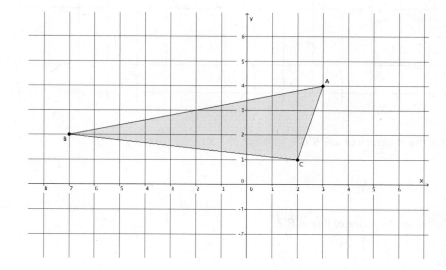

Name _____   Date_____

Lesson 7: Informal Proofs of Properties of Dilations

Exit Ticket

Dilate $\angle ABC$ with center O and scale factor $r = 2$. Label the dilated angle $\angle A'B'C'$.

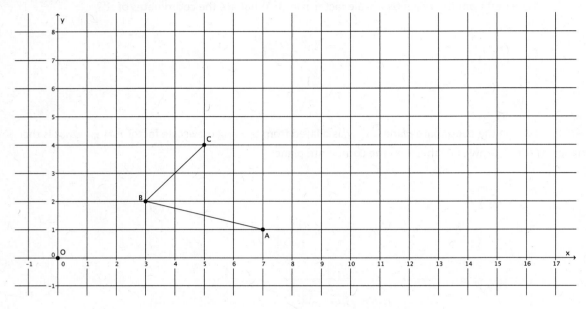

1.   If $\angle ABC = 72°$, then what is the measure of $\angle A'B'C'$?

2.   If segment AB is 2 cm. What is the measure of line $A'B'$?

3.   Which segments, if any, are parallel?

Name _____   Date _____

1. Use the figure below to complete parts (a) and (b).

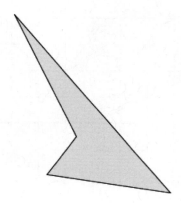

a. Use a compass and ruler to produce an image of the figure with center O and scale factor $r = 2$.

b. Use a ruler to produce an image of the figure with center O and scale factor $r = \frac{1}{2}$.

2. Use the diagram below to answer the questions that follow.

Let D be the dilation with center O and scale factor $r > 0$ so that $D(P) = P'$ and $D(Q) = Q'$.

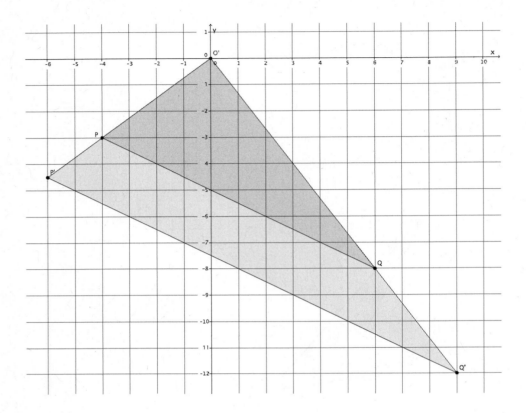

a. Use lengths $|OQ| = 10$ units and $|OQ'| = 15$ units, to determine the scale factor r, of dilation D. Describe how to determine the coordinates of P' using the coordinates of P.

b. If $|OQ| = 10$ units, $|OQ'| = 15$ units, and $|P'Q'| = 11.2$ units, determine the length of $|PQ|$. Round your answer to the tenths place, if necessary.

3. Use a ruler and compass, as needed, to answer parts (a) and (b).

   a. Is there a dilation D with center O that would map figure $PQRS$ to figure $P'Q'R'S'$? If yes, describe the dilation in terms of coordinates of corresponding points.

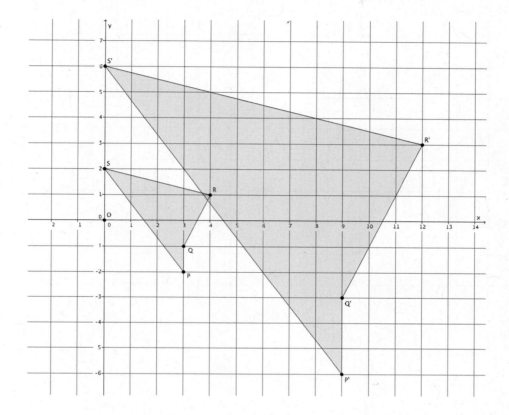

b.   Is there a dilation D with center O that would map figure $PQRS$ to figure $P'Q'R'S'$?   If yes, describe the dilation in terms of coordinates of corresponding points.

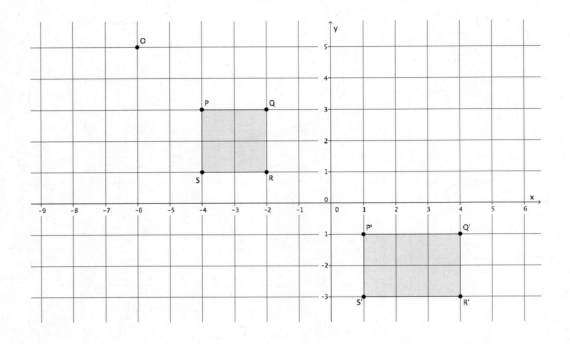

c.   Triangle ABC is located at points $A = (-4, 3)$, $B = (3, 3)$, and $C = (2, -1)$ and has been dilated from the origin by a scale factor of 3. Draw and label the vertices of triangle ABC. Determine the coordinates of the dilated triangle $A'B'C'$ and draw and label it on the coordinate plane.

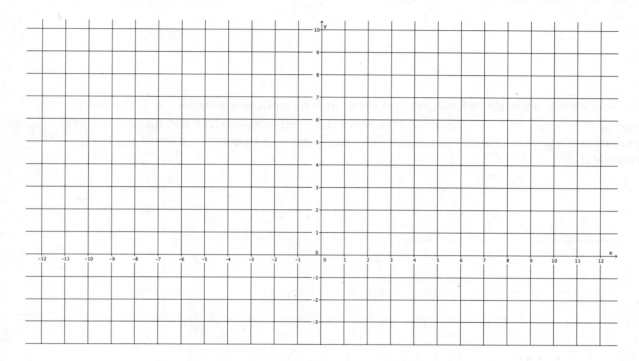

Name_____   Date_____

Lesson 8: Similarity

Exit Ticket

In the picture below, we have a triangle DEF that has been dilated from center O, by scale factor $r = \frac{1}{2}$. The dilated triangle is noted by $D'E'F'$. We also have a triangle $D''EF$, which is congruent to triangle DEF (i.e., $\triangle DEF \cong \triangle D''EF$). Describe the sequence of a dilation followed by a congruence (of one or more rigid motions) that would map triangle $D'E'F'$ onto triangle $D''EF$.

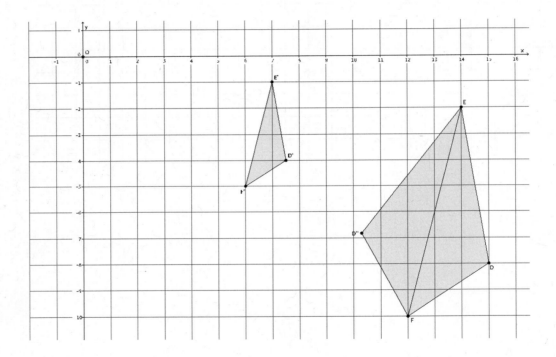

Name _____   Date_____

Lesson 9: Basic Properties of Similarity

Exit Ticket

Use the diagram below to answer questions 1 and 2.

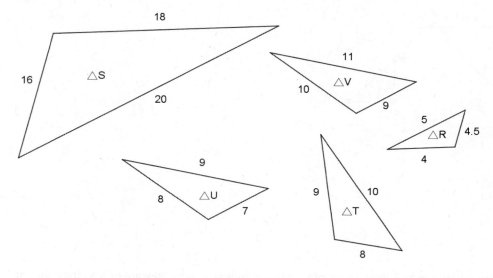

1.   Which triangles, if any, have similarity that is symmetric?

2.   Which triangles, if any, have similarity that is transitive?

Name _____   Date_____

Lesson 10: Informal Proof of AA Criterion for Similarity

Exit Ticket

1. Are the triangles shown below similar? Present an informal argument as to why they are or why they are not.

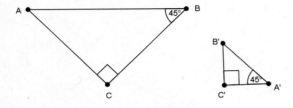

2. Are the triangles shown below similar? Present an informal argument as to why they are or why they are not.

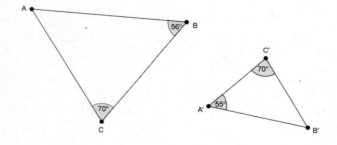

Name_____   Date_____

Lesson 11: More About Similar Triangles

Exit Ticket

1. In the diagram below, you have △ ABC and △ $A'B'C'$. Based on the information given, is △ $ABC \sim$ △ $A'B'C'$?
    Explain.

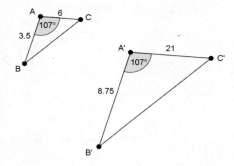

2. In the diagram below, △ $ABC \sim$ △ DEF. Use the information to answer parts (a)–(b).

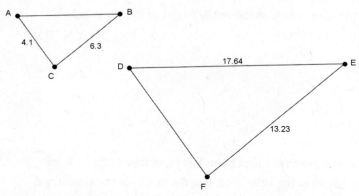

a.   Determine the length of AB. Show work that leads to your answer.

b.   Determine the length of DF. Show work that leads to your answer.

Name _____   Date_____

Lesson 12: Modeling Using Similarity

Exit Ticket

1. Henry thinks he can figure out how high his kite is while flying it in the park. First, he lets out 150 feet of string and ties the string to a rock on the ground. Then he moves from the rock until the string touches the top of his head. He stands up straight, forming a right angle with the ground. He wants to find out the distance from the ground to his kite. He draws the following diagram to illustrate what he has done.

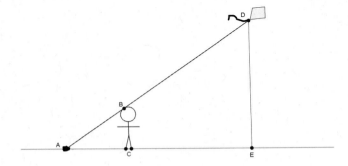

a.   Has Henry done enough work so far to use similar triangles to help measure the height of the kite? Explain.

b.   Henry knows he is $5\frac{1}{2}$ feet tall. Henry measures the string from the rock to his head and found it to be 8 feet. Does he have enough information to determine the height of the kite? If so, find the height of the kite. If not, state what other information would be needed.

Name _____   Date _____

1. Use the diagram below to answer the questions that follow.

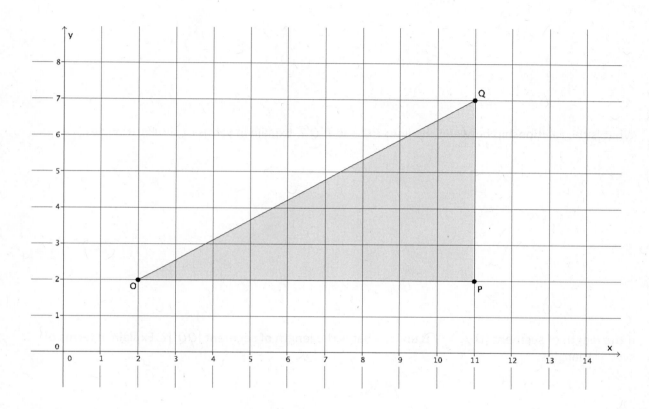

a. Dilate triangle $\triangle OPQ$ from center O and scale factor $r = \frac{4}{9}$. Label the image $\triangle OP'Q'$.

b. Find the coordinates of P' and Q'.

c.   Are $\angle OQP$ and $\angle OQ'P'$ equal in measure? Explain.

d.   What is the relationship between the lines PQ and $P'Q'$? Explain in terms of similar triangles.

e.   If the length of segment $|OQ| = 9.8$ units, what is the length of segment $|OQ'|$? Explain in terms of similar triangles.

2. Use the diagram below to answer the questions that follow. The length of each segment is as shown: segment OX is 5 units, segment OY is 7 units, segment XY is 3 units, and segment $X'Y'$ is 12.6 units.

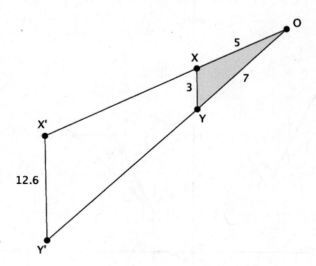

a. Suppose XY is parallel to $X'Y'$. Is triangle $\triangle OXY$ similar to triangle $\triangle OX'Y'$? Explain.

b. What is the length of segment OX'? Show your work.

c. What is the length of segment OY'? Show your work.

3. Given $\triangle ABC \sim \triangle A'B'C'$ and $\triangle ABC \sim \triangle A''B''C''$ in the diagram below, answer parts (a)–(c).

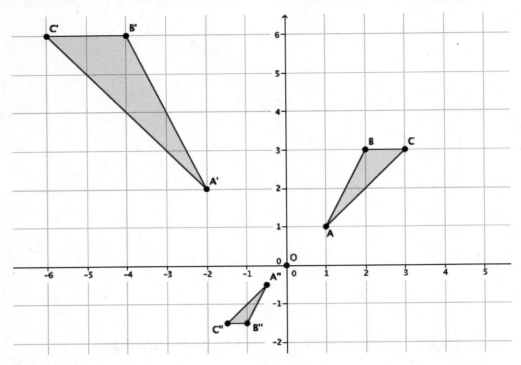

a. Describe the sequence that shows the similarity for $\triangle ABC$ and $\triangle A'B'C'$.

b. Describe the sequence that shows the similarity for $\triangle ABC$ and $\triangle A''B''C''$.

c. Is $\triangle A'B'C'$ similar to $\triangle A''B''C''$? How do you know?

Name _____   Date_____

Lesson 13: Proof of the Pythagorean Theorem

Exit Ticket

Determine the length of side BD in the triangle below.

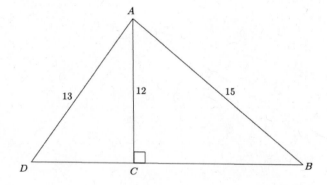

Name _____   Date_____

Lesson 14: The Converse of the Pythagorean Theorem

Exit Ticket

1. The numbers in the diagram below indicate the lengths of the sides of the triangle. Bernadette drew the following triangle and claims it a right triangle. How can she be sure?

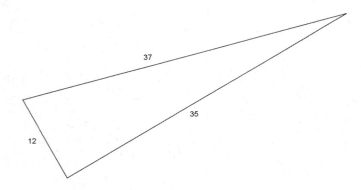

2. Will the lengths 5, 9, and 14 form a right triangle? Explain.